HISTORY OF THE

OSCARS®

HISTORY OF THE OSCARS®

DANIEL & SUSAN COHEN

This book is neither authorized nor endorsed
by the Academy of Motion Picture Arts and Sciences.

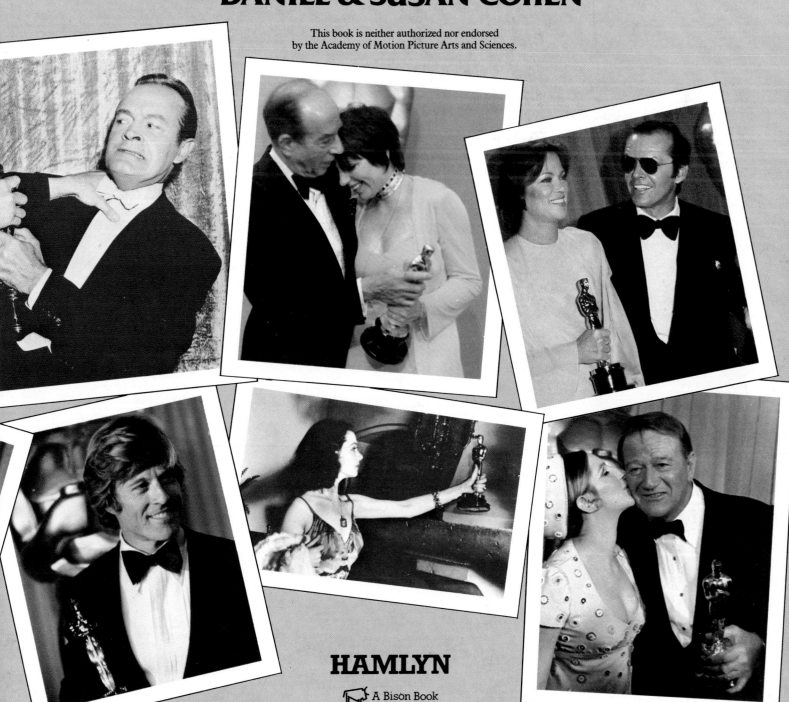

HAMLYN

A Bison Book

Published by Bison Books Ltd
176 Old Brompton Road
London SW5

Copyright © 1986 Bison Books Ltd

Distributed by Hamlyn Publishing
A Division of The Hamlyn Publishing Group Ltd.
Bridge House, London Road,
Twickenham, Middlesex

ISBN 0 600 50329 1
Printed in Hong Kong

PAGE 2-3: Clockwise from top right; Barbra Streisand, *Funny Girl* (1968); Marlon Brando, *On The Waterfront* (1954) with Bob Hope; Liza Minnelli, *Cabaret* (1972) with her father, Vincente Minnelli; Louise Fletcher, Jack Nicholson, *One Flew Over The Cuckoo's Nest* (1975); John Wayne, *True Grit* (1969), with Barbra Streisand; Vivien Leigh, *Gone With The Wind* (1939); Robert Redford, *Ordinary People* (1980); Jane Fonda accepts for her father, Henry Fonda, *On Golden Pond* (1981); Gene Hackman, *The French Connection*, Jane Fonda, *Klute* (1971); Simone Signoret, *Room At The Top* (1959); Ray Milland, *The Lost Weekend* (1945), with Ingrid Bergman.

ABOVE: Cedric Gibbons, the art director at M-G-M is credited with the design of the Oscar statuette.

DEDICATION
To Barbara Alimonti

'The Envelope Please'

That is a phrase that immediately evokes the Academy Awards the most popular and influential entertainment awards in the world. Each year thousands gather in Los Angeles to watch Hollywood honor itself. Millions more watch the ceremony on TV. There are weeks of speculation beforehand, and weeks of grumbling and second guessing afterward. Academy Award winners are better known than the winners of most elections, and the Awards are certainly more fun.

The film industry was giving awards even before there was an Academy of Motion Picture Arts and Sciences. *Photoplay Magazine* began giving popularity Photoplay Awards to stars in 1921 and soon the Western Association of Motion Picture Advertisers (WAMPA) began handing out *Wampas* awards to promising new stars, popularly called Wampas Babies. Clara Bow was a Wampas Baby, so was Joan Crawford. But all of these were eclipsed by the Academy Awards.

The Academy of Motion Picture Arts and Sciences was developed in the late 1920s, primarily at the urging of movie mogul Louis B Mayer. Whether Mayer envisioned a genuine 'academy' that would further artistic and technical progress in the industry or whether the crafty Mayer was simply trying to create a company union and keep out genuine unions, as some have charged, is unclear. But today the Academy is neither, it has evolved primarily into an organization that gives awards and works for the preservation of film. The membership is made up of people working in the motion picture industry.

Voting procedures have changed over the years but today the members of each of the several branches of the Academy select, by secret vote, five nominees. Then, also by secret vote, all the members of the Academy select the winners in each category. The one exception is Best Picture where the nominees and the final selection are chosen by the general membership. The categories have changed, as the business has changed, for example separate awards are no longer given for black and white and color films.

Generally only films officially released between 1 January and 31 December of a year are eligible for competition in that year, but there are exceptions, particularly in the area of foreign films where release dates vary. Perhaps the most extreme example was

Charlie Chaplin's film *Limelight* which was actually made in 1952, but not officially released in the Los Angeles area until 1972 when the music from it won an award for Best Original Score.

Since an award or even a nomination can mean big money to a studio and a huge boost to a performer's career, there have been well-founded charges of pressure, log-rolling and the influence of personal popularity rather than performance. The Academy has tried to limit these influences, so that the awards are more representative, but electioneering among voting members of the Academy is still intense around voting time.

Not everyone wants an Academy Award. George Bernard Shaw was insulted when he was given one for the scenario for the movie *Pygmalion* in 1938. George C Scott tried to have his name withdrawn from nomination in 1970. He couldn't do it and received the

INTRODUCTION

Award as Best Actor for *Patton* anyway.

In the end the selection of the 'best' or even the five top nominees in any category is really a matter of personal opinion, for which there can be no objective measure. The Academy members do seem to prefer a certain type of serious, middle brow, film like *Gandhi* over an entertainment like *ET*, or *How Green Was My Valley* over *Citizen Kane*, and *The Maltese Falcon*. Comedy has a tough time winning, so do adventure films. Fantasy, westerns, science fiction and horror are almost completely excluded from top awards. Box office success is not a guarantee of success at the Awards, otherwise Steven Spielberg and George Lucas would have a number of Oscars by now, but they don't. However, it is also extremely difficult for a small, independently made film to get the sort of attention needed for an award or a nomination. The Academy has its favorites, Katharine Hepburn, Meryl Streep, and those who never seem to win an Oscar, Cary Grant, for example,

but then he played primarily in comedies. (Grant was given an honorary award after he retired.)

A lot of the winners are forgettable – when was the last time you saw *Mrs Miniver*? We are fans, not computers, and in preparing this book we often found ourselves cursing the blindness and stupidity of the Awards. 'Why has Stanley Kubrick been denied an Oscar?' 'Why has Marsha Mason received so many undeserved nominations?' We assume that you, the reader, will have the same reaction, and will disagree not only with the judgment of the Academy, but with many of our judgments as well.

Most of all, however, we found real pleasure in recalling some of the great films, and performances of the past that are reflected in the Academy Awards. We assume that you will feel a similar pleasure. Recall that in 1934, a film that nobody wanted to make called *It Happened One Night*, made an unprecedented sweep of the Awards. And what about 1939, perhaps the best year Hollywood ever had, with pictures like *Gone With The Wind*, *The Wizard of Oz*, *Wuthering Heights*, *Stagecoach*!

A word about the Oscar. The Academy Award statuette was designed in 1928 by MGM Art Director Cedric Gibbons, and the trophy was created by Los Angeles sculptor George Stanley. The figure represents a knight holding a crusader's sword standing on a reel of film whose spokes represent the five original branches of the Academy – Actors, Directors, Producers, Technicians and Writers. The statuette is thirteen and one half inches tall and weighs eight and a half pounds. It is made of britannium plated with gold. The nickname Oscar started in the 1930s, and no one knows who thought it up or what it means. Among others, Bette Davis and Hollywood columnist Sidney Skolsky have claimed credit, as did a secretary who worked for the Academy office and said that the statuette looked like her uncle Oscar.

For the first eleven years the winners names were given to the newspapers ahead of time, the papers pledging they would not reveal the winners until the ceremony. The Los Angeles *Times* broke the pledge in 1939, after which the names were kept in sealed envelopes until their contents could be read on stage during the Academy presentations. America heard that fateful phrase 'The envelope please' for the first time in 1940.

1927/28

Best Picture: *Wings.*
Actor: Emil Jannings, *The Last Command* and *The Way Of All Flesh.*
Actress: Janet Gaynor, *Seventh Heaven, Street Angel* and *Sunrise.*
Director: Frank Borzage, *Seventh Heaven.*
Writing (Original Story): Ben Hecht, *Underworld.*
Special Awards: Warner Brothers for producing *The Jazz Singer.* Charles Chaplin, *The Circus.*

The immortal words, 'You ain't heard nothin' yet,' could have been the motto of the first Academy Awards presentation even though neither the man who uttered them, Al Jolson, nor the movie he uttered them in, *The Jazz Singer,* were nominated. However, Warner Brothers did receive a Special Award for producing the film, described as 'the pioneer talking picture, which has re-

RIGHT: Clara Bow and Buddy Rogers in *Wings,* a film about fliers in World War I.
BELOW: Al Jolson in *The Jazz Singer,* the first film with sound.

volutionized the industry.' Revolutionized is an understatement but to many in Hollywood it was sheer hyperbole and talking pictures an oddity which would represent little more than a passing phase. On 16 May 1929 the date of the second anniversary and the first awards banquet of the Academy of Motion Picture Arts and Sciences those honored were the creators and stars of silent movies, the idols of that prosperous and wild decade, the twenties.

Charles Chaplin won a Special Award for his genius and versatility in writing, acting, directing and producing *The Circus* but another great silent film clown, Buster Keaton, whose classic, *The General,* was released in 1927, received no nomination. King Vidor's disturbing and pessimistic movie about the anonymity of city life, *The Crowd,* didn't make it to the Best Picture list of nominations and he lost out in the directing category though today *The Crowd* is acknowledged to be one of the greatest of all silent films.

What did win against *The Last Command, The Racket, Seventh Heaven* and *The Way of All Flesh* was *Wings,* a dashing war movie which had excitement, romance, and the 'It' girl, Clara Bow. The cast of *Wings* also included

Charles 'Buddy' Rogers, Richard Arlen and a good-looking young fellow whose name had been linked to Bow's in the gossip columns, Gary Cooper.

Another of those ironies which would pepper the Academy Awards over the years was the omission of William Wellman, the director of *Wings*, from the list of directing nominees. Yet *Wings* owed much of its verve and the excitement of its airborne action to Wellman's experiences as a World War I flier.

Emil Jannings, star of stage and screen in Germany, an actor of international reputation won the Best Actor category for his first two American films, *The Last Command* and *The Way Of All Flesh* over Richard Barthelmess in *The Noose* and *The Patent Leather Kid* and Chaplin in *The Circus*. Unfortunately for Jannings, his Germanic accent destroyed any chance of his making a transition to talkies in Hollywood and he returned to Germany where he made *The Blue Angel*. Jannings stayed in Germany making propaganda movies during the Third Reich, ultimately receiving the title of 'Artist of the State.'

The superstar of the occasion was

Janet Gaynor who hit a triple, winning Best Actress for *Seventh Heaven*, *Street Angel* and *Sunrise*. The petite Gaynor was the opposite of Clara Bow, vulnerable and pure even when playing prostitutes, no mean feat but then she was

BELOW: Janet Gaynor starred in *Seventh Heaven*.
BOTTOM: Emil Jannings with Evelyn Brent in *The Last Command*.

always more victim than vampire. *Seventh Heaven*, which teamed Gaynor with her frequent film partner Charles Farrell, was a box office smash, a sentimental love story directed by the romantic and lyrical Frank Borzage, who won the award for Best Director for the movie. *Street Angel*, again with Farrell was similar to *Seventh Heaven* in plot while Gaynor played a good wife tossed aside by her husband for a bad girl in *Sunrise*. Losing out to Gaynor was Louise Dresser in *A Ship Comes In* and Hollywood glamour queen, Gloria Swanson, who appeared in *Sadie Thompson* which was based on Somerset Maugham's novella, *Rain*.

The winner of the Best Writer (original story) award was Ben Hecht for *Underworld* and he would remain one of Hollywood's most skillful screenwriters for decades. The coming of talkies held no fears for him. But the award for writing titles, which went to Joseph Farnham for *Fair Co-Ed*, *Laugh, Clown, Laugh* and *Telling The World*, would never be given again and the high-point of the banquet was a filmed conversation between Douglas Fairbanks, President of the Academy and Adolph Zukor, producer of *Wings*.

1928/29

Best Picture: *Broadway Melody.*
Actor: Warner Baxter, *In Old Arizona.*
Actress: Mary Pickford, *Coquette.*
Director: Frank Lloyd, *The Divine Lady.*
Art Director: Cedric Gibbons, *The Bridge Of San Luis Rey.*

The most important thing about the second Academy Awards was the choice of Best Picture. *Broadway Melody*, a comeback movie for Bessie Love was trite, clichéd and silly, but it was the right winner for its time. *Broadway Melody* was the first honest-to-goodness movie musical, an art form Hollywood would grow to appreciate and the public would grow to love.

There had been silent musicals in the past though they often boasted canned music and sound effects. As a matter of fact one of the movies nominated for cinematography in 1928/29, was *Our Dancing Daughters*, basically a silent musical despite the dance scenes starring a very lovely flapper named Joan Crawford. *Broadway Melody*, drenched in sound, was a breakthrough, a pivotal event. Sad to say Hollywood rarely honored later more deserving musicals and musical stars with Academy Awards.

ABOVE: *In Old Arizona* starred Warner Baxter, here with Dorothy Burgess.
LEFT: Mary Pickford won for *Coquette.*

Rounding out the cast of *Broadway Melody* were Anita Page and Charles King and though the movie was an original the plot was not. It told the already hackneyed story of small town girls trying to make it to stardom on Broadway. Appropriately enough the movie was a creation of MGM, which would later produce some of the best musicals in Hollywood. The film was the brain child of Irving Thalberg, MGM's production chief, with music by a pair of upstarts named Nacio Herb Brown and Arthur Freed. Freed would later become the producer of many MGM musicals. The movie's most enduring song was 'You Were Meant for Me.' *Broadway Melody* introduced the big musical production number with 'The Wedding of the Painted Doll' which was shot both in black and white and in color. The film's dialogue was silly and the sets were tacky. The chorus girls were distinctly plump and

their costumes simplistic. But from little acorns oak trees grow and the basic structure of better musicals was first put in place in *Broadway Melody*.

Warner Baxter was voted best actor for his role as the Cisco Kid in *In Old Arizona*. The use of sound in *In Old Arizona* made him a popular leading man because Baxter had a good speaking voice besides being darkly handsome. The other nominees were Chester Morris in *Alibi*, Lewis Stone for *The Patriot*, George Bancroft for *Thunderbolt* and Paul Muni in *The Valiant*. Stone would be fondly remembered for his role as the judge in The Andy Hardy series later in his career and Morris, a former child actor making his adult debut in *Alibi*, would play Boston Blackie in a number of the action films in that particular series.

The Best Actress Award went to Mary Pickford, America's Sweetheart, who came out of retirement to make *Coquette*. But her bobbed hair and adult personality didn't work. The public preferred her in ringlets and the Award did not resurrect her career. But she

won it over Ruth Chatterton in *Madame X*, Betty Compson in *The Barker*, Jeanne Eagels in *The Letter*, and *Broadway Melody's* Bessie Love.

Frank Lloyd took directing honors for *The Divine Lady* and was also nominated for directing *Weary River* and *Drag*, leaving Lionel Barrymore, nominated for director of *Madame X*, in the cold. Ernst Lubitsch, who directed *The Patriot*, received his first 'always a bridesmaid' nomination that year. This highly gifted director of sophisticated comedy and an innovator of camera techniques never did win an Academy Award. Perhaps had the Academy not dropped the category of comedy direction won by Lewis Milestone in 1927/28 for *Two Arabian Knights*, Lubitsch would eventually have received a much deserved Oscar.

The most sensitive movie of the 1928/29 season, *The Bridge Of San Luis Rey*, wasn't nominated for Best Picture though it did bring Cedric Gibbons the Art Direction Award. The superb film, an adaptation of Thornton Wilder's novel, starred Lili Damita, Ernest

Torrence, and Duncan Renaldo. It had everything going for it except sound. Between the introduction and epilogue the movie was silent and in Hollywood silence was no longer golden.

ABOVE: *Broadway Melody* starred Anita Page, Bessie Love and Charles King.

BELOW: Tully Marshall and Henry B Wathall in *The Bridge Of San Luis Rey*.

1929/30

Best Picture: *All Quiet On The Western Front.*
Actor: George Arliss, *Disraeli.*
Actress: Norma Shearer, *The Divorcée.*
Director: Lewis Milestone, *All Quiet On The Western Front.*
Writing: *The Big House.*
Cinematography: Willard Van Der Veer and Joseph T Rucker, *With Byrd At The South Pole.*
Sound Recording: Douglas Shearer, *The Big House.*

The great anti-war film, *All Quiet On The Western Front*, based on the famous novel by Erich Maria Remarque, won the Award for Best Picture. It was a very human movie, far from the glorified, romanticized image of war which would so often roll across theater screens in the future and had so often rolled across them in the past. Here was life in the trenches in all its ugliness at a time when the memory of World War I was very fresh and very real.

Though the director, Lewis Milestone, won an Academy Award for the film not a single actor in *All Quiet On The Western Front* received a nomination for Best Actor, and that included Lew Ayres. Yet his brilliant portrayal of a young German soldier disillusioned with the war marked the critical high point of his movie career.

The actors who were nominated represented a cross section of types and talents. George Arliss, *Disraeli*, had been a Broadway star who turned to films when he was middle-aged, playing the same kind of roles he had on stage, notably great statesmen. He had made an earlier silent version of *Disraeli* in 1921. The homely but popular Wallace Beery received a nomination for *The Big House*, a movie of major historical significance because it was one of a new breed of films which came in on the wings of sound, the tough guy-gangster genre. Robert Montgomery and Chester Morris were also in the movie which brought a Best Writing Achievement Award (not given after this year) to Frances Marion and a Best Sound Recording Award (new category) to Douglas Shearer.

The gallant Maurice Chevalier was nominated for the light-hearted *The Love Parade* with Jeanette MacDonald, directed by Ernst Lubitsch who received a Best Director nomination, and *The Big Pond* with another delightful film heroine, Claudette Colbert. Singer Lawrence Tibbett was nominated for *The Rogue Song* and the elegant Ronald Colman for *Bulldog Drummond*. But it was Arliss who won the Academy Award thanks to the added dimension sound brought to his characterization of the witty, sharp tongued Benjamin Disraeli.

The big upset of the evening came in the Best Actress category. Norma Shearer walked away with the prized statuette for her role in a scarcely remembered film, *The Divorcée*. Shearer was also nominated for *Their Own Desire*. She was up against Nancy

Lew Ayres as Paul Baumer, with Raymond Griffith in *All Quiet On The Western Front.*

greatest playwrights, *Anna Christie* had been carefully selected as Garbo's debut into talkies.

The studio brass at MGM had been forced to contemplate the horrible possibility that Garbo might not be able to make the transition to talking pictures. When it turned out that she had a nice sexy voice advertisements for *Anna Christie* blazed the glorious words, 'Garbo Speaks!' And speak she did, sending shivers down movie goers' spines with lines like 'Gimme a vhiskey' and 'Dot suits me down to de groun'...'

Despite the limitations of filming dramas in the early days of sound, because of the microphone stationed so that it practically hit actors on the head, the sound camera confined in a large booth and the need to shoot outdoor scenes with a silent camera, *Anna Christie* managed to achieve a brooding poetry. Garbo played a Swedish-born character totally lacking in glamour. There were no fancy sets or beautiful

LEFT: Mr George Arliss in *Disraeli*.
BELOW: Leila Hyams and Chester Morris in *The Big House*, which also starred Wallace Beery and Robert Montgomery.

Carroll for *The Devil's Holiday*, Ruth Chatterton in *Sarah And Son* and Gloria Swanson in *The Trespasser*. Had this been the entire list her win would have seemed perfectly reasonable though Swanson's mystique, Carroll's bubbling charm, and Chatterton's position as a mature actress could easily have given Shearer a run for the money. But it was the loss by the remaining female nominee that caused a furor. Her name was Greta Garbo.

Garbo was nominated for two films, *Anna Christie* and *Romance*. Considering the success of *Anna Christie* and the fuss made over it the public expected Garbo to win. Based on the play by Eugene O'Neill, one of America's

costumes to carry her along. There was just Garbo's beautiful face and impressive talent.

Two other movies are worthy of mention, both in the category of Cinematography. One is *With Byrd At The South Pole* which won the award for Willard Van Der Veer and Joseph T

Rucker. The film combined footage from the actual expedition with scenes shot in the studio which created an inspiring and innovative movie. Its competition was *Hell's Angels*, the brain child of millionaire movie mogul Howard Hughes. This was the breakthrough movie for a rather remarkable

Norma Shearer won the Award for Best Actress for *The Divorcee*.

platinum blonde, destined to triumph in talkies, Jean Harlow. Whatever the Academy thought the public would soon discover her and turn her into a legend.

1930/31

Best Picture: *Cimarron*.
Actor: Lionel Barrymore, *A Free Soul*.
Actress: Marie Dressler, *Min And Bill*.
Director: Norman Taurog, *Skippy*.
Writing (Original Story): John Monk Saunders, *The Dawn Patrol*.
Writing (Adaptation): Howard Estabrook, *Cimarron*.
Cinematography: Floyd Crosby, *Tabu*.
Art Director: Max Ree, *Cimarron*.

The dashing and the beautiful went down to defeat this year when middle-aged Lionel Barrymore won the Award for Best Actor for *A Free Soul* and elderly Marie Dressler routed four Hollywood lovelies, Norma Shearer in *A Free Soul*, Ann Harding in *Holiday*, Irene Dunn in *Cimarron* and Marlene Dietrich in *Morocco* to take home the prize. It was pay-off time for character actors.

Lionel Barrymore was the first of the famous theatrical family to appear in films. He had already had a long movie career as actor, scriptwriter, and director before playing the free-thinking lawyer fond of drink in *A Free Soul*. It was a sensitive perceptive performance but the movie is best remembered today as the film which made Clark Gable's career. Audiences got such a kick out of

ABOVE: Lionel Barrymore as the lawyer Steve Ashe in *A Free Soul*.

LEFT: Marie Dressler starred in *Min And Bill*.

the way Gable pushed Norma Shearer around that he became a sex symbol on the spot. The film's cast included James Gleason and British actor Leslie Howard, who had recently arrived in Hollywood.

Fellow nominees for Best Actor were the dapper Adolphe Menjou for *The Front Page*; a real gem, based on the Broadway play written by Ben Hecht and Charles Mac Arthur; all-round talent Fredric March for *The Royal Family Of Broadway*, adapted from the stage play *The Royal Family*; ex-silent film hero, Richard Dix in *Cimarron*; and Jackie Cooper in *Skippy*. Curiously, the character nominee March played in *The Royal Family Of Broadway* was

based on winning nominee Lionel Barrymore's brother John.

As for Jackie Cooper he was a child star with several episodes from the 'Our Gang' series in his past and a long line of tear jerkers in his future. *Skippy* was directed by Norman Taurog, Cooper's uncle, who won the Best Director Award for it over Clarence Brown (*A Free Soul*); Lewis Milestone (*The Front Page*); Wesley Ruggles (*Cimarron*); and the great Josef Von Sternberg (*Morocco*, which paired two hot stars, Dietrich and Gary Cooper).

Seasoned veteran Marie Dressler who titled her autobiography 'The Life Story Of An Ugly Duckling' was an unlikely superstar but superstar she was, winning for the very popular *Min And Bill*, a comedy which cast her opposite Wallace Beery, as two waterfront characters. The Best Picture Award went to *Cimarron*, a splashy saga of the Old West based on the Edna Ferber novel, starring, besides nominees Richard Dix and Irene Dunne, Edna May Oliver. Howard Estabrook won Best Adaptation for the movie and Max Ree, Best Art Director. It was one

of the rare occasions when the Academy would give due recognition to a western.

Other movies up for Best Picture were *East Lynne; The Front Page*, a hard-boiled comedy about journalistic hi-jinx with Menjou as editor and Pat O'Brien as the reporter; *Skippy*; *The Royal Family of Broadway*; *Trader Horn*, and *A Free Soul*. *The Front Page* was remade in 1940 as *His Girl Friday*, starring Rosalind Russell as the reporter and Cary Grant as the editor. There was a later version, too, made in 1974 starring Jack Lemmon and Walter Matthau. But the original is definitely the best.

The Dawn Patrol, a melodrama about World War I aviators which was filmed again in 1938 as a vehicle for Errol Flynn, starred Richard Barthelmess, Neil Hamilton, and Douglas Fairbanks, Jr, and it won John Mark Saunders the Academy Award for Best Original Story. *Tabu*, a beautiful film, directed by Robert Flaherty and F W Murnau, brought a Cinematography Award to Floyd Crosby, deservedly so. Unfortunately, that's all *Tabu* won

ABOVE: Richard Dix in *Cimarron*.
OPPOSITE: Richard Barthelmess and Douglas Fairbanks Jr in *The Dawn Patrol*.

because it was silent with only a musical score for background.

If *Tabu* represented the way Hollywood neglected the old, *Little Caesar*, *The Public Enemy* and *Scarface* (1932) were examples of Hollywood's myopic reaction to the new. *Little Caesar*, the tale of a Chicago hoodlum reminiscent of Al Capone, made Edward G Robinson a major star, cinema's king of the killers and Robinson was consistently ignored by the Academy throughout his career despite many fine serious performances. The only nomination *Little Caesar* received was for Original Story. The same was true for *The Public Enemy*, a finer, more enduring film about a Prohibition gangster. It starred a tough, pugnacious little guy named James Cagney. The movie's success has become legendary and few scenes from any movie are more famous than the one in *The Public Enemy* where Cagney violently pushes a grapefruit in Mae Clarke's face.

1931/32

Best Picture: *Grand Hotel.*
Actor: Fredric March, *Dr Jekyll And Mr Hyde*, and Wallace Beery, *The Champ.*
Actress: Helen Hayes, *The Sin Of Madelon Claudet.*
Director: Frank Borzage, *Bad Girl.*
Writing (Original Story): Frances Marion, *The Champ.*
Writing (Adaptation): Edwin Burke, *Bad Girl.*
Cinematography: Lee Garmes, *Shanghai Express.*
Short Subjects (Cartoon): *Flowers And Trees*, Walt Disney.
Short Subjects (Comedy): *The Music Box*, Hal Roach, (Laurel and Hardy).
Short Subjects (Novelty): *Wrestling Swordfish*, Mack Sennett-Educational.
Special Award: Walt Disney, for the creation of Mickey Mouse.
Scientific And Technical Award: Technicolor Motion Picture Corporation, for their color cartoon process.

What do you get if you put an all-star cast consisting of Lionel Barrymore, John Barrymore, Greta Garbo, Joan Crawford, Wallace Beery, Lewis Stone, and Jean Hersholt together with plenty of opportunity for showing off, then put them in the hands of versatile director, Edmund Goulding, a man skilled at coping with temperamental stars? You get a wonderful movie mosaic called *Grand Hotel*. Throw in a grand romance between John Barrymore and Garbo and you've got a surefire winner. And win it did, both the Best Picture Academy Award and enormous popularity with fans. It still holds up beautifully.

1931/32 was a landmark year for Hollywood. For the first time the Academy was unable to choose between two performances in the Best Actor category and so a tie was declared between Wallace Beery for *The Champ* and Fredric March for the twin roles of *Dr Jekyll And Mr Hyde*. Beery had played comedy parts in silents, moving on to play villains, thanks to his homely face and rough appearance but in talking pictures he became the screen's most lovable rogue, and was frequently cast as a buffoon or a tough with a heart

BELOW: Frederic March in *Dr Jekyll And Mr Hyde*.
BOTTOM: Wallace Beery, Edward Brophy, Jackie Cooper, Roscoe Ates in *The Champ*.

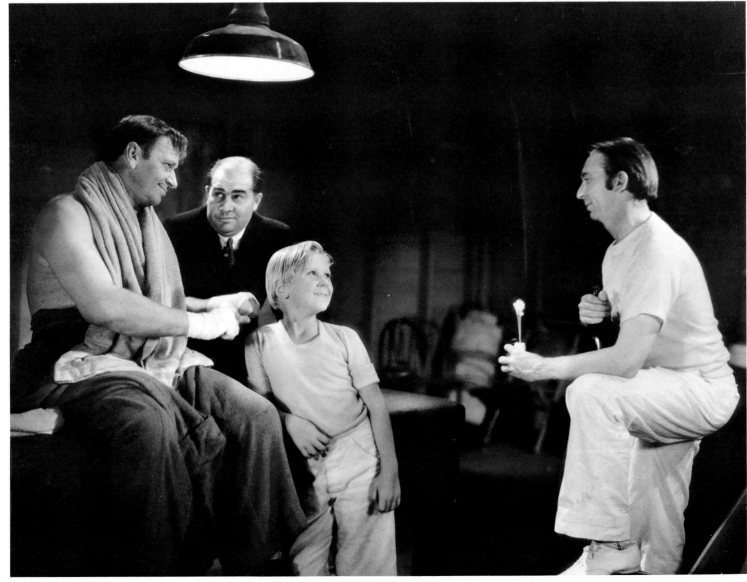

of gold. His portrayal of an ex-heavy-weight champion boxer on the skids with Jackie Cooper as his loyal son made *The Champ* such a ferocious hit with the public that Beery moved into the top ten list of box-office draws and remained a major money maker for some years. King Vidor was nominated for directing the film which had audiences happily weeping oceans of tears.

The Fredric March version of *Dr Jekyll And Mr Hyde*, directed by Rouben Mamoulian, a master of light and shadow, striking imagery, camera work at its most fluid, and sharp cutting, is considered by many critics to be the greatest adaptation of the Robert Louis Stevenson story ever brought to the screen. Though March relied on make-up in the transformation scenes, unlike John Barrymore who developed his 1920 silent screen characterization

LEFT: Greta Garbo in *Grand Hotel*, with Robert McWade and Ferdinand Gottschalk. BELOW: Helen Hayes in *The Sin Of Madelon Claudet*, with Lewis Stone.

without any such help, March and co-star Miriam Hopkins emphasized sexual tension rather than horror in interpreting their roles. Unfortunately, neither Hopkins nor Mamoulian were rewarded with nominations by the Academy. Neither were Spencer Tracy or Ingrid Bergman nominated for their creepy sado-masochistic version of *Dr Jekyll and Mr Hyde* (1941).

Now that it was obvious that talkies were here to stay Hollywood studios raided New York's Broadway looking for actors and actresses who wouldn't need crash courses in voice and elocution. The famous acting team of Alfred Lunt and Lynn Fontanne appeared together in *The Guardsman*, garnering

nominations. Neither won. But another great theatrical star did, Helen Hayes, who won as Best Actress for *The Sin Of Madelon Claudet*. The only real Hollywood star in contention for Best Actress was Marie Dressler in *Emma*.

Frank Borzage of *Seventh Heaven* fame won his second Best Director Award for *Bad Girl*. The movie also brought Edwin Burke a Best Writing Award (Adaptation). The Best Writing (Original Story) Award went to Frances Marion for *The Champ*. Boxers would prove a popular subject in Hollywood for decades to come. Josef von Sternberg's *Shanghai Express* starring a very mysterious Marlene Dietrich, with Clive Brook, Anna May Wong, and

Warner Oland received several nominations, including Best Picture and Best Director but it won only for Cinematography and that it took easily since Lee Garmes's camera caught the flavor of China in ferment even though the entire film was shot in safe and sunny California.

Perhaps the biggest news at the Awards Ceremony this year was the blossoming of animation. A Scientific And Technical Award went to the Technicolor Motion Picture Corporation for its color cartoon process and a

Marlene Dietrich as Shanghai Lilly in *Shanghai Express* directed by Joseph von Sternberg.

Special Award was given to Walt Disney for the creation of Mickey Mouse. This was the first year Awards were given for Short Subjects and Disney won in the Cartoon category for *Flowers And Trees*.

In 1923 Walt Disney had gone into partnership with his brother Roy. Working with Disney was a creative artist with the unlikely name of Ub Iwerks who played a major role in the development of the character, Mickey Mouse, receiving 'drawn by' screen credits in the early Mickey Mouse and Silly Symphony cartoons. Disney himself provided Mickey's distinctive high-pitched voice in the first Mickey Mouse sound cartoon, *Steamboat Willie* (1929). Entrepreneurial and technically innovative Disney oversaw the creation of an entire zoo's worth of cartoon creatures including Minnie Mouse, Donald Duck, Goofy (originally Dippy Dawg) and Pluto, all destined to become mythic American characters. 1931 saw major advances in color from Disney and further advances would follow soon. It wouldn't be long before the Disney Studio would be a massive organization, a virtual factory of animated fantasy, with hundreds of

RIGHT: Walt Disney with the Oscar for *Flowers And Trees* and an early version of Mickey Mouse.
BELOW: Mickey Mouse in *Steamboat Willie*.

employees, and a wide range of merchandized products, based on Disney characters.

Short features had been an important phase of films during the silent era, especially in the realm of comedy. Mack Sennett, the 'King of Comedy' was one of the shining names associated with the genre, along with Charles Chaplin, Buster Keaton, W C Fields and Laurel and Hardy among others. Though no longer the power he had been in the past, Sennett went on working in the sound era as did many other major figures from the days of the silents. So it is only fitting that Sennett's *The Loud Mouth* received a nomination in the Short Subjects (Comedy) category and his *Wrestling Swordfish* won the Short Subjects (Novelty) category. *The Music Box* with Laurel and Hardy won the Award for Short Subjects (Comedy).

1932/33

Best Picture: *Cavalcade.*
Actor: Charles Laughton, *The Private Life of Henry VIII.*
Actress: Katharine Hepburn, *Morning Glory.*
Director: Frank Lloyd, *Cavalcade.*
Writing (Original Story): Robert Lord, *One Way Passage.*
Writing (Adaptation): Sarah Y Mason and Victor Heerman, *Little Women.*
Cinematography: Charles Bryant Lang, Jr, *A Farewell To Arms.*
Art Director: William S Darling, *Cavalcade.*
Sound Recording: Harold C Lewis, *A Farewell To Arms.*
Assistant Director: Charles Dorian, Metro-Goldwyn Mayer; Gordon Hollingshead, Warner Brothers; Dewey Starkey, RKO Radio; Charles Barton, Paramount; Scott Beal, Universal; Fred Fox, United Artists; William Tummel, Fox.
Short Subjects (Cartoon): *The Three Little Pigs,* Walt Disney.
Short Subjects (Comedy): *So This Is Harris.*
Short Subjects (Novelty): *Krakatoa.*

It was a gold-spangled season for Best Picture. Up for consideration was *State Fair*, a charming bit of Americana in its first incarnation, starring Will Rogers, Lew Ayres, Janet Gaynor and Sally Eilers; *Smilin' Thru*, a sentimental remake of a 1922 silent film starring Sidney Franklin, Norma Shearer, Leslie Howard, and Fredric March, and *Lady For A Day*. Directed by Frank Capra who received a Best Director nomination for the movie, *Lady For A Day* told the Damon Runyon tale of an old flowerseller aided and abetted by benevolent gangsters. It featured a hearty performance by May Robson which gained her a nomination as Best Actress. Lovable heartwarming foolishness, the film was vintage Hollywood. It was remade in 1961 as *Pocketful Of Miracles*.

Forty-Second Street, one of the best movie musicals ever made, was also nominated. This tune-filled show about a young girl's quick trip from the chorus line to star billing had a glowing cast. Warner Baxter, Ruby Keeler, Dick Powell, a very peppery and sexy Ginger Rogers, and Bebe Daniels brought this most famous of Broadway back-stage musicals to life. Production numbers were directed by the one and only Busby Berkeley. Another Best Picture nominee was *She Done Him Wrong*, a comic gem, with Mae West making eyes at Cary Grant while tossing off some of her immortal one-liners. *The Private Life Of Henry VIII*, the first English picture to play successfully in the States, was a robust romp, starring a larger-than-life Charles Laughton, with Robert Donat, Elsa Lanchester, and Binnie Barnes. It brought Laughton the Best Actor Award and the film a nomination as Best Picture, but unfairly director Alexander Korda wasn't nominated.

A Farewell To Arms was also a contender. Based on the Ernest Hemingway novel the movie was directed by Frank Borzage and starred Gary Cooper and Helen Hayes. *I Am A Fugitive From A Chain Gang* was a great Depression film, brimming with compassion and social consciousness. In

Charles Laughton in *The Private Life Of Henry VIII* with Binnie Barnes.

ABOVE: Una O'Connor, Diana Wynyard and Clive Brook welcome the new century in *Cavalcade*
RIGHT: Gary Cooper and Helen Hayes as the ill-fated lovers in *A Farewell To Arms*.

addition to being nominated for Best Picture its star Paul Muni received a Best Actor nomination for his sensitive portrayal of a man driven to crime by a ruthless society. Unfairly Director Mervyn Le Roy wasn't even nominated. George Cukor did earn a Best Director nomination for Best Picture nominee *Little Women*. Starring Katharine Hepburn, Joan Bennett, Paul Lukas, and Spring Byington, it is considered to be the definitive movie version of the Louisa May Alcott novel.

Considering the competition it's rather startling to realize the Academy gave the Best Picture Award to Noel Coward's *Cavalcade*, a patriotic epic starring Clive Brook and a mainly British cast. An American film, directed by Frank Lloyd who won Best Director for it, the movie covered thirty years in the life of a British family searching for dignity, peace, and meaning in a time of turmoil. It was the kind of uplifting movie the Academy has always liked. *Cavalcade* also won William S Darling the Academy Award for Art Direction.

In addition to Laughton and Muni, Leslie Howard received a Best Actor nomination for his performance in *Berkeley Square* which was also directed by Frank Lloyd. A delicately romantic fantasy about a modern man who goes back in time to the eighteenth century, *Berkeley Square*, was based on Henry James's 'The Sense Of The Past.'

Along with May Robson, Diana Wynyard was nominated for Best Actress for her role in *Cavalcade*. However, so was a refreshing young star by the name of Katharine Hepburn. She turned a rather thin film with a shopworn plot, *Morning Glory*, into a shining triumph. Hepburn was sincerely touching as a stagestruck girl who, after arduous searching, wangles a job as an understudy and replaces the star on opening night.

A new category was established this year, Assistant Director, resulting in the unique and rather extraordinary choice of six people representing different studios winning a Multiple Award. Charles Dorian of Metro-Goldwyn-Mayer, Gordon Hollingshead of Warner Brothers, Dewey Starkey of RKO Radio, Charles Barton of Paramount, Scott Beal of Universal, Fred Fox of United Artists and William Tummel of Fox shared the honors. The Sound Recording Award went to Harold C Lewis for *A Farewell To Arms* which also gained the Cinematography Award for Charles Bryant Lang, Jr. However, the nomination of *Forty-Second Street* in this category shows how far sound had come in only a few brief years. Musicals were beginning to sound good, becoming more than just an interesting novelty. Nominated in the sound category was another famous musical choreographed by Busby Berkeley, *Golddiggers of 1933*, the first of a series of popular Warner Brothers musicals.

Sarah Y Mason and Victor Heerman won the Award for their adaptation of the classic, *Little Women* and Robert Lord received the Award for Best Writer (Original Story) for *One Way Passage*, a crowd-pleasing tear jerker with Kay Francis and William Powell about a dying woman and a convicted murderer who, hiding their secret, fall in love on an ocean liner. Walt Disney won the Short Subjects (Cartoons) category again, this time for *The Three Little Pigs*, while *Krakatoa* won Novelty and Award for Comedy went to *So This Is Harris*. One absolutely fabulous trail-blazing movie of the year wasn't nominated for anything. *King Kong*, starring Robert Armstrong and Fay Wray was ignored by the Academy just as Bela Lugosi's *Dracula* and Boris Karloff's *Frankenstein* had been in 1931.

Katharine Hepburn won her first Academy Award as Best Actress for her performance as Eva Lovelace, the stage-struck heroine of *Morning Glory*, costarring Adolphe Menjou and Douglas Fairbanks Jr.

1934

Best Picture: *It Happened One Night.*
Actor: Clark Gable, *It Happened One Night.*
Actress: Claudette Colbert, *It Happened One Night.*
Director: Frank Capra, *It Happened One Night.*
Writing (Original Story): Arthur Caesar, *Manhattan Melodrama.*
Writing (Adaptation): Robert Riskin, *It Happened One Night.*
Cinematography: Victor Milner, *Cleopatra.*
Art Director: Cedric Gibbons and Frederic Hope, *The Merry Widow.*
Music: (From 1934 to 1937 presented to studio Music Department head instead of to composer.)
Music (Score): Louis Silvers, *One Night Of Love,* Columbia. Thematic Music by Victor Schertzinger and Gus Kahn.
Music (Song): Herb Magidson (Lyrics), Con Conrad (Music), 'The Continental' from *The Gay Divorcée.*
Short Subjects (Cartoon): *The Tortoise And The Hare,* Walt Disney.
Special Award: Shirley Temple, presented in grateful recognition of her outstanding contribution to screen entertainment during the year 1934.

Twelve movies were nominated for Best Picture in 1934, which might be taken as a sure sign that Hollywood had entered its vintage years. Categories were expanding, nominees increasing, and new awards were the order of the day. What with the addition of Best Song, Best Score, and the nomination of Ginger Rogers's and Fred Astaire's *The Gay Divorcée* for Best Picture, a gorgeous splash of froth with champagne dancing, the Academy Awards took a light-hearted turn.

Comedy got its due at this particular ceremony. One nominee was *The Thin Man* starring William Powell and Myrna Loy as Nick and Nora Charles in the mystery-comedy movie based on Dashiell Hammett's popular detective novel. Powell was elegant and unflappable while Loy played her role as an ultra-chic good sport becomingly. In the running, too, was *One Night Of Love* with opera star Grace Moore and *Flirtation Walk* with Dick Powell and Ruby Keeler. Of these four pictures either *The Gay Divorcée* or *The Thin Man* was favored to win. The other two films were considered long shots.

One Night Of Love brought Moore an Oscar nomination for Best Actress. Norma Shearer in *The Barretts Of*

Wimpole Street was also nominated for Best Actress as the movie was for Best Picture. William Powell was nominated for Best Actor for his performance in *The Thin Man*, Frank Morgan for his in *Affairs Of Cellini. The Thin Man* also brought nominations to writers (Adaptation) Frances Goodrich and Albert Hackett and to director W S Van Dyke.

But life isn't always predictable and neither are the Academy Awards. *It Happened One Night*, an outrageous madcap comedy torpedoed the opposi-

Clark Gable and Claudette Colbert try to thumb a ride in *It Happened One Night,* directed by Frank Capra.

tion. It collected Best Picture, won leads Clark Gable and Claudette Colbert Best Actor and Best Actress Oscars, captured the Best Director Award for Frank Capra who was considered at that time simply another Hollywood director. And it gave Robert Riskin the Writing (Adaptation) award over even the ubiquitous Ben

ABOVE: Shirley Temple with Adolphe Menjou in *Little Miss Marker*.
RIGHT: Norma Shearer was nominated for *The Barretts Of Wimpole Street*.

Hecht, nominated for *Viva Villa* which was also up for Best Picture.

Movies rarely clobber everything in sight unless they have important studio backing, including a massive publicity campaign. But *It Happened One Night* was a fluke, an accident, a sleeper, a Cinderella movie with MGM's Louis B Mayer cast in the role of wicked stepmother. The picture started out as Mayer's way of punishing Gable for asking for a raise. To humble the rising star Mayer loaned him out to struggling Columbia Pictures to make a silly little film nobody would go see. Leading ladies were far from willing to co-star and at last Colbert agreed to appear with Gable but only under duress.

The cast and the director had a good time filming the movie because they knew it didn't count. The results were terrific, and the two stars proved charismatic together and comically

adept. The film established Colbert as one of Hollywood's leading lights of light sophisticated comedy. The screen-play about an heiress turned runaway and her run-in with a journalist crackled with charm. The scenes on the night bus, the hitch-hiking scene, and the final 'Walls of Jericho' scene set the pattern for future comedies. The film opened without fanfare and became an enormous success, thanks to the best press agent of all, word-of-mouth. It made Columbia rich and got Gable his raise.

1934 was a big year for Colbert who was the star of another movie nomin-ated for Best Picture, *Cleopatra*, a Cecil B De Mille production. At first glance Colbert seemed an odd choice for the exotic Cleo. But the cute, saucy, round-faced, petite Colbert, assisted by a cast of thousands and Warren William as Caesar and Henry Wilcoxon as Antony, carried it off. *Cleopatra* was cited in several categories and won Victor Milner the Cinematography Award. It was classic epic De Mille, touting virtue while flaunting sex, a different picture altogether from *It Happened One Night* with its snappy irreverent suggestive-ness.

The Gay Divorcée lost the Best Score Award to *One Night Of Love* but 'The Continental' also from the movie *The Gay Divorcée* won Best Song. Also nominated for Best Song was 'Carioca' from Astaire and Rogers's first film together, *Flying Down To Rio*. *The Gay Divorcée* was the pair's first starring venture. Choreographed by Hermes Pan, the film featured Eric Blore and Edward Everett Horton. From the start the Rogers/Astaire chemistry, sex and class, was very much in evidence. *The Gay Divorcée's* dialogue was dumb but appealing, the costumes were pretty, and the movie was a bright spot in a dark world. Even today it can turn a small television set into a silver screen.

Another dancing darling of 1934 won a Special Academy Award, this one in miniature. Dimpled, golden-haired Shirley Temple, child star *extraordin-aire*, gained it for her performances in *Little Miss Marker* with Adolphe Menjou, *Now And Forever* with Gary Cooper and Carole Lombard, and *Stand Up And Cheer* with James Dunn. Little Shirley was a phenomenon. Millions adored her and the movies she made in the Depression are still popular on television. She wasn't Fred Astaire but her baby feet could really tap and she knew how to put across a song.

For the third year running Walt Disney took home an Oscar for *The Tortoise And The Hair*, easily beating *Jolly Little Elves* from Universal and Columbia's *Holiday Land*. It was a wonderful funny Awards year. It is a pity the Academy wasn't amused more often.

Maurice Chevalier as Prince Danilo steals a slipper from Jeanette MacDonald as *The Merry Widow*.

1935

Best Picture: *Mutiny On The Bounty.*
Actor: Victor McLaglen, *The Informer.*
Actress: Bette Davis, *Dangerous.*
Director: John Ford, *The Informer.*
Writing (Original Story): Ben Hecht, Charles MacArthur, *The Scoundrel.*
Writing (Best Written Screenplay): Dudley Nichols, *The Informer.*
Cinematography: Hal Mohr, *A Midsummer Night's Dream.*
Art Director: Richard Day, *The Dark Angel.*
Music (Score): Max Steiner, *The Informer,* RKO Radio. Score by Max Steiner.
Music (Song): Al Dubin (Lyrics), Harry Warren (Music), 'Lullaby Of Broadway' from *Golddiggers Of 1935.*
Dance Director: Dave Gould, 'I've Got A Feeling You're Fooling' number from *Broadway Melody Of 1936* and the 'Straw Hat' number from *Folies Bergere.*
Short Subjects (Cartoon): *Three Orphan Kittens,* Walt Disney.
Special Award: David Wark Griffith for his distinguished creative achievements as director and producer and his invaluable initiative and lasting contributions to the progress of the motion picture arts.

The 1935 list of Best Picture nominees is varied, impressive, and exciting. It reads like an honor role of some of Hollywood's finest films. *Captain Blood*, a historical costume drama and adventure movie starred the handsome roguish Errol Flynn who was consistently underrated as an actor. Yet Flynn's droll characterizations have stood the test of time and the bold and colorful *Captain Blood* is still great entertainment. One of the best Astaire/Rogers musicals, *Top Hat*, had the couple dancing cheek to cheek. The movie's song 'Cheek To Cheek,' music and lyrics by Irving Berlin, was nominated for Best Song. *Alice Adams* was a touching film about the cruelty of small town American snobbery, starring Katharine Hepburn. She received a Best Actress nomination for her portrayal of a sensitive young woman on the outs with the 'in' clique.

David Copperfield was a Dickensian triumph directed by George Cukor. A distinguished cast included Freddie Bartholomew, Frank Lawton, Edna May Oliver, Basil Rathbone, Roland Young, and an American comic genius, W C Fields, as Mr Micawber. Though he made many wonderful films Fields was never nominated for an Oscar. After all Fields was unswervingly anti-establishment and anti-respectable, both in his life and in his work and the Academy was and is distinctly respectable. Still, it's nice to know that *David Copperfield* brought Fields at least some of the recognition he so thoroughly deserved.

The third American version of *Les Miserables* starred Fredric March and Charles Laughton. Gary Cooper and Franchot Tone starred in the great adventure movie, *Lives Of A Bengal Lancer.* Charles Laughton appeared in *Ruggles Of Red Gap*, about an English butler on an American ranch. Max Reinhardt's *A Midsummer Night's Dream* succeeded beautifully, thanks partly to the imaginative casting of James Cagney as Bottom and Mickey Rooney as Puck. Dick Powell, Anita Louise, Arthur Treacher, and Olivia de Havilland also appeared. Jeanette McDonald and Nelson Eddy's *Naughty Marietta* and another musical, *Broadway Melody of 1936* were also nominated.

Two stunning nominees for Best Picture remain, both big winners. The remakes of *Mutiny On The Bounty* have never even come close to equalling the

ABOVE: Victor MacLaglen and J M Kerrigan in *The Informer*.
LEFT: Charles Laughton and Clark Gable in *Mutiny On The Bounty*.

In addition to Hepburn's nomination for Best Actress the list of candidates included the gifted Polish actress Elisabeth Bergner for the British film, *Escape Me Never*; 1934's winner, Claudette Colbert in *Private Worlds*; Miriam Hopkins for *Becky Sharp* and Merle Oberon for *The Dark Angel*. There was one other entrant, a clever highly talented young actress who should have been nominated the year before for her role as the waitress, Mildred, in the movie *Human Bondage*, Bette Davis. To make up for their mistake the Academy gave her not only a nomination but the Oscar for *Dangerous*, in which she played an actress hooked on liquor and sex. It is somehow fitting that Hepburn won her first Oscar in 1932/33 and Davis's turn came so soon after.

Walt Disney, as regular as clockwork, again won his inevitable Award for Best Cartoon. *A Midsummer Night's Dream* was deservedly honored for Cinematography with the Oscar going to Hal Mohr. A superb horror movie, *The Bride Of Frankenstein*, starring Karloff, Elsa Lanchester and Ernest Thesiger and directed by James Whale was nominated for Best Sound Recording. It deserved lots more. A Special Award went to David Wark (D W) Griffith, the great silent film director and innovative movie pioneer responsible for *The Birth Of A Nation*, *Intolerance*, *Way Down East*, and *Orphans Of The Storm*.

version starring Charles Laughton as the brutal and monstrous Captain Bligh; Clark Gable as Fletcher Christian, the Bounty's first mate, who led the rebellious crew members to Pitcairn Island; and Franchot Tone as the midshipman tried for mutiny at a naval court-martial in England. Tone, Gable, and Laughton were all nominated for Best Actor for their performances. They lost to Victor McLaglen for *The Informer*.

Though *Mutiny On The Bounty* won the Award for Best Picture, *The Informer* occupies a higher position in the archives of film. Director John Ford won the Best Director Award over

Bounty director Frank Lloyd. *The Informer* also brought Max Steiner an Oscar for Best Score. A new category, Best Written Screenplay, replaced Writing (Adaption) this year and was won by *Informer* scriptwriter Dudley Nichols. Based on the Liam O'Flaherty novel *The Informer*, set in Dublin, takes place on a single night in the life of Gypo Nolan, played by McLaglen, popularly known as 'The Beloved Brute.' The story concerns the slow-witted Gypo's betrayal of a fellow Irish rebel and the movie confronts the themes of guilt and terror, redemption, repentence, and death.

Another new category was added this year, in the realm of Music. The Award for Best Dance Director was Hollywood's way of cheering on good choreography. The category was essentially fashioned for Busby Berkeley, known for achieving kaleidoscopic effects with gorgeous girls. Ironically, Berkeley didn't win. He was nominated for two numbers in *Golddiggers Of 1935*. They are 'Lullaby Of Broadway' and 'The Words Are In My Heart.' Among the Dance Director nominees was Hermes Pan for 'Piccolino' from *Top Hat* and the movie's song 'Top Hat.' The winner was Dave Gould for 'I've Got A Feeling You're Fooling' from *Broadway Melody Of 1936* and the 'Straw Hat' number from *Folies Bergère*.

The Marx Brother's glorious farce, *A Night At The Opera* was also released in 1935 and like *Duck Soup, Horse Feathers, Monkey Business* and *Animal Crackers* before it was snubbed by the Academy. Posterity is smarter.

RIGHT: D W Griffiths and his cameraman Wilhelm (Billy) Bitzer on location for *Way Down East* (1920).
BELOW: Bette Davis and Franchot Tone in *Dangerous*.

1936

Best Picture: *The Great Ziegfeld.*
Actor: Paul Muni, *The Story Of Louis Pasteur.*
Actress: Luise Rainer, *The Great Ziegfeld.*
Supporting Actor: Walter Brennan, *Come And Get It.*
Supporting Actress: Gale Sondergaard, *Anthony Adverse.*
Director: Frank Capra, *Mr Deeds Goes To Town.*
Writing (Original Story): Pierre Collings and Sheridan Gibney, *The Story Of Louis Pasteur.*
Writing (Best Written Screenplay): Pierre Collings, and Sheridan Gibney, *The Story Of Louis Pasteur.*
Cinematography: Tony Gaudio, *Anthony Adverse.*
Art Director: Richard Day, *Dodsworth.*
Assistant Director: Jack Sullivan, *The Charge Of The Light Brigade.*
Music (Score): Leo Forbstein, *Anthony Adverse*, Warner Bros. Score by Erich Wolfgang Korngold.
Music (Song): Dorothy Fields (Lyrics), Jerome Kern (Music), 'The Way You Look Tonight' from *Swingtime.*
Dance Director: Seymour Felix, 'A Pretty Girl Is Like A Melody' number from *The Great Ziegfeld.*
Short Subjects (Cartoon): *Country Cousin*, Walt Disney.
Short Subjects (Color): *Give Me Liberty.*
Short Subjects (1-Reel): *Bored Of Education*, Hal Roach, 'Our Gang.'
Special Awards: The March Of Time, for its significance to motion pictures and for having revolutionized one of the most important branches of the industry — the newsreel. W Howard Greene and Harold Rosson, for the color cinematography of the Selznick international production, *The Garden of Allah.*

The big news at the Awards Ceremony this year wasn't *The Great Ziegfeld* which won Best Picture or Paul Muni who won Best Actor for *The Story Of Louis Pasteur*, nor was it the Best Actress category, the Oscar going to Luise Rainer for *The Great Ziegfeld*. The most important event at the Academy Awards of 1936 was the inclusion of two new categories, Best Supporting Actor and Best Supporting Actress. This opened the Awards up to a whole raft of talented character actors otherwise dwarfed by the stars.

The contest for Best Picture had no firm favorite but biographies seemed to have the extra edge. *The Great Ziegfeld* was a giant of a film, three hours long, starring William Powell in the title role of Flo Ziegfeld, Broadway's titan of a showman. A musical melodrama with lavish production numbers the film's cast included Myrna Loy as Ziegfeld's wife Billie Burke, a Hollywood star in her own right, Fannie Brice, Eddie Cantor and Will Rogers. Luise Rainer, fresh from Austria, played Ziegfeld's first wife, singer Anna Held. 'Follies' production numbers famous for gorgeous girls helped keep film fans enthralled.

The Story Of Louis Pasteur, the tale of the great pioneer of medical science doesn't sound like the sort of movie that would raise cheers but it proved exciting and popular. It ignited a whole series of Warner Brothers historical biographical films and further enhanced Muni's reputation as an actor. Also nominated for Best Picture was *Anthony Adverse*, a giant spectacle with more feet of film, more speaking roles, and more sets than seemed possible or perhaps even desirable. The cast included Fredric March, Olivia de Havilland, Anita Louise, Donald Woods, Edmund Gwenn, Claude Rains, and Louis Hayward. Also in contention was the sweeping *A Tale Of Two Cities* with Ronald Colman; the dizzy screwball comedy *A Libeled Lady* with Myrna Loy, William Powell, Jean Harlow and Spencer Tracy; *Three Smart Girls*, the first feature film of box-office sensation Deanna Durbin; the lavish, all-star *San Francisco* a romanticized vision of the 1906 earthquake that devastated the city; *Romeo And Juiet*, starring Leslie Howard and Norma Shearer, who as usual was rewarded with a Best Actress nomination, and two intelligent films, *Dodsworth* and *Mr Deeds Goes To Town*.

Directed by William Wyler, who received a Best Director nomination for it *Dodsworth* was a mature perceptive interpretation of Sinclair Lewis's novel

Claude Rains in *Anthony Adverse* with Gale Sondergaard, the first winner of the Best Supporting Actress Award.

ABOVE: 'A Pretty Girl Is Like A Melody,' from *The Great Ziegfeld*.
RIGHT: Lionel Stander, Jean Arthur and Gary Cooper in *Mr Deeds Goes To Town*.

about a small-town businessman and his selfish wife. What made the movie outstanding was lead actor Walter Huston's performance which earned him a nomination for Best Actor. *Mr Deeds Goes To Town* is a Depression classic about a young man who is considered crazy because he tries to give away an unexpected inheritance to the poor and needy. Gary Cooper won a Best Actor nomination for his role as the innocent philanthropist who proves his sanity and gets the girl, engagingly portrayed by Jean Arthur. It was a case of perfect casting for Cooper and won director Frank Capra his second Oscar.

William Powell was nominated for Best Actor, not for *Ziegfeld*, but for *My Man Godfrey*, another socially conscious thirties film which also starred one of Hollywood's most beautiful and

talented comediennes, Carole Lombard. She gained a Best Actress nomination for her role as a bored and wacky rich girl brought to heel by the family butler, well played by Powell. One of Hollywood's greatest masters of understated acting, Spencer Tracy, received his first nomination for Best Actor this year, as the priest who met saloon keeper Gable head on in *San Francisco*. The remaining actresses who received Best Actress nominations were Irene Dunne in *Theodora Goes Wild* and Gladys George in *Valiant Is The Word For Carrie*.

Nominees for Best Supporting Actress were a sensational group. They included the exceptionally skillful and ever familiar Beulah Bondi in *The Gorgeous Hussy*; Alice Brady a leading lady in the silent era who became an important featured actress in sound films after a decade away from movies in *My Man Godfrey*; popular child star Bonita Granville in *These Three*, and the Russian actress Maria Ouspenskaya who recreated her stage role of the baroness in the screen version of *Dodsworth*. But the winner was darkly exotic, glamourous Gale Sondergaard for her debut movie role as Faith in *Anthony Adverse*. This epic picture also brought the Cinematography Award to Tony Gaudio; the Film Editing Award to Ralph Dawson, and the Award for Best Music Score to the head of Warner Brothers Studio Music Department, Leo Forbstein. The score was by Erich Wolfgang Korngold, the Czech composer and conductor who wrote many of Hollywood's finest romantic scores.

The nominees for Best Supporting Actor were also well regarded. Russian emigré Mischa Auer played the wild Carlo in *My Man Godfrey*. The eternally awkward boyish-looking Stu Erwin was Judy Garland's corn-ball brother in *Pigskin Parade*. Energetic and expressive Akim Tamiroff, a graduate of the Moscow Art Theater played the Chinese bandit, General Yang, in *The General Died At Dawn*. Basil Rathbone, intelligent and brooding, was Tybalt in *Romeo And Juliet*. The Award went to Walter Brennan who made a career out of playing old men. It was Brennan's first of three Best Supporting Actor Awards and he took this one for the role of Swan Bostrom in *Come And Get It*, based on a novel by Edna Ferber with Frances Farmer.

Nominees for Best Song included Cole Porter's 'I've Got You Under My Skin' from *Born To Dance* and 'Pennies From Heaven' from the movie of the same name. Both lost to 'The Way You Look Tonight' from the irresistable *Swing Time* with Fred Astaire and Ginger Rogers. Busby Berkeley was again nominated for an Oscar, this time for the 'Love And War' number in *Gold Diggers Of 1937*. Nominated, too, was Hermes Pan for the smashing 'Bojan-gles' number from *Swing Time*. The Award went instead to Seymour Felix for 'A Pretty Girl Is Like a Melody' a mind-boggling glitzy production number from *The Great Ziegfeld*.

The first supporting actor award was won by Walter Brennan, with Frances Farmer in *Come And Get It.*

1937

Best Picture: *The Life of Emile Zola.*

Actor: Spencer Tracy, *Captains Courageous.*

Actress: Luise Rainer, *The Good Earth.*

Supporting Actor: Joseph Schildkraut, *The Life Of Emile Zola.*

Supporting Actress: Alice Brady, *In Old Chicago.*

Director: Leo McCarey, *The Awful Truth.*

Writing (Original Story): Robert Carson, William A Wellman, *A Star Is Born.*

Writing (Best Written Screenplay): Norman Reilly Raine, Heinz Herald, Geza Herczeg, *The Life Of Emile Zola.*

Cinematography: Karl Freund, *The Good Earth.*

Art Director: Stephen Goosson, *Lost Horizon.*

Music (Score): Charles Previn, *One Hundred Men And A Girl*, Universal. No composer credit.

Music (Song): Harry Owens (Lyrics and Music), 'Sweet Leilani' from *Waikiki Wedding.*

Dance Director: Hermes Pan, 'Fun House' number from *A Damsel In Distress.*

Short Subjects (Cartoon): *The Old Mill*, Walt Disney.

Short Subjects (Color): *Penny Wisdom.*

Special Awards: The Museum Of Modern Art Film Library for making available to the public the means of studying the development of the motion picture as one of the major arts, collection of films dating from 1895. Mack Sennett for his lasting contribution to the comedy technique of the screen. Edgar Bergen for his outstanding comedy creation, Charlie McCarthy. W Howard Greene, for the color cinematography of *A Star Is Born.*

Janet Gaynor in *A Star Is Born* with Eddie Kane and Bud Flannigan.

The Awful Truth, a picture about a couple toying with divorce, was one of the first film comedies to combine utter lunacy with sophistication and romance. It was nominated for Best Picture. The film's female star, Irene Dunne, was nominated for Best Actress. Cast member Ralph Bellamy was nominated for Best Supporting Actor. Leo McCarey received nominations in both the Directing and Screenplay Writing categories, winning Best Director. The awful truth is that the movie's male lead, Cary Grant, wasn't nominated for Best Actor. Nor would he be nominated for *Holiday* or *Bringing Up Baby* the following year, great pictures co-starring Katharine Hepburn who wouldn't be nominated

either. Rarely did the Academy consider the urbane, charming Grant more than another temporary pretty face.

One superb actor who did receive a nomination, his second in a row, was Spencer Tracy who played Manuel, the Portugese fisherman in *Captains Courageous*, directed by Victor Fleming and based on the novel by Rudyard Kipling. Tracy won the Best Actor Academy Award for his portrayal and the movie was nominated for Best Picture. However, director Fleming did not receive a Best Director nomination.

Among the Best Picture nominations was *Dead End*, with Claire Trevor as Humphrey Bogart's ex-girlfriend turned prostitute. She literally stole the movie with one great scene and received

a Best Supporting Actress nomination. *Lost Horizon*, based on the James Hilton novel about a mysterious Tibetan Utopia was a popular film starring Ronald Colman. It quite literally put Shangri-La on the map. *One Hundred Men And A Girl* had teenager Deanna Durbin fighting to form an orchestra to help unemployed musicians and there were lots of songs along the way. *Stage Door* reworked the old young-actresses-dreaming-of-stardom routine with Katharine Hepburn and Ginger Rogers, among them and it brought a Best Director nomination to Gregory La Cava and a Best Supporting Actress nomination to Andrea Leeds.

Charming Don Ameche, charming Alice Faye, and charming Tyrone Power appeared in *In Old Chicago*. The movie was not only nominated for Best Picture, it won Alice Brady the Best Supporting Actress Award for her role as cow keeper Mrs O'Leary. It also won Assistant Director Robert Webb an Oscar, the last time an award was given in this category.

One of the most enduring movies of the year was *A Star Is Born*. In addition to a Best Picture nomination it brought Fredric March a Best Actor nomination, Janet Gaynor a Best Actress nomination, director William Wellman a Best Director nomination, and Eric Stacey a nomination for Best Assistant Director. Wellman and Robert Carson

RIGHT: Joseph Schildkraut as Captain Dreyfus in *The Life Of Emile Zola*.
BELOW: Shangri-La was the mysterious valley in *Lost Horizon*, with Ronald Colman.

based on Pearl S Buck's novel. Filmed partly on location in China *The Good Earth* brought director Sidney Franklin a nomination and cinematographer Karl Freund an Oscar. Luise Rainer took Best Actress, her second in a row, for her role as O-lan, the patient Chinese woman devoted to her family, facing storms, starvation, and revolution bravely for their sake.

French matinee idol Charles Boyer was nominated for Best Actor for *Conquest*. Nominated, too, was Robert Montgomery in what was perhaps his finest performance as the psychopathic killer in the suspenseful *Night Must Fall*. Dame May Whitty received a Best Supporting Actress nomination for her role as the woman he terrified.

A Best Actress nomination went to Greta Garbo for her role as the dying courtesan in *Camille* with Robert Taylor. Barbara Stanwyck, solid, consistent, and always professional, received her first nomination for Best Actress for *Stella Dallas*, which also brought a Supporting Actress nomination to Anne Shirley. Character actor Thomas Mitchell won a Best Supporting Actor nomination for his role as Dr Kersaint in John Ford's *The Hurricane*. A Best Supporting Actor nomination went, too, to Roland Young as the bumbling, lovable banker haunted by a ghostly pair, Constance Bennett and Cary Grant, in the delicious Hal Roach production, *Topper*.

It was the last chance for Busby Berkeley to win the Dance Direction Award. He didn't. His 'The Finale' number from *Varsity Show* went down to defeat before Hermes Pan's 'Fun House' number from *A Damsel In Distress*. The Award was abolished after this year. *Lost Horizon* was in the running for Best Score as were *Maytime*, *In Old Chicago*, and *The Prisoner Of Zenda*, but *One Hundred Men And A Girl* came in first and the Award went to Universal Studio Music Department head, Charles Previn. Ira and George Gershwin's 'They Can't Take That Away From Me' from *Shall We Dance?* received a nomination but lost, along with several other good songs to the treacly 'Sweet Leilani' from *Waikiki Wedding*.

This was a big year for Special Awards. Director, producer, and

won the Oscar for Writing (Original Story), for *A Star Is Born* and Alan Campbell, Robert Carson, and Dorothy Parker received a Best Screenplay nomination for it. This tale of a rising and a falling star whose marriage goes sour was based on a 1930 film called *What Price Hollywood?* and would be remade by two of Hollywood's biggest names, Judy Garland in 1954, and Barbra Streisand in 1976.

The winning movie was *The Life Of Emile Zola* with Paul Muni crusading this time, not for science as he had as

Louis Pasteur, but for literature and liberty. Muni was nominated for Best Actor for his portrayal of Zola and the film's director, William Dieterle received a Best Director nomination. Joseph Schildkraut won the Best Supporting Actor category for his role as Captain Alfred Dreyfus, a victim of anti-Semitism, falsely accused of treason. The movie brought Best Screenplay Awards to Heinz Herald, Geza Herczeg, and Norman Reilly Raine.

Muni also appeared in *The Good Earth*, an epic movie about China,

entrepreneur Mack Sennett of silent pictures and Keystone Kops days received one, as did ventriloquist Edgar Bergen for dummy Charlie McCarthy. His statuette was made of wood. The Museum Of Modern Art Film Library received a certificate in recognition of its great film collection and W Howard Greene was given an Award for the color photography of *A Star Is Born*. In honor of Irving G Thalberg, the production executive of MGM who died in 1936 at the age of thirty-seven the Academy established a new category, the Irving G Thalberg Memorial Award, given for the most consistent high level of production achievement by an individual producer. This first Award went to Twentieth Century Fox's Darryl F Zanuck.

And if ignoring Cary Grant in *The Awful Truth* was a mistake then consider that Walt Disney's first full-length feature *Snow White And The Seven Dwarfs* received only one nomination, despite its magnificent color, fabulous animation, and wonderful songs. It was nominated for Best Score, which it lost. One year, and bundles of money for Disney later, the movie won a Special Award but strictly as a cartoon. It should have been considered for Best Picture.

Freddie Bartholomew and Spencer Tracy in *Captains Courageous*.

1938

Best Picture: *You Can't Take It With You.*
Actor: Spencer Tracy, *Boys Town.*
Actress: Bette Davis, *Jezebel.*
Supporting Actor: Walter Brennan, *Kentucky.*
Supporting Actress: Fay Bainter, *Jezebel.*
Director: Frank Capra, *You Can't Take It With You.*
Writing (Original Story): Eleanor Griffin and Dore Schary, *Boys Town.*
Writing (Adaptation): W P Lipscomb, Cecil Lewis, Ian Dalrymple, *Pygmalion.*
Writing (Best Written Screenplay): George Bernard Shaw, *Pygmalion.*
Cinematography: Joseph Ruttenberg, *The Great Waltz.*
Art Director: Carl Weyl, *The Adventures Of Robin Hood.*
Music (Score): Alfred Newman, *Alexander's Ragtime Band.*
Music (Original Score): Erich Wolfgang Korngold, *The Adventures Of Robin Hood.*
Music (Song): Leo Robin (Lyrics), Ralph Rainger (Music), 'Thanks For The Memory' from *Big Broadcast Of 1938.*
Short Subjects (Cartoon): *Ferdinand The Bull*, Walt Disney.
Irving G Thalberg Memorial Award: Hal B Wallis.
Special Awards: Deanna Durbin and Mickey Rooney for their significant contribution in bringing to the screen the spirit and personification of youth. Walt Disney, for *Snow White And The Seven Dwarfs*, a significant screen innovation which has charmed millions and pioneered a great new entertainment field for the motion picture cartoon. Oliver Marsh and Allen Davey for the color cinematography of the MGM production, *Sweethearts.*

Uniformity was definitely not the hallmark of this year's awards, with entries running the gamut from light froth to deeply serious and a high proportion of films from across the Atlantic were included in the nominees. Nominated for Best Picture were *The Adventures Of Robin Hood*; *Alexander's Ragtime Band*; *Boys Town*; *The Citadel*; *Four Daughters*; *Grand Illusion*; *Jezebel*; *Pygmalion*; *Test Pilot*, and *You Can't Take It With You.* Of these, *Grand Illusion* ranks as a masterpiece, one of the finest anti-war films ever made, directed by one of the world's greatest film artists, Jean Renoir, son of the Impressionist painter, Auguste Renoir.

On a different scale but flawlessly brilliant was *Pygmalion*, screenplay by the great playwright, George Bernard Shaw, based on his original stage play. Wendy Hiller, nominated for Best Actress, played Eliza perfectly. Leslie Howard, in top form as Henry Higgins received a much deserved best Actor nomination for his performance.

Robert Donat won a Best Actor nomination for *The Citadel* which described a doctor's rise from an impoverished Welsh community to London's Harley Street, with much disillusionment and corruption paving the route. *The Citadel's* director, King Vidor, also received a nomination. The movie that won wasn't in the same league as these pictures yet in its own way it was a real treat. *You Can't Take It With You* based on the stage play by George S Kaufman and Moss Hart offered advice for surviving the Depression leavened with a strong dose of comedy in the tale of a slightly lunatic family that had abandoned the rat race to live happily ever after.

Frank Capra won the Award as Best Director for it, his third in five years. The movie starred Lionel Barrymore, Jean Arthur, James Stewart and Spring Byington, who received a Best Supporting Actress nomination for her performance, as well as Edward Arnold, Mischa Auer, Ann Miller,

Spencer Tracy as Father Flanagan, with Mickey Rooney in *Boys Town.*

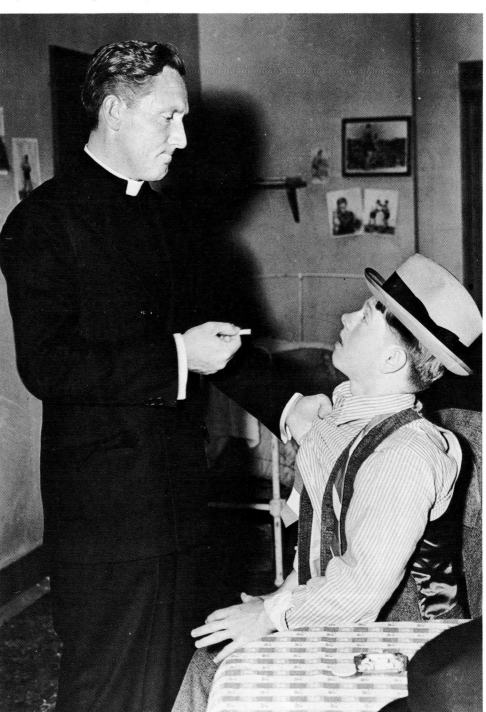

Samuel S Hinds, Donald Meek, H B Warner and Halliwell Hobbes.

The feisty James Cagney received a nomination as Best Actor in *Angels With Dirty Faces*. The film's director Michael Curtiz picked up a nomination as well. A gangster melodrama with a moral the brave Cagney pretended to be a coward as he went to the electric chair so the Dead End Kids wouldn't make a hero out of him. Apparently, his message got through since the Dead End Kids quickly turned to comedy, many later regrouping as the Bowery Boys. Michael Curtiz was also nominated for Best Director for *Four Daughters*, a cheery movie which introduced a handsome, sexy, talented actor who would play meatier roles, John Garfield. He received a Best Supporting Actor nomination for *Four Daughters* which eventually spawned several movies, including *Four Wives*, *Four*

Mothers and *Four Sons*.

Charles Boyer was nominated for Best Actor for *Algiers* though in the movie he didn't actually say 'Come with me to the casbah' to gorgeous Hedy Lamarr. The man who won Best Actor was Spencer Tracy again, this time for his role as Father Flanagan in *Boys Town*, a three-handkerchief-tear-jerker which, though it may have proved that 'there is no such thing as a bad boy,' cannot be said to have proved that there is no such thing as bad judgment at least when it comes to the Academy of Motion Picture Arts and Sciences. Despite Tracy's performance and the nomination of director Norman Taurog for Best Director the movie is distinctly sentimental by modern standards.

Fay Bainter, nominated for Best Actress for *White Banners* lost to Bette Davis who won Best Actress for *Jezebel* but Fay Bainter did win the Best Sup-

Bette Davis as Julie Morrison, with George Brent as Buck Cantrell in *Jezebel*.

porting Actress Oscar for her role in *Jezebel*. This movie about a headstrong belle of the Old South may have been Davis's way of getting a leg up on the role of Scarlett O'Hara, Hollywood's juiciest part. Best Actress nominations also went to Norma Shearer in *Marie Antoinette* and Margaret Sullavan, one of Hollywood's most appealing actresses for *Three Comrades*.

Basil Rathbone in *If I Were King*, Robert Morley in *Marie Antoinette*, Gene Lockhart in *Algiers*, and Walter Brennan in *Kentucky* completed the list of Best Supporting Actor nominees. Brennan won. The remaining nominees for Best Supporting Actress were Beulah Bondi in *Of Human Hearts*, Billie Burke in *Merrily We Live* and Polish opera singer, Miliza Korjus for

from *Going Places*, music by Harry Warren, lyrics by Johnny Mercer and Irving Berlin's 'Change Partners And Dance With Me' from *Carefree*. The winning song was 'Thanks For The Memory' from *Big Broadcast Of 1938*, sung by comic Bob Hope and Shirley Ross. Ralph Rainger wrote the music, Leo Robin wrote the lyrics and Hope made 'Thanks For The Memory' immortal by turning it into his theme song.

By now the Academy was passing out Special Awards by the bushel in recognition of Hollywood's burgeoning achievements in technical areas such as Color Cinematography. A Special Award also went to two young performers. Graceful singer Deanne Durbin and pint-sized all round-dynamite personality Mickey Rooney took home miniature statuettes for 'bringing to the screen the spirit and personification of youth.' Walt Disney was similarly honored. But he got seven miniature Oscars and one full-sized Oscar for his full-length animated masterpiece, *Snow White And The Seven Dwarfs*.

LEFT: *Snow White And The Seven Dwarfs* was the first full length cartoon from the Disney studio.
BELOW: James Stewart and Edward Arnold in *You Can't Take It With You*.

The Great Waltz, the film biography of Johann Strauss. It was Korjus's first and last Hollywood movie.

Thanks to *Pygmalion*, George Bernard Shaw had the Best Screenplay category all locked up. Original Story, however, went to Eleanor Griffin and Dore Schary for *Boys Town*. The splendid swashbuckling romance, *The Adventures Of Robin Hood* starring Errol Flynn, one of the most delightful movies of its kind ever made won several production awards and the Alice Faye, Don Ameche, Tyrone Power, Ethel Merman, Jack Haley musical *Alexander's Ragtime Band* beat all comers in the Best Score category. The popular Gary Cooper-Merle Oberon comedy *The Cowboy And The Lady* won the Sound Recording category but lost out for the Best Song.

The song 'The Cowboy And The Lady,' with music by Lionel Newman, lyrics by Arthur Quenzer was joined in defeat by such hits as 'Jeepers Creepers'

1939

Best Picture: *Gone With The Wind.*
Actor: Robert Donat, *Goodbye, Mr. Chips.*
Actress: Vivien Leigh, *Gone With The Wind*
Supporting Actor: Thomas Mitchell, *Stagecoach.*
Supporting Actress: Hattie McDaniel, *Gone With The Wind.*
Director: Victor Fleming, *Gone With The Wind.*
Writing (Original Story): Lewis R Foster, *Mr Smith Goes To Washington.*
Writing (Best Written Screenplay): Sidney Howard, *Gone With The Wind.*
Cinematography (Black and White): Greg Toland, *Wuthering Heights.*
Cinematography (Color): Ernest Haller, Ray Rennahan, *Gone With The Wind.*
Art Director: Lyle Wheeler, *Gone With The Wind.*
Special Effects: *The Rains Came.*
Music (Score): Richard Hageman, Franke Harling, John Leipold, Leo Shuken, *Stagecoach.*

Music (Original Score): Herbert Stothart, *The Wizard Of Oz.*
Music (Song): E Y Harburg (Lyrics), Harold Arlen (Music), 'Over The Rainbow' from *The Wizard Of Oz.*
Short Subjects (Cartoon): *The Ugly Duckling*, Walt Disney.
Irving G Thalberg Memorial Award: David O Selznick.
Special Awards: Douglas Fairbanks (Commemorative Award), recognizing the unique and outstanding contribution of this first President of the Academy to the international development of the motion picture. Motion Picture Relief Fund, acknowledging outstanding service to the industry, presented by Jean Hersholt. Judy Garland for her outstanding performance as a screen juvenile during the past year (Miniature Statuette). William Cameron Menzies for use of color for the enhancement of dramatic mood in *Gone With The Wind.* Technicolor Company for contributions in successfully bringing three-color feature production to the screen.

There has never been a better year for movies than 1939. In addition to its other claims to glory it was the first year that comedian Bob Hope emceed a portion of an Academy Awards Ceremony. The majority of films nominated for Best Picture are unforgettable, needing no introduction. They were: *Dark Victory*; *Goodbye, Mr Chips*; *Ninotchka*; *Of Mice And Men*; *Stagecoach*; *The Wizard Of Oz*, and *Wuthering Heights*. Not in the top class but still solid Best Picture nominations were *Love Affair*, starring Irene Dunne and Charles Boyer and *Mr Smith Goes to Washington.*

The title of *Love Affair* tells all.

Vivien Leigh as Scarlett O'Hara leaves the Tarleton twins (George Reeves and Fred Crane) on the steps of Tara in the opening moments of *Gone With The Wind.*

Hattie McDaniel (Best Supporting Actress) joins Clark Gable for a celebratory drink in *Gone With The Wind.*

Dunne and Boyer meet, love and part with élan and style. *Mr Smith Goes To Washington*, directed by Frank Capra, put James Stewart in the first rank of movie stars. The film bears a strong resemblance to Capra's 1936 Academy Award winner *Mr Deeds Goes To Town*, starring Gary Cooper. This time it was Stewart who played the innocent idealist, a young senator fresh from Wisconsin who took on corrupt fellow senator, Claude Rains.

To show just how good 1939 was the following movies received nominations in various categories but never made it to Best Picture: *Beau Geste* starring Gary Cooper and Brian Donlevy; *The Hunchback Of Notre Dame* starring Charles Laughton; *The Private Lives Of Elizabeth And Essex*, in color with Bette Davis and Errol Flynn; *Golden Boy* with Lee J Cobb and introducing William Holden; *Intermezzo* which introduced a beautiful young Swedish actress, Ingrid Bergman, and *Young Mr Lincoln*, an example of pure Americana, with an excellent performance by Henry Fonda. Not nominated at all was

the best of the Basil Rathbone/Nigel Bruce Sherlock Holmes films, *The Hound Of The Baskervilles*; Claudette Colbert's charming *Midnight* with Don Ameche, and the immortal *Gunga Din*, starring Douglas Fairbanks, Jr, Cary Grant, and Victor McLaglen.

The sweeping romance *Gone With The Wind* swept up most of the Awards including Best Picture, earning a total of nine regular Oscars and two special citations. The movie, based on the Margaret Mitchell novel of the Civil War and its aftermath in Georgia, was an extraordinary much-heralded cinema event. At the New York City opening hundreds of police were needed to control the crowd and in Atlanta, Mitchell's hometown, the movie was the stuff of instant legend. Even today Atlanta tour bus drivers still talk of *Gone With The Wind.*

The search for the actress who would play the movie's heroine, the beautiful, spoiled, but determined and fascinating Scarlett O'Hara, literally turned Hollywood upside down. In the end the role went to British actress Vivien Leigh who played Scarlett perfectly. Impressive, too, was Clark Gable as Rhett Butler, the dashing adventurer and hero. An outstanding cast helped make

Gone With The Wind a spectacular triumph.

If there is one dark side to the brightness of *Gone With The Wind* it's the film's total domination of the Awards Ceremony. Only rarely did the colorful epic lose out as in the Best Actor category when Robert Donat took the Award for his sensitive portrayal of the gentle Mr Chips, beating out Clark Gable. Donat was superb as Chips, aging on screen from twenty-five to eighty-three. But for most nominees it was no contest and that raises some questions. For instance, even though Leigh was lovely as Scarlett was Davis not dazzling as Judith Traherne, the doomed but inspiring heroine of *Dark Victory?* Marvelous, too, was Greta Garbo in *Ninotchka*, a departure into comedy for Hollywood's greatest star and possibly the best picture she ever made. Director Ernst Lubitsch didn't even receive a nomination for it though the sparkle and glamor of *Ninotchka* reveal 'the Lubitsch touch,' at its most assured.

Is *Gone With The Wind* a better movie than *The Wizard Of Oz*, the wonderful fantasy based on the book by L Frank Baum and didn't Judy Garland deserve a Best Actress nomination for her role as Dorothy? Deserving of nominations, too, were Scarecrow Ray Bolger, the Tin Man Jack Haley, Wicked Witch Margaret Hamilton and Cowardly Lion Bert Lahr, especially. Director Vincent Fleming did win the Best Director Oscar but for *Gone With The Wind* though so many directors worked on that film no one director could really take credit for it.

Fleming's win denied John Ford an Oscar for directing *Stagecoach*, virtually the prototype of the serious, mature western. *Stagecoach* rescued a dying genre, propelled John Wayne into stardom and did a lot for the career of a very fine actress, Claire Trevor. As a romance, is *Gone With The Wind* better than *Wuthering Heights*, a haunting and brooding film with Laurence Olivier at his most handsome as Heathcliff and Merle Oberon at her most beautiful as Cathy? Based on Emily Bronte's novel of love and vengeance on the Yorkshire moors the movie *Wuthering Heights* was so popular, the name Heathcliff became a household word from Maine to California. Filmed in luminous black and white it was a stunning example of the kind of lyrical romantic picture which would flourish during the following decade.

Davis in *Dark Victory*; Dunne in *Love Affair*; Garbo in *Ninotchka*; Irish-born actress Greer Garson for her brief role as Mrs Chips in her debut film, *Goodbye, Mr. Chips*, and Vivien Leigh, the winner for *Gone With The Wind*. The Best Supporting Actor nominees were British actor Brian Aherne in *Juarez*; ex-silent film western star Harry Carey for his role as Senate president in *Mr Smith Goes To Washington*; Brian Donlevy for his portrayal of the sadistic sergeant in *Beau Geste*; Claude Rains in *Mr Smith Goes To Washington*, and Thomas Mitchell for the part of Doc Boone, the tipsy doctor in *Stagecoach*. Mitchell, who also played Scarlett's father in *Gone With The Wind*, won.

Nominess for Best Supporting Actress were Olivia de Havilland as the gentle but strong as steel Melanie in *Gone With The Wind*; Geraldine Fitzgerald as Isabel Linton in *Wuthering Heights*; Edna May Oliver as the pioneer widow, Mrs McClennan in *Drums*

ABOVE: George Bancroft and John Wayne give Best Supporting Actor Thomas Mitchell a cup of coffee in *Stagecoach*.
RIGHT: Robert Donat with Terry Kilburn in *Goodbye Mr Chips*.

1939 was the only year horror film star Lon Chaney, Jr stood a chance of being nominated for an Oscar thanks to his moving portrayal of Lennie in *Of Mice And Men* from the John Steinbeck novel. Had there been less competition he might have made it. But who can blame the Academy for failing to satisfy everyone in a year when there was an embarrassment of riches on screen.

The Best Actor category alone shows why it was a tough time to make choices. Besides winner Donat in *Goodbye, Mr. Chips*; Gable in *Gone With The Wind*; Stewart, the Mr Smith of *Mr Smith Goes To Washington*, and Olivier in *Wuthering Heights*; Mickey Rooney received a Best Actor nomination for his performance in *Babes In Arms*. Directed by Busby Berkeley *Babes In Arms* was an important musical, representing the first pairing of Mickey Rooney and Judy Garland. The movie established Judy as a star as surely as *The Wizard Of Oz* did.

The Best Actress nominees were

Dorothy (Judy Garland), The Scarecrow (Ray Bolger), The Cowardly Lion (Bert Lahr) and The Tin Woodman (Jack Haley), in *The Wizard Of Oz.*

Along The Mohawk; Maria Ouspenskaya in *Love Affair*, and winner Hattie McDaniel for her role as Mammy in *Gone With The Wind*, the first black actress to win an Oscar. Best Director nominees were Frank Capra for *Mr Smith Goes To Washington*; John Ford for *Stagecoach*; Sam Wood for *Goodbye, Mr. Chips*; William Wyler for *Wuthering Heights*, and winner Victor Fleming for *Gone With The Wind*.

The Wizard Of Oz had to wait for Original Score to score and Harold Arlen and E Y Harburg won the Best Song category for 'Over The Rainbow.' However, the choice of *The Rains Came*, based on Louis Bromfield's novel of British India, starring Myrna Loy and Tyrone Power, over *The Wizard of Oz* in the newly created Special Effects category seems ludicrous if not downright criminal. Also losing to *The Rains Came* for Special Effects were *Gone With The Wind*, *Topper Takes A Trip* (the sequel to *Topper* and big on camera trickery), *The Private Lives of Elizabeth And Essex*, *Union Pacific* and *Only Angels Have Wings* which rescued Rita Hayworth from the 'B' pictures which seemed to be her fate at that moment.

There were only two nominees in the Black and White Cinematography category, *Wuthering Heights* and *Stagecoach* with its magnificent locale of Utah's Monument Valley, destined to be used again and again by John Ford in future movies. Though *Wuthering Heights* won this was a time they could have given out two Oscars and called it a tie. 1939 saw the release of a charming full-length feature cartoon from Walt Disney's chief rivals, Max and Dave Fleischer, called *Gulliver's Travels*. The movie should have won recognition from the Academy but didn't.

A Commemorative Award went to Douglas Fairbanks, first President of the Academy. Judy Garland, the kid with the grown-up sized talent who would become one of Hollywood's most widely loved stars, and ultimately one of its tragic victims also won a Special Award. A Special Award went, too, to the Motion Picture Relief Fund and to its founder Jean Hersholt. The Irving G Thalberg Memorial Award went, and justly so, to David O Selznick, the wizard behind *Gone With The Wind*.

1940

Best Picture: *Rebecca*.
Actor: James Stewart, *The Philadelphia Story*.
Actress: Ginger Rogers, *Kitty Foyle*.
Supporting Actor: Walter Brennan, *The Westerner*.
Supporting Actress: Jane Darwell, *The Grapes Of Wrath*.
Director: John Ford, *The Grapes Of Wrath*.
Writing (Original Story): Benjamin Glazer and John S Toldy, *Arise, My Love*.
Writing (Original Screenplay): Preston Sturges, *The Great McGinty*.
Writing (Best Written Screenplay): Donald Ogden Stewart, *The Philadelphia Story*.
Cinematography (Black And White): George Barnes, *Rebecca*.
Cinematography (Color): George Perrinal, *The Thief Of Bagdad*.
Art Director (Black And White): Cedric Gibbons, Paul Groesse, *Pride And Prejudice*.
Art Director (Color): Vincent Korda, *The Thief Of Bagdad*.
Sound Recording: Douglas Shearer, *Strike Up The Band*.
Special Effects: Lawrence Butler (Photographic), Jack Whitney (Sound), *The Thief Of Bagdad*.
Music (Best Score): Alfred Newman, *Tin Pan Alley*.
Music (Original Score): Leigh Harline, Paul J Smith, Ned Washington, *Pinocchio*, Walt Disney.
Music (Song): Ned Washington (Lyrics), Leigh Harline (Music), 'When You Wish Upon A Star' from *Pinocchio*.
Short Subjects (Cartoon): *The Milky Way*, M-G-M.
Short Subjects (2-Reel): *Teddy, The Rough Rider*.
Special Awards: Bob Hope, in recognition of his unselfish services to the Motion Picture Industry. Colonel Nathan Levinson, for making possible the efficient mobilization of the Motion Picture Industry facilities for the production of Army training films.

What could producer David O Selznick do to equal his 1939 triumph *Gone With The Wind*? Probably nothing but he came close by giving the world *Rebecca*, a glamorous movie filled with romance, suspense, and psychological drama which won the Oscar for Best Picture. Based on the best-selling novel by Daphne du Maurier, *Rebecca* was a historic first. It marked the American

debut of British director Alfred Hitchcock who had already achieved greatness with *The Man Who Knew Too Much* (1934), *The Thirty-Nine Steps* (1935) and *The Lady Vanishes* (1938).

Rebecca brought Hitchcock a nomination for Best Director but on the whole he did not fare well with the Academy. Like Ernst Lubitsch, Hitchcock was viewed by many as a creator of escapist stuff, light entertainment, too lacking in substance to be worthy of an Academy Award. Today Hitchcock is seen differently, widely recognized as one of the most technically innovative, influential, and exciting directors in the history of film. Add to that list, unpretentious. Totally lacking in self-indulgence Hitchcock kept his eye on the audience. If they squirmed it was from tension not boredom.

Up against *Rebecca* for Best Picture were *All This, And Heaven Too* with Bette Davis and Charles Boyer, about a governess in love with the master of the house; *Foreign Correspondent*, a thriller also directed by Hitchcock; *The Grapes Of Wrath* based on John Steinbeck's novel about the migration of poor farmers from the Dust Bowl during the Depression, compellingly directed by John Ford; *The Great Dictator*, Charles Chaplin's scathing satire on Adolf Hitler and the Nazis, and *Kitty Foyle*, with Ginger Rogers as a long-suffering Irish girl whose love life did not run smoothly.

Also in the running were *The Letter*,

Macaulay Connor (James Stewart) brings Tracy Lord (Katharine Hepburn) back from a midnight swim in *The Philadelphia Story*.

for *Kitty Foyle*. It is a pity she and Astaire never won Oscars for their musicals.

The Best Supporting Actor category gave Jack Oakie a shot at an Award for his hilarious performance as the Mussolini-like character, Benzini Napolini. But Walter Brennan won his third Award for his role as Judge Roy Bean in *The Westerner*. Judith Anderson was magnificent as the malignant Mrs Danvers, the housekeeper of Manderley, madly loyal to the memory of the dead Rebecca. Though Anderson was nominated for *Rebecca* she lost to Jane Darwell, outstanding as Ma Joad in *The Grapes Of Wrath*.

In addition to Hitchcock the other nominations for Best Director included George Cukor for *The Phladelphia Story*. Nominated, too, were John Ford for his stark yet compassionate direction of *The Grapes Of Wrath*, a film which turned downtrodden wanderers into heroes and symbols of endurance; Sam Wood for *Kitty Foyle*, and William Wyler for *The Letter*. John Ford won.

The Great McGinty, a great irreverent spoof that poked fun at American politics, starring Brian Donlevy and Akim Tamiroff, should have been festooned with nominations but wasn't. Still the controversial film turned out to be a huge success and writer/director Preston Sturges won the Writing (Original Screenplay) Award for it. The following

LEFT: Best Supporting Actress Jane Darwell as Ma Joad in *The Grapes Of Wrath*.
BELOW: Mrs Danvers (Judith Anderson) and the second Mrs de Winter (Joan Fontaine) in *Rebecca*.

with Bette Davis at her best being calculating, hypocritical, and self-protective in the steamy tropics of Somerset Maugham; *The Long Voyage Home*, adapted from four one-act plays by Eugene O'Neill, with John Wayne, directed by John Ford; the simple and moving *Our Town*, based on the play by Thornton Wilder starring William Holden as George and Martha Scott repeating her Broadway role as Emily, and the sophisticated *The Philadelphia Story* with Katharine Hepburn as society girl Tracy Lord, costarring with James Stewart and Cary Grant.

Among the Best Actor nominees was Charles Chaplin in *The Great Dictator*. Chaplin played two roles in the film, a gentle Jewish barber and Adenoid Hynkel, dictator of Tomania. Chaplin's portrayal of Hynkel was more than a simple parody. It was a work of art. Henry Fonda, generally neglected by the Academy, was nominated for Best Actor for his role as Tom Joad in *Grapes Of Wrath*. Nominated, too, was Raymond Massey who played the title role in *Abe Lincoln In Illinois*, and Laurence Olivier for his portrayal of the tortured Max de Winter in *Rebecca*. Though it's hard to believe, Chaplin didn't win. The Award went instead to James Stewart, for his role as Macaulay Connor in *The Philadelphia Story*.

Not surprisingly Bette Davis was nominated for Best Actress in *The Letter*. Joan Fontaine was also nominated for her role as Olivier's timid young wife in *Rebecca*. Katharine Hepburn was nominated for *The Philadelphia Story*, Martha Scott for *Our Town*, and the winner Ginger Rogers

year Sturges made an even better film, *Sullivan's Travels* which received no nominations.

George Barnes won the Cinematography (Black And White) Award for *Rebecca* with its haunting images of the great house and the sea, demolishing competition like *Boom Town*, starring Clark Gable, Spencer Tracy, and Claudette Colbert. Among the films nominated for Cinematography (Color) was *Down Argentine Way* which made a star out of starlet Betty Grable but the Award went to the gorgeous Arabian Nights fantasy, *The Thief Of Bagdad* which glowed with magical special effects. The movie boasted impish star Sabu, a former stable boy from the court of an Indian Maharajah. The picture also took the Art Direction (Color) Award and the Award for Special Effects. The movie is still a joy to see. Up against it for Special Effects was a wide range of films including the Richard Rodgers, Lorenz Hart musical, *The Boys From Syracuse*; *One Million BC* with Victor Mature, Carol

Landis and so-called dinosaurs; *Swiss Family Robinson*; *Typhoon*; *The Invisible Man Returns*, and Errol Flynn's swashbuckling pirate film, *The Sea Hawk*.

The Art Direction (Black And White) Award went to *Pride And Prejudice*, an elegant romance, based on Jane Austen's novel, script by Aldous Huxley, starring Greer Garson and Laurence Olivier. In competition was the comedy/drama *Arise, My Love*, with Claudette Colbert and Ray Milland. This movie, an early attempt to get the American public to wake up and face the reality of World War II received nominations in several categories and won for Best Writing (Original Story). Also in the running for Art Direction were the melodrama *My Son, My Son*; *Lillian Russell*; *My Favorite Wife* with Cary Grant and Irene Dunne, and *Arizona*. This year's classic unnominated gem was *The Bank Dick*, W C Field's comedy.

Walt Disney's *Pinocchio* won the Award for Best Original Score and its

Gary Cooper as Cole Hardin and Best Supporting Actor Walter Brennan as Judge Roy Bean in *The Westerner*.

charming 'When You Wish Upon A Star' won Best Song. However, for the first time since the 1931/32 Awards Disney did not win the cartoon category. M-G-M's *Milky Way* (Rudolph Ising Series) did. *Teddy, The Rough Rider*, one of the many historical featurettes of the era, took the Best 2-Reel Short Subject category. Special Awards went to Bob Hope for his unselfish services to the Motion Picture Industry, and to Colonel Nathan Levinson for making possible the efficient mobilization of the Industry facilities for the production of Army Training Films. Pearl Harbor was still many months away on the night of 27 February 1941 when the banquet dispensed with an emcee and instead was addressed by President Franklin Delano Roosevelt, via radio. But the spirit of World War II was in the air and by 1942 would permeate Hollywood movies.

1941

Best Picture: *How Green Was My Valley.*
Actor: Gary Cooper, *Sergeant York.*
Actress: Joan Fontaine, *Suspicion.*
Supporting Actor: Donald Crisp, *How Green Was My Valley.*
Supporting Actress: Mary Astor, *The Great Lie.*
Director: John Ford, *How Green Was My Valley.*
Writing (Original Story): Harry Segall, *Here Comes Mr Jordan.*
Writing (Original Screenplay): Herman J Mankiewicz, Orson Welles, *Citizen Kane.*
Writing (Best Written Screenplay): Sidney Buchman, Seton I Miller, *Here Comes Mr Jordan.*
Cinematography (Black And White): Arthur C Miller, *How Green Was My Valley.*
Cinematography (Color): Ernest Palmer, Ray Rennahan, *Blood And Sand.*
Art Director (Black And White): Richard Day and Nathan Juran, *How Green Was My Valley.*
Art Director (Color): Cedric Gibbons, Urie McCleary, *Blossoms In The Dust.*
Sound Recording: Jack Whitney, *That Hamilton Woman.*
Special Effects: Farciot Edouart and Gordon Jennings (Photographic), Louis Mesenkop (Sound), *I Wanted Wings.*
Music (Scoring Dramatic Picture): Bernard Hermann, *All That Money Can Buy.*
Music (Scoring Musical Picture): Frank Churchill and Oliver Wallace, *Dumbo.*
Music (Song): Oscar Hammerstein II (Lyrics) and Jerome Kern (Music), 'The Last Time I Saw Paris' from *Lady Be Good.*
Short Subjects (Cartoon): *Lend A Paw,* Walt Disney.
Documentary (New Category): *Churchill's Island.*
Irving G Thalberg Memorial Award: Walt Disney.
Special Awards: Rey Scott, for his extraordinary achievement in producing *Kuhan*, the film record of China's struggle, under the most difficult and dangerous conditions. The British Ministry of Information for its vivid and dramatic presentation of the heroism of the RAF in the documentary film, *Target For Tonight.* Leopold Stokowski and his associates for their unique achievement in the creation of a new form of visualized music in Walt Disney's production of *Fantasia.* Walt Disney and the RCA Manufacturing Company for their contribution to the advancement of sound in motion pictures through the production of *Fantasia.*

This was the year of *Citizen Kane*, the remarkable and original creation of a remarkable and original talent, Orson Welles. And shame on the Academy since *Citizen Kane* should have captured most of the Awards, yet received only one. *Citizen Kane*, according to Welles 'a portrait of a public man's private life' was based on newspaper magnate William Randolph Hearst. It was Welles's first film and he made it on a shoestring. RKO Radio allowed him total artistic control and he not only played the title role but produced and directed the film as well and was involved in its creation at every level.

In 1941 Welles was the 'boy wonder' of Hollywood and *Citizen Kane* proved a critical though not a commercial success. Today many critics consider it the finest movie ever made and it is certainly one of the most famous. This inspired masterpiece broke all the conventional rules of movie-making. There were few close-ups, whole scenes were played with the actors' faces in shadow, and lighting was used to heighten drama rather than illuminate performers. The entire structure of the movie with its bold newsreel 'March Of Time' style and frequent flashbacks was innovative. Even the sound track was creatively used and the casting from Welles's Mercury Theater Company was flawless. At least the film picked up many nominations.

Another great movie released in 1941 was *The Maltese Falcon*, based on Dashiell Hammett's suspense story involving detective Sam Spade. It represented the directing debut of John Huston, who also wrote the script, and the screen debut of Sydney Greenstreet. The matchless trio of Humphrey Bogart, Greenstreet and Peter Lorre was so good it's hard to see why, if the Academy was going to bypass *Citizen Kane*, it didn't offer a few awards to *The Maltese Falcon*. Greenstreet at least was given a Best Supporting Actor nomination and the movie was also nominated for Best Picture. But Huston wasn't even nominated for Best Director, only for Screenplay, and Bogart and Lorre weren't nominated at all. The Academy would eventually give Bogart his due but Lorre was never nominated for an Award, an absolutely myopic blunder.

Also nominated for Best Picture was *Blossoms In The Dust* with Greer Garson

Charles Foster Kane (Orson Welles) and Jed Leland (Joseph Cotton) with an early run of The New York Inquirer in *Citizen Kane*.

Grant in the sentimental but exquisitely done series of vignettes entitled *Penny Serenade*; Walter Huston, brilliant as the Devil in *All That Money Can Buy*, and the winner, Gary Cooper in *Sergeant York*. It was Cooper's first Academy Award.

Bette Davis was nominated for Best Actress in *The Little Foxes*; Olivia de Havilland in *Hold Back The Dawn*, and Olivia's sister Joan Fontaine in *Suspicion*. De Havilland's and Fontaine's fierce rivalry, either real or publicity inspired, added juice to this particular competition. Greer Garson was nominated for *Blossoms In The Dust* as was Barbara Stanwyck for her delightful

LEFT: Best Actor Gary Cooper in *Sergeant York* with Margaret Wycherly as his mother.
BELOW: Mickey Mouse as 'The Sorcerer's Apprentice' in *Fantasia*.

and Walter Pidgeon and the superb *Here Comes Mr Jordan* with Robert Montgomery and Claude Rains, the story of a boxer who dies because of a heavenly screw-up and returns to earth, winding up in somebody else's body with many weird and hilarious results. The picture was remade in 1978 as *Heaven Can Wait* starring Warren Beatty. *Hold Back The Dawn*, starred Olivia de Havilland and Charles Boyer. He was a suave refugee looking for a US passport, not love and she was the shy schoolteacher he manipulated into marriage but discovered he loved.

Bette Davis starred in Lillian Hellman's *The Little Foxes* about a greedy Southern family after the Civil War grasping for all they could get. *Sergeant York* was Gary Cooper at his best as a pacifist country boy who became a hero in World War I. *Suspicion*, directed by Albert Hitchcock and starring Joan Fontaine and Cary Grant, was based on a mystery novel by Francis Iles. The movie was hurt badly by a studio imposed ending which knocked a hole in the plot as wide as the Grand Canyon just to keep Cary Grant from playing a villian. Also nominated for Best Picture was *One Foot In Heaven*, *Citizen Kane* and the winning film, *How Green Was My Valley*, based on Richard Llewellyn's novel, a powerfully moving evocation of life in a Welsh mining village starring a very young but very talented Roddy McDowall. Director John Ford won the Oscar for it.

Nominated for Best Actor was Orson Welles for *Citizen Kane*; Robert Montgomery in *Here Comes Mr Jordan*; Cary

The Welsh coal mining village in *How Green Was My Valley*.

performance in *Ball of Fire* as a show-girl chewing gum and making eyes at a meek professor played by Gary Cooper. Stanwyck was also outstanding that year in *Lady Eve*. Fontaine won, probably as a consolation for not winning the year before in *Rebecca*.

Donald Crisp won Best Supporting Actor for his role as Mr Morgan the father in *How Green Was My Valley* making losers not only of Greenstreet, but of Walter Brennan in *Sergeant York*, Charles Coburn as the millionaire masquerading as a clerk in *The Devil And Miss Jones* and flinty James Gleason in *Here Comes Mr Jordan*. Best Supporting Actress nominees were Sara Allgood as the mother in *How Green Was My Valley*, Patricia Collinge who recreated her stage role as the frightened Aunt Birdie Hubbard in *The Little Foxes*, Teresa Wright for her debut performance in *The Little Foxes*, and Margaret Wycherley in *Sergeant York*. Mary Astor won Best Supporting Actress for her portrayal of a sharp-tongued woman with style in the Bette Davis vehicle, *The Great Lie*. Astor stole the picture from Davis but is best remembered as the treacherous Brigid O'Shaughnessy in *The Maltese Falcon*.

Rouben Mamoulian's visually gorgeous *Blood And Sand*, starring Tyrone Power, Linda Darnell and Rita Hayworth took the Cinematography (Color) Award. 'The Last Time I Saw Paris' from *Lady Be Good*, won Best Song over stiff competition like 'Blues In The Night' from *Blues In The Night*, 'Boogie Woogie Bugle Boy Of Company B' from Abbott and Costello's *Buck Privates*, and 'Chattanooga Choo Choo' from *Sun Valley Serenade*. *Churchill's Island* won the new Documentary category over several nominees including the British Ministry of Information's *Christmas Under Fire* and *Letter From Home*, but the British Ministry of Information won a Special Award for *Target For Tonight*. *The Sea Wolf*, with an outstanding performance by Edward G Robinson, *That Hamilton Woman*, and *A Yank In The RAF* were nominees in the Special Effects category, but the winner was *I Wanted Wings*.

Walt Disney's *Fantasia* was honored only in the Special Awards category. *Dumbo*, the world's favorite elephant movie won an Oscar for the Scoring Of A Musical Picture in the Music category. One of the most competitive categories this year was Black And White Cinematography which among other pictures included *Sundown*, *The Chocolate Soldier*, and the fine Spencer Tracy/Ingrid Bergman version of *Dr Jekyll And Mr Hyde*. Nominated in this category as in so many others was *Citizen Kane*, thanks to cinematographer Gregg Toland's brilliant work but the winner was *How Green Was My Valley*.

Worthy of mention, too, was *Citizen Kane's* nomination in the Art Direction (Black And White) category in appreciation of gifted Art Directors Perry Ferguson and Van Nest Polglase, and in the Sound Recording category in honor of John Aalberg's extraordinary sound achievement. Herman J Mankiewicz only received credit as co-author of the screenplay for *Citizen Kane* after the Writers Guild forced Welles into it and that was the only Award *Citizen Kane* won.

1942

Best Picture: *Mrs Miniver.*

Actor: James Cagney, *Yankee Doodle Dandy.*

Actress: Greer Garson, *Mrs Miniver.*

Supporting Actor: Van Heflin, *Johnny Eager.*

Supporting Actress: Teresa Wright, *Mrs Miniver.*

Director: William Wyler, *Mrs Miniver.*

Writing (Original Story): Emeric Pressburger, *The Invaders.*

Writing (Original Screenplay): Ring Lardner, Jr and Michael Kanin, *Woman Of The Year.*

Writing (Best Written Screenplay): Arthur Wimperis, George Froeschel, James Hilton, and Claudine West, *Mrs Miniver.*

Cinematography (Black And White): Joseph Ruttenberg, *Mrs Miniver.*

Cinematography (Color): Leon Shamroy, *The Black Swan.*

Art Director (Black And White): Richard Day and Joseph Wright, *This Above All.*

Art Director (Color): Richard Day and Joseph Wright, *My Gal Sal.*

Special Effects: Gordon Jennings, Farciot Edouart, William L Pereira (Photographic), Louis Mesenkop (Sound), *Reap The Wild Wind.*

Music (Scoring Dramatic Or Comedy Picture): Max Steiner, *Now Voyager.*

Music (Scoring Musical Picture): Ray Heindorf and Heinz Roemheld, *Yankee Doodle Dandy.*

Music (Song): Irving Berlin (Lyrics And Music), 'White Christmas' from *Holiday Inn.*

Short Subjects (Cartoon): *Der Fuehrer's Face*, Walt Disney.

Documentary (Short Subject): *Kokoda Front Line, Battle Of Midway,* and *Moscow Strikes Back.*

Documentary (Feature Length): *Prelude To War.*

Irving G Thalberg Memorial Award: Sidney Franklin.

Special Awards: Charles Boyer for his progressive cultural achievement in establishing the French Research Foundation in Los Angeles. Noel Coward for his outstanding production achievement *In Which We Serve.* MGM for its achievement in representing the American Way Of Life in the production of the 'Andy Hardy' series of films.

Greer Garson comforts the wounded Teresa Wright, her daughter-in-law in *Mrs Miniver.*

Mrs Miniver was a war movie but not about men in battle. It told the story of a British family going bravely about the business of life in the midst of World War II. The movie was a box office smash in America which entered the War while the movie was in production. Since the American people felt a special kinship with the British *Mrs Miniver* was more than just another movie. Greer Garson played the title role with grace and strength and whether she was tending the roses, capturing a German parachutist played by Helmut Dantine in the garden, or quietly reading to the children during the Blitz she was an inspirational example of muted heroism for American audiences minding the 'home front.'

The movie was voted Best Picture and Greer Garson won the Award as Best Actress for the title role. Walter Pidgeon who played her husband received a best Actor nomination. Teresa Wright had the rare dual distinction of being nominated for Best Actress in *The Pride Of The Yankees* and Best Supporting Actress in *Mrs Miniver.* She won the latter Award over, among others, Gladys Cooper in *Now, Voyager,* Susan Peters in *Random Harvest,* and Dame May Whitty, also nominated for *Mrs Miniver.* William Wyler won the Best Director Award for *Mrs Miniver,* and the movie brought the Best Written Screenplay Award to a quartet of writers including James Hilton who was primarily known for his novels *Lost Horizon, Goodbye Mr Chips,* and *Random Harvest* which were all

turned into fine films. *Mrs Miniver* also won Joseph Ruttenberg the Cinematography (Black And White) Oscar.

The Magnificent Ambersons, Orson Welles's flawed masterpiece (it was badly butchered by the studio) was nominated for Best Picture and brought Agnes Moorehead a Supporting Actress nomination for her magnificent portrayal of the repressed and sometimes hysterical spinster, Fanny Minifer. *The Pride Of The Yankees,* possibly the best sports movie ever made, starred Gary Cooper as Lou Gehrig, the great baseball player who had died the previous year. Cooper was nominated for Best Actor and the movie for Best Picture. James Cagney was charisma personified as the versatile, musical, and colorful George M Cohan in *Yankee Doodle Dandy* with Walter Huston and Joan Leslie. Though the movie lost Best Picture Huston's performance won him a Best Supporting Actor nomination. Cagney won the Best Actor Award, and Michael Curtiz picked up a Best Director nomination for the film.

Ronald Colman, a tender, romantic, elegant film idol since the silent era played the amnesiac who married Greer Garson twice without realizing it in *Random Harvest* and made the implausible plot work. Colman was nominated for Best Actor, *Random Harvest* for Best Picture, director Mervyn LeRoy, Best Director. Colman was also in another Best Picture nominee, *The Talk Of The Town* with Cary Grant and Jean Arthur. The remaining movies nominated for Best Picture were an action war film

James Cagney as George M Cohan in a number from 'Little Johnny Jones' in *Yankee Doodle Dandy.*

Wake Island which brought director John Farrow a Best Director nomination; the British film *The Invaders*; the excellent drama *Kings Row*, directed by Sam Wood who was also nominated for Best Director, and *The Pied Piper* starring Monty Wooley who was nominated for Best Actor.

Bette Davis was nominated for Best Actress for *Now, Voyager*, the movie in which she uttered the immortal words, 'Don't let's ask for the moon – we have the stars.' Katharine Hepburn was up for Best Actress in *Woman Of The Year*, the first of the great Hepburn/Tracy pairings. She and Spencer Tracy played journalists on the edge of divorce and the movie was an urbane delight. Also delightful was Rosalind Russell as the brainy sister in *My Sister Eileen*, based on the Broadway hit, which earned her a Best Actress nomination.

Frank Morgan, often underrated as a serious actor, won a Best Supporting Actor nomination for his role as 'The Pirate' in *Tortilla Flat*. Henry Travers was nominated for Best Supporting Actor for his portrayal of the rose-growing station master in *Mrs Miniver*. Nominated, too, was William Bendix, a tough marine in *Wake Island*. But the winner was Van Heflin, the cerebral but drunken stooge in *Johnny Eager*

which starred Robert Taylor and Lana Turner.

Richard Day and Joseph White won both Oscars for Art Direction for *This Above All* (Black And White) and *My Gal Sal* (Color).

One of the greatest comedy series in the history of Hollywood was launched this year with the first of the famous Bob Hope/Bing Crosby Road pictures, *The Road To Morocco*, nominated for Writing (Original Story) and Sound

Donald Duck salutes in *Der Fuehrer's Face.*

Recording. Crosby showed up again in the music department with his hit *Holiday Inn*, nominated for Scoring Of A Musical Picture. The Irving Berlin song 'White Christmas' from *Holiday Inn* took the Best Song category over 'Dearly Beloved' from *You Were Never Lovelier* with the very lovely Rita Hayworth who was also in *My Gal Sal* and the very agile Fred Astaire who was also in *Holiday Inn*; 'How About You?' from *Babes On Broadway*; 'It Seems I Heard That Song Before' from *Youth On Parade*, and 'I've Got A Gal In Kalamazoo' from *Orchestra Wives*, great songs all.

Rene Clair's *I Married A Witch* starring Fredric March and adorable Veronica Lake was nominated for Scoring Of A Dramatic Or Comedy Picture only but today it is as fresh and charming as it was then which can hardly be said of many of the movies nominated. 1942 was the year of Walt Disney's *Bambi*, nominated in several musical and technical categories and in contrast a very long list of war related Documentary nominees. War related, too, were the Special Awards which went to Charles Boyer for establishing the French Research Foundation; Noel Coward for the partriotic *In Which We Serve*, and M-G-M for representing the American Way Of Life in the production of the 'Andy Hardy' series of films. This was the last year the Awards were presented at a banquet. Henceforth hotels were out and theaters were in since only theaters could accommodate the increased attendance.

1943

Best Picture: *Casablanca.*

Actor: Paul Lukas, *Watch On The Rhine.*

Actress: Jennifer Jones, *The Song Of Bernadette.*

Supporting Actor: Charles Coburn, *The More The Merrier.*

Supporting Actress: Katina Paxinou, *For Whom The Bell Tolls.*

Director: Michael Curtiz, *Casablanca.*

Writing (Original Story): William Saroyan, *The Human Comedy.*

Writing (Original Screenplay): Norman Krasna, *Princess O'Rourke.*

Writing (Best Written Screenplay): Julius J Epstein, Phillip G Epstein, and Howard Koch, *Casablanca.*

Cinematography (Black And White): Arthur G Miller, *The Song Of Bernadette.*

Cinematography (Color): Hal Mohr and W Howard Greene, *The Phantom Of The Opera.*

Art Director (Black And White): James Basevi and William Darling, *The Song Of Bernadette.*

Art Director (Color): Alexander Golitzen and John B Goodman, *The Phantom Of The Opera.*

Special Effects: Fred Sersen (Photographic), Roger Herman (Sound), *Crash Dive.*

Music (Scoring Dramatic Or Comedy Picture): Alfred Newman, *The Song Of Bernadette.*

Music (Scoring Musical Picture): Ray Heindorf, *This Is The Army.*

Music (Song): Mack Gordon (Lyrics), Harry Warren (Music), 'You'll Never Know' from *Hello, Frisco, Hello.*

Short Subjects (Cartoon): *Yankee Doodle Mouse*, MGM.

Documentary (Short Subject): *December 7th.*

Documentary (Feature Length): *Desert Victory.*

Irving G Thalberg Memorial Award: Hal B Wallis.

Special Award: George Pal, for the development of novel methods and techniques in the production of short subjects known as Puppetoons.

Casablanca was a little movie about people whose lives were changed by war, yet it has outlived all the big, splashy, epic war movies ever made. It just may be the most popular movie in the world. Making the movie was sheer chaos and nobody involved realized that the idealistic anti-Nazi melodrama with *film noir* overtones would turn out

to be a masterpiece. Humphrey Bogart played the American nightclub owner Rick Blaine. Paul Henreid was Victor Laszlo, the resistance leader who escaped from a concentration camp. Ingrid Bergman played Ilsa, Laszlo's wife, who was also in love with Rick. Claude Rains was the charming un-scrupulous police chief, Captain Renault who, along with the tormented Rick, behaved heroically at film's end. Also featured were Peter Lorre, Sydney Greenstreet, S Z Sakall, and Dooley Wilson singing 'As Time Goes By.' Since *Casablanca* is the best and most stirring movie of its kind and seems to sum up an era it's nice to know that it also won the Academy Award for Best Picture.

Casablanca brought Humphrey Bogart a Best Actor nomination,

Claude Rains a Best Supporting Actor nomination and Michael Curtiz the Best Director Oscar. *Casablanca* also took the Best Screenplay Award and picked up nominations in several other categories. Ingrid Bergman was also nominated for Best Actress that year but for her performance in *For Whom The Bell Tolls*, based on Ernest Hemingway's novel about an American fighting with a band of guerillas during the Spanish Civil War. The movie gained a Best Picture nomination; brought a Best Actor nomination to Gary Cooper; a Best Supporting Actor nomination to Akim Tamiroff for his role as the guerrilla leader, and brought the Best Supporting Actress Award to Greek actress Katina Paxinou who played Pilar.

Ernst Lubitsch was nominated for his

Claude Rains orders a round-up of the usual suspects in *Casablanca*, watched by Paul Henreid, Humphrey Bogart and Ingrid Bergman.

John Mills, Richard Attenborough and Celia Johnson, with Coward playing the captain of the doomed ship. In 1942 Coward had received a Special Academy Award for *In Which We Serve* and the movie was nominated for Best Picture the following year.

Greet Garson and Walter Pidgeon had proved a successful duo in 1942's Best Picture selection *Mrs Miniver* with Garson as Mrs and Pidgeon as Mr Miniver. This time round they were paired in *Madame Curie* with Garson as Madame and Pidgeon as Monsieur Curie, husband of the discoverer of radium. Garson received a Best Actress nomination for *Madame Curie*, Pidgeon received a Best Actor nomination, and the movie was up for Best Picture. *The More The Merrier* was a timely and funny wartime comedy set in overcrowded Washington, DC where hotels were bursting at the seams with new arrivals. It took a Best Picture nomination; brought a Best Actress nomination to petite scratchy-voiced Jean Arthur,

one of Hollywood's most engaging leading ladies; got George Stevens nominated for Best Director, and brought Charles Coburn the Best Supporting Actor Award for his role as millionaire Benjamin Dingle, merrily sharing a Washington apartment with Jean Arthur and Joel McCrea.

The Ox-Bow Incident was a failure at the box-office but deservedly was nominated for Best Picture. This outstanding movie about an 1885 Western frontier lynching of three innocent victims was based on a novel by Walter Van Tilburg Clark. The picture's highly deserving cast, however, led by Henry Fonda, received no nominations at all. Today *The Ox-Bow Incident* is considered by many critics to be one of the finest movies Hollywood ever produced. But wartime audiences were in need of inspiration or escape and the film's daringly downbeat tone was just too much for them.

The Song Of Bernadette starred Jennifer Jones, an exquisite young woman from Tulsa, Oklahoma who won the Best Actress Award for her performance as a French peasant girl who saw

Jennifer Jones in *The Song Of Bernadette*.

direction of Best Picture nominee *Heaven Can Wait*, a polished gem of a movie, lavishly done in beautiful color. The film starred Don Ameche as an elegant but deceased gentleman telling his troubles to a congenial Satan in a Hell so luxurious it would tempt an angel. Gene Tierney was the movie's charming female star. Warren Beatty borrowed the title for his 1978 remake of the 1941 *Here Comes Mr Jordan*.

The Human Comedy, nominated for Best Picture, was based on the work by William Saroyan. The movie brought a Best Actor nomination to Mickey Rooney and a Best Director nomination to Clarence Brown. Noel Coward produced, co-directed, and wrote the script and music for *In Which We Serve*, a British movie about a British destroyer in World War II, starring Bernard Miles,

visions of the Virgin. The movie was publicized as Jones's debut film, ignoring the 'B' movies she made in 1939. A huge hit, *The Song Of Bernadette* launched a new cycle of sentimental religious films. It also gained a Best Picture nomination; brought Best Supporting Actress nominations to Anne Revere and Gladys Cooper; a Best Supporting Actor nomination to rugged Charles Bickford, and earned director Henry King a best Director nomination. The most controversial casting in the picture was sex goddess Linda Darnell as the Virgin Mary.

Paul Lukas won the Award for Best Actor for his role as a dedicated anti-Nazi undercover agent in *Watch On The Rhine*, based on the play by Lillian Hellman, adapted for the screen by Dashiell Hammett who was given a Best Screenplay nomination for it. *Watch On The Rhine* also brought Lucille Watson a Best Supporting Actress nomination for her role as Bette Davis's mother. Other nominees included Joan Fontaine for Best Actress for her portrayal of a teenager in *The Constant Nymph* with Charles Boyer. J Carrol Naish was in the running for Best Supporting Actor for his performance as a confused Italian prisoner of war in *Sahara*, and Paulette Goddard earned a Best Supporting Actress nomination for *So Proudly We Hail* with Claudette Colbert and Veronica Lake.

Grauman's Chinese Theater was the site of the Awards Ceremony this year which was broadcast overseas with Jack Benny as emcee. Benny had starred in the 1942 bitter comedy *To Be Or Not To Be*, co-starring Carole Lombard which sank under the weight of the war because it was far too farcical to be accepted by a home-front audience. Mel Brooks remade the movie in 1983, starring in it with his wife, Anne Bancroft.

1943 movies which received nominations in various categories but were not really given the credit they deserved included Albert Hitchcock's thriller *Shadow Of A Doubt*, starring Joseph Cotton and Theresa Wright, which revealed the danger lurking beneath the surface of ordinary life. Billy Wilder's thriller *Five Graves To Cairo* featured Erich Von Stroheim in top form as Rommel. *Lassie Come Home* was a touching film, with little Liz Taylor, already gorgeous, and a male collie named Pal in the title role. *The Moon And Sixpence* was based on Somerset Maugham's novel of the life of painter Gauguin. *Cabin In The Sky*, a musical

drama with an all black cast directed by Vincent Minnelli, starred Eddie Anderson, Ethel Waters, and Lena Horne. That movie produced a Best Song nominee, 'Happiness Is A Thing Called Joe,' which lost to 'You'll Never Know' from *Hello, Frisco, Hello* starring Alice Faye.

Claude Rains starred in *Phantom Of The Opera* with Susanna Foster, a good film and a winner in several production categories but not up to the Lon Chaney 1925 silent original version of the tale of a disfigured madman driven by love as

he haunted the Paris Opera House. Tyrone Power, Dana Andrews, and Anne Baxter starred in *Crash Dive*, whose scenes aboard a submarine, won the Special Effects Award. MGM's patriotic *Yankee Doodle Mouse* won in the cartoon category.

BELOW: Best Supporting Actress Katina Paxinou, Ingrid Bergman and Gary Cooper in *For Whom The Bell Tolls*.
BOTTOM: Bette Davis, Paul Lukas in *Watch On The Rhine*.

1944

Best Picture: *Going My Way.*
Actor: Bing Crosby, *Going My Way.*
Actress: Ingrid Bergman, *Gaslight.*
Supporting Actor: Barry Fitzgerald, *Going My Way.*
Supporting Actress: Ethel Barrymore, *None But The Lonely Heart.*
Director: Leo McCarey, *Going My Way.*
Writing (Original Story): Leo McCarey, *Going My Way.*
Writing (Original Screenplay): Frank Butler and Frank Cavett, *Going My Way.*
Cinematography (Black And White): Joseph La Shelle, *Laura.*
Cinematography (Color): Leon Shamroy, *Wilson.*
Art Director (Black And White): Cedric Gibbons and William Ferrari, *Gaslight.*
Art Director (Color): Wiard Ihnen, *Wilson.*
Special Effects: A Arnold Gillespie, Donald Jahraus, Warren Newcombe (Photographic), Douglas Shearer (Sound), *Thirty Seconds Over Tokyo.*
Music (Scoring Dramatic Or Comedy Picture): Max Steiner, *Since You Went Away.*
Music (Scoring Musical Picture): Morris Stoloff and Carmen Dragon, *Cover Girl.*
Music (Song): Johnny Burke (Lyrics) and James Van Heusen (Music), 'Swinging On A Star' from *Going My Way.*
Short Subjects (Cartoon): *Mouse Trouble*, MGM.
Documentary (Short Subject): *With The Marines At Tarawa.*
Documentary (Feature Length): *The Fighting Lady.*
Irving G Thalberg Memorial Award: Darryl F Zanuck.
Special Awards: Margaret O'Brien, outstanding child actress of 1944. Bob Hope, for his many services to the Academy, a Life Membership in the Academy Of Motion Picture Arts And Sciences.

Five movies received Best Picture nominations this year, down from ten and even more in past years. The one movie which trounced the opposition was *Going My Way*, an episodic and immensely popular bit of sweetness and light starring Bing Crosby as young Father O'Malley, singing his way

TOP: Cary Grant and Ethel Barrymore in *None But The Lonely Heart.*
RIGHT: Bing Crosby, Barry Frizgerald, Risë Stevens and Frank McHugh in *Going My Way.*

Stanwyck murdered Stanwyck's husband for his insurance money, hence the film's title. Edward G Robinson was in top form as the claims investigator but neither Robinson nor McMurray received nominations for their performances. Stanwyck was nominated for Best Actress and Billy Wilder for Best Director. Though Wilder and *Double Indemnity* co-writer Raymond Chandler earned a Screenplay nomination, credit for the story belongs to James M Cain who wrote the original novel.

Nominated for Best Picture was *Gaslight*, a suspenseful thriller set in the Victorian era about a woman whose husband deliberately attempts to drive her insane. Ingrid Bergman won the Best Actress Award for her portrayal of the deluded wife and Charles Boyer received a Best Actor nomination for his role as the villainous husband. Teenager Angela Lansbury was marvelous as the Cockney maid, gaining a Best Supporting Actress nomination for her first performance.

Since You Went Away, a big dramatic movie nominated for Best Picture was producer David O Selznick's tribute to the women left at home by the men who went off to war. Claudette Colbert starred and the cast included Jennifer Jones, Monty Woolley and Robert Walker. The movie brought Colbert a

LEFT: Spencer Tracy as Col James P Doolittle in *Thirty Seconds Over Tokyo*.
BELOW: Ingrid Bergman, Charles Boyer and Barbara Everest in *Gaslight*.

through poor St Dominic's parish with Barry Fitzgerald as the lovable but stubborn older priest. Crosby won the Best Actor Award for the picture which also brought both a Best Actor and Best Supporting Actor nomination to Barry Fitzgerald. Fitzgerald won Best Supporting Actor. Not only did *Going My Way* win Best Picture but producer/director Leo McCarey won the Best Director Oscar and the Writing (Original Story) Award. The picture brought Frank Butler and Frank Cavett the Best Screenplay Award and Johnny Burke and James Van Heusen's 'Swinging On A Star' won the Award for Best Song.

The losing pictures were an interesting lot. Best picture nominee *Double Indemnity*, a classic *film noir*, featured a surprisingly sexy Fred McMurray in a convincing performance as the man seduced by *femme fatale* Barbara Stanwyck. Together McMurray and

Gene Kelly, Rita Hayworth and Phil Silvers
eat oysters served by Edward S Brophy in
Cover Girl.

Best Actress nomination, Jones a Best
Supporting Actress nomination, and
Woolley a Best Supporting Actor nomination. Canadian-born actor Alexander
Knox portrayed Woodrow Wilson in
Wilson, and received a Best Actor
nomination. *Wilson*, which earned a
nomination for Best Picture, also
brought director Henry King a Best
Director nomination and went on to
win Awards in several categories.

Cary Grant was nominated for Best
Actor for his role as the Cockney hero in
None But The Lonely Heart, based on
the novel by Richard Llewellyn, with
Barry Fitzgerald and Ethel Barrymore,
directed by Clifford Odets who wrote
the screenplay. *None But The Lonely
Heart* won Barrymore the Award for
Best Supporting Actress. *Mr Skeffing-
ton* brought Bette Davis a Best Actress
nomination for her role as the fading
selfish beauty who lets husband Claude
Rains come back to her once he's too
blind to see that she has lost her looks.
Still the movie was enjoyable and
Rains, too, received a nomination, in
this case for Best Supporting Actor.
Greer Garson was nominated for Best

Actress for the family saga *Mrs Parkington*, once more opposite Walter Pidgeon who by now must have dreamed of
being in a movie with Mr in the title.

Aline MacMahon earned a Best Supporting Actress nomination for her
portrayal of the matriarch in *Dragon
Seed*. The movie also had Agnes
Moorehead playing a Chinese virago
but Moorehead's Best Supporting
Actress nomination came for *Mrs
Parkington*, where she played the lively
witty French woman who taught a
gauche Greer Garson the ways of a lady.
Hume Cronyn received a Best Support-
ing Actor nomination in *The Seventh
Cross*, a good anti-Nazi chase film set in
pre-war Germany starring Spencer
Tracy. Tracy's *A Guy Named Joe* with
Irene Dunne was nominated in the
Cinematography (Black And White)
category and he also starred in *Thirty
Seconds Over Tokyo* which won the
Special Effects Oscar.

The real best picture of the year
wasn't even nominated in the Best
Picture category though Otto Premin-
ger received a Best Director nomination
for it and it won Cinematography
(Black And White). The movie was
Laura, a haunting film with a beautiful
score, starring Dana Andrews and Gene
Tierney, Vincent Price and Judith
Anderson. Clifton Webb did win a Best

Supporting Actor nomination for his
portrayal of the sarcastic love-lorn
Waldo Lydecker. If *Laura* was a
mystery with supernatural overtones
and a naturalistic ending *The Uninvited*
was a superb delicately done ghost story
starring Ray Milland. It won only one
nomination, Cinematography (Black
And White).

'The Trolley Song' from the colorful
turn-of-the-century period musical
Meet Me In St Louis, starring Judy
Garland with child star Margaret
O'Brien, was nominated for Best Song.
So was 'Long Ago And Far Away' from
Cover Girl with Rita Hayworth and
Gene Kelly. *Lady In The Dark* with
Ginger Rogers at least won a Scoring Of
A Musical Picture nomination.

Lifeboat managed to achieve sus-
pense under the most claustrophobic of
conditions, in a lifeboat at sea. John
Steinbeck wrote the script and Tallulah
Bankhead and Walter Slezak won
praise for their acting. Director Alfred
Hitchcock earned a Best Director
nomination for the film. A Special
Award was given to little Margaret
O'Brien in the form of a miniature
Oscar for being the outstanding child
actress of 1944. Bob Hope won a
Special Award, too, in the form of a Life
Membership in the Academy for his
many services to it.

1945

Best Picture: *The Lost Weekend.*
Actor: Ray Milland, *The Lost Weekend.*
Actress: Joan Crawford, *Mildred Pierce.*
Supporting Actor: James Dunn, *A Tree Grows In Brooklyn.*
Supporting Actress: Anne Revere, *National Velvet.*
Director: Billy Wilder, *The Lost Weekend.*
Writing (Original Story): Charles G Booth, *The House On 92nd Street.*
Writing (Original Screenplay): Richard Schweizer, *Marie-Louise.*
Writing (Best Written Screenplay): Charles Brackett and Billy Wilder, *The Lost Weekend.*
Cinematography (Black And White): Harry Stradling, *The Picture Of Dorian Gray.*
Cinematography (Color): Leon Shamroy, *Leave Her To Heaven.*
Art Director (Black And White): Wiard Ihnen, *Blood On The Sun.*

Art Director (Color): Hans Dreier and Ernst Fegte, *Frenchman's Creek.*
Special Effects: John Fulton (Photographic), Arthur W Johns (Sound), *Wonder Man.*
Music (Scoring Dramatic Or Comedy Picture): Miklos Rozsa, *Spellbound.*
Music (Scoring Musical Picture): Georgie Stoll, *Anchors Aweigh.*
Music (Song): Oscar Hammerstein II (Lyrics) and Richard Rodgers (Music), 'It Might As Well Be Spring' from *State Fair.*
Short Subjects (Cartoon): *Quiet, Please,* MGM.
Documentary (Short Subject): *Hitler Lives?*
Documentary (Feature Length): *The True Glory.*
Special Awards: Walter Wanger, for his six years' service as President of the Academy. Peggy Ann Garner, outstanding child actress of 1945. *The House I Live In*, a short subject about tolerance starring Frank Sinatra.

A lively musical, an uplifting tear-jerker, a melodrama, a mystery and a major dramatic motion picture received the nominations for Best Picture this time round. *Anchors Aweigh* starred Gene Kelly, Frank Sinatra, Kathryn Grayson and José Iturbi with Kelly and Sinatra playing sailors on leave. Kelly's dance with a cartoon mouse proved very popular. The movie, a forerunner of the even better *On The Town* (1949), made Kelly a star and earned him a Best Actor nomination.

Bing Crosby and Ingrid Bergman teamed up in *The Bells Of Saint Mary's*, in essence a sequel to last year's Oscar winning *Going My Way* with Crosby as Father O'Malley again and Bergman as a nun. Even more successful at the box-

Ray Milland tries to pawn his typewriter on a Sunday in *The Lost Weekend*. Both Milland and the film won awards.

ABOVE: Joan Crawford in *Mildred Pierce* with Zachary Scott.
RIGHT: James Dunn and Peggy Ann Garner as Johnny and Francie Nolan in *A Tree Grows In Brooklyn.*

office than its predecessor the picture garnered a Best Actor nomination for Crosby, a Best Actress nomination for Bergman and a Best Director nomination for Leo McCarey. 1945 was also the year a brilliant Italian director Roberto Rossellini unleashed a totally unsentimental movie, *Open City*, upon the world, signalling the post-war European movement of neo-realistic films. *Open City* wasn't nominated for an Oscar this year but it certainly had impact, not least on Bergman who would link both her life and career to Rossellini in the following decade, much to the horror of millions of American movie-goers who perpetually saw her as the devoted nun in *The Bells Of Saint Mary's*.

Mildred Pierce reestablished Joan Crawford as a top star and earned her the Best Actress Oscar. The movie, about a devoted mother, had a plot which included murder, larceny,

blackmail, adultery and tips on running the restaurant business. Eve Arden was Crawford's knowing friend and Ann Blyth played Crawford's daughter. Both received Best Supporting Actress nominations for the film. Gregory Peck and Ingrid Bergman starred in *Spellbound*. The plot device was an old one, amnesia, but the treatment was modern, a preview of the post-war interest in psychiatric explanations of behavior. The dream sequence designed by Salvador Dali was and still is fascinating. Alfred Hitchcock and character actor Michael Chekhov, nephew of playwright Anton Chekhov, both received nominations for the movie; Hitchcock as Best Director and Chekhov as Best Supporting Actor.

Like Bergman, Peck, too, was nominated for a movie other than *Spellbound*, receiving a Best Actor nomination for the role of Chinese missionary Father Chisholm, in *The Keys Of The Kingdom*. Peck was also in *The Valley Of Decision* with Greer Garson who earned a Best Actress nomination for that movie. Jennifer Jones received a Best Actress nomination for *Love Letters*, its plot, like *Spellbound's* turning on amnesia. A Best Actor nomination went to handsome Cornel Wilde as the romantic composer Chopin in *A Song To Remember*. Gene Tierney won a nomination for Best Actress for her portrayal of Hollywood's brand of the evil woman in *Leave Her To Heaven*, also with Wilde.

The movie that won the Best Picture Oscar was the outstanding *Lost Weekend* which catapulted light comedy leading man Ray Milland into serious stardom. The movie, with Philip Terry and Jane Wyman, took the audience through three tortured days in the life of an alcoholic. It won Milland the Best Actor Award and Billy Wilder Best Director. *Lost Weekend*, unsentimental and disturbing, yet moving is still very much worth seeing today.

John Dall gained a Best Supporting Actor nomination for *The Corn Is Green*, based on the play by Emlyn Williams, starring Bette Davis which also brought young Joan Lorring a Best Supporting Actress nomination. Robert Mitchum was a tough but tired captain in *The Story Of GI Joe*, winning a Best Supporting Actor nomination. A Best Supporting Actor nomination also went to J Carroll Naish for his portrayal of a Mexican father in *A Medal For Benny*. Naish appeared too in Jean Renoir's fine film about a poor Texas family, *The Southerner*, which brought

Renoir a Best Director nomination. However, it was James Dunn who won the Best Supporting Actor Award for his touching performance as the loving but vacillating father in *A Tree Grows In Brooklyn* with talented child star Peggy Ann Garner.

Angela Lansbury was nominated for Best Supporting Actress in *The Picture Of Dorian Gray*, for her role as the vulnerable young singer. The movie, based on Oscar Wilde's strange fantasy about a man who remains young and handsome while his portrait ages was a splendid film, beautifully directed by Albert Lewin. Unfortunately star Hurd Hatfield did not receive a deserved Best Actor nomination. Lansbury was also in *National Velvet*, the story of a girl who races her horse to glory which made a superstar of young Elizabeth Taylor. Anne Revere won the Best Supporting Actress Award for her portrayal of Liz's mother and the film brought Clarence Brown a Best Director nomination.

Hurd Hatfield as Dorian Gray and George Sanders as Lord Henry Wotton, his cynical mentor, in *The Picture of Dorian Gray*.

The Best Song Oscar went to 'It Might As Well Be Spring' from the delightful *State Fair*, a remake of the 1933 movie with Will Rogers, Lew Ayres, and Janet Gaynor. The new version starred Charles Winninger, Dick Haymes, Jeanne Craine and Vivian Blaine. Also in the running for Best Song was 'Accentuate The Positive' from *Here Comes The Waves*; 'So In Love' from the whacky irresistible *Wonder Man* starring comic wonder man Danny Kaye, and 'Linda' from *GI Joe*. Winning an original screenplay was *Music For Millions* starring Jimmy Durante and the very popular Margaret O'Brien. It was Peggy Ann Garner's turn to win the laurels as the outstanding child actress of the year and she was given a special miniature statuette as a Special Award.

1946

Best Picture: *The Best Years Of Our Lives.*

Actor: Fredric March, *The Best Years Of Our Lives.*

Actress: Olivia de Havilland, *To Each His Own.*

Supporting Actor: Harold Russell, *The Best Years Of Our Lives.*

Supporting Actress: Anne Baxter, *The Razor's Edge.*

Director: William Wyler, *The Best Years Of Our Lives.*

Writing (Original Story): Clemence Dane, *Vacation From Marriage.*

Writing (Original Screenplay): Muriel Box and Sydney Box, *The Seventh Veil.*

Writing (Best Written Screenplay): Robert E Sherwood, *The Best Years Of Our Lives.*

Cinematography (Black And White): Arthur C Miller, *Anna And The King Of Siam.*

Cinematography (Color): Charles Rosher, Leonard Smith, Arthur Arling, *The Yearling.*

Art Director (Black And White): Lyle Wheeler and William Darling, *Anna And The King Of Siam.*

Art Director (Color): Cedric Gibbons and Paul Groesse, *The Yearling.*

Special Effects: Thomas Howard (Photographic), *Blithe Spirit.*

Music (Scoring Dramatic Or Comedy Picture): Hugo Friedhofer, *The Best Years Of Our Lives.*

Music (Scoring Musical Picture): Morris Stoloff, *The Jolson Story.*

Music (Song): Johnny Mercer (Lyrics) and Harry Warren (Music), 'On The Atchison, Topeka And Santa Fe' from *The Harvey Girls.*

Short Subjects (Cartoon): *The Cat Concerto*, MGM.

Irving G Thalberg Memorial Award: Samuel Goldwyn.

Special Awards: Laurence Olivier, for his outstanding achievement as actor, producer and director in bringing *Henry V* to the screen. Harold Russell, for bringing hope and courage to his fellow veterans through his appearance in *The Best Years Of Our Lives.* Ernst Lubitsch, for his distinguished contributions to the art of the motion picture. Claude Jarman, Jr, outstanding child actor of 1946.

The Best Years Of Our Lives was Hollywood's way of telling the world that the war was over. It was also a perfect Academy Award winning Best Picture, timely, but not timeless, respectable but not remarkable, serious but not original. *Blithe Spirit*, starring Rex Harrison as the writer haunted by the women in his life and Margaret Rutherford as the well-meaning medium, earned only one Oscar, but the movie is pure champagne, totally watchable today while *The Best Years Of Our Lives*, though covered with Oscars is distinctly dated. Another Best Picture nominee, Laurence Olivier's *Henry V*, represents perhaps the finest film version of a Shakespearean play in the history of cinema.

The Best Years Of Our Lives told the story of three returning veterans trying to adjust to post-war life. The picture brought Oscars to director William Wyler; actor Fredric March; support-

Harold Russell, Teresa Wright, Dana Andrews, Myrna Loy, Fredric March, with Hoagy Carmichael in *The Best Years Of Our Lives.*

ing actor Harold Russell, an amputee who never made another movie and who also received a Special Award for the film; screenplay writer Robert E Sherwood; film editor Daniel Mandell, and Hugo Freidhofer for Best Musical Score.

Also in the running for Best Picture was director Frank Capra's own favorite achievement *It's A Wonderful Life* starring James Stewart as a would-be suicide who comes to see how much his life has meant to his friends and family. A good mix of sentiment and comedy the picture earned Stewart a Best Actor nomination and Capra a Best Director nomination. Service in the marines had interrupted Tyrone Power's film career but he was back pulling in the crowds as Larry in *The Razor's Edge*, based on Somerset Maugham's last major novel. Gene Tierney played Isobel and Anne Baxter the tragic Sophie. John Payne, Herbert Marshall and Clifton Webb rounded out the cast. The movie received a Best Picture nomination and brought Webb a Best Supporting Actor nomination and Baxter the Best Supporting Actress Award.

Gregory Peck, Jane Wyman, and Claude Jarman, Jr starred in Best Picture nominee *The Yearling* from Marjorie Kinnan Rawlings' homespun novel. The movie gained Peck a Best Actor nomination, Wyman a Best Actress nomination, Clarence Brown a Best Director nomination, and won Jarman a miniature statuette Special Award for being the outstanding child actor of 1946. A Special Award went, too, to Laurence Olivier for the magnificent achievement of bringing *Henry V* to the screen. Olivier also received a Best Actor nomination for his portrayal of the ideal warrior king.

The Jolson Story, a box-office smash, was Hollywood's sanitized version of the life of charismatic performer Al Jolson. Star Larry Parks was given a Best Actor nomination for his impersonation of Jolson and William Demarest was nominated for Best Supporting Actor for his role as Jolson's old burlesque buddy. Also up for Best Supporting Actor were Charles Coburn as Alexander 'Dandy' Gow in *The Green Years* and Claude Rains for his role as Ingrid Bergman's treacherous husband

Larry Parks as the legendary Al Jolson in *The Jolson Story.*

in Hitchcock's spy thriller *Notorious*.

Brief Encounter, an excellent romantic British post-war movie starring Trevor Howard and Celia Johnson brought Johnson a Best Actress nomination and director David Lean a Best Director nomination. *Duel In The Sun* was a western filled with raw violence and raw passion, the longest movie since *Gone With The Wind*. Jennifer Jones received a Best Actress nomination for her portrayal of the tempestuous half-breed Pearl desired by Joseph Cotton and Gregory Peck. Rosalind Russell was nominated for Best Actress for *Sister Kenny*, an idealized film biography of the nurse who developed a controversial method of treating polio victims. But the Best Actress Award went to Olivia de Havilland for *To Each His Own*, about an unwed mother who gives up her child rather than have it face the stigma of illegitimacy.

The Spiral Staircase, a scary suspense film featuring Dorothy McGuire as a deaf-mute brought a Supporting Actress nomination to Ethel Barrymore who stole the picture. Nominated also for Best Supporting Actress were ex-silent film star Lillian Gish for her role as Lionel Barrymore's consumptive wife in *Duel In The Sun*, Flora Robson as Ingrid Bergman's maid in *Saratoga Trunk*, and Gale Sondergaard for her role as Lady Thiang in *Anna And The King Of Siam*. *Anna And The King Of Siam* was notable, too, for Rex Harrison's performance as the king, opposite Irene Dunne, a role later dominated by Yul Brynner in the musical version of the story of Anna, *The King And I*. The film did win several production awards.

The Killers introduced Burt Lancaster

Tyrone Power and Anne Baxter in *The Razor's Edge*.

and brought director Richard Siodmak a Best Director nomination. Up for Original Screenplay was Raymond Chandler's *The Blue Dahlia* starring the well matched team of Alan Ladd and Veronica Lake, *The Road To Utopia* with trio Hope, Crosby, and Lamour, and the winner, the romantic *The Seventh Veil* with James Mason the irresistible villain/hero who hits pianist Ann Todd's hands with his cane but wins her love anyways, despite or maybe because of the cane.

Violins were in order for *Humoresque* nominated for Scoring Of A Dramatic Or Comedy Picture with Joan Crawford and John Garfield, male sex symbol par excellence. Best song nominee included Hoagy Carmichael and Jack Brook's 'Ole Buttermilk Sky' from *Canyon Passage* which lost to 'The Atchison,

Topeka And Santa Fe' from *The Harvey Girls* with Judy Garland.

Caesar And Cleopatra deserved a lot but took only one nomination, Interior Decoration (Color), despite a fine performance by Claude Rains and the delightful kittenish performance of Vivien Leigh. One of the hottest, sexiest, and most exciting pictures of the year *Gilda* with Rita Hayworth, Glenn Ford, and George Macready received no nominations, a sign that though audiences steamed *Gilda* left the Academy lukewarm. The dazzling Ernst Lubitsch at last won recognition for his directing via a Special Award, and a British movie *Perfect Strangers* with Glynis Johns and Deborah Kerr as Wrens won the Writing (Original Story) Award under its US title *Vacation From Marriage*.

1947

Best Picture: *Gentleman's Agreement.*

Actor: Ronald Colman, *A Double Life.*

Actress: Loretta Young, *The Farmer's Daughter.*

Supporting Actor: Edmund Gwenn, *Miracle On 34th Street.*

Supporting Actress: Celeste Holm, *Gentleman's Agreement.*

Director: Elia Kazan, *Gentleman's Agreement.*

Writing (Original Story): Valentine Davies, *Miracle On 34th Street.*

Writing (Original Screenplay): Sidney Sheldon, *The Bachelor And The Bobby-Soxer.*

Writing (Best Written Screenplay): George Seaton, *Miracle On 34th Street.*

Cinematography (Black And White): Guy Green, *Great Expectations.*

Cinematography (Color): Jack Cardiff, *Black Narcissus.*

Art Director (Black And White): John Bryan, *Great Expectations.*

Art Director (Color): Alfred Junge, *Black Narcissus.*

Special Effects: A Arnold Gillespie, Warren Newcombe (Visual), Douglas Shearer, Michael Steinore (Audible), *Green Dolphin Street.*

Music (Scoring Dramatic Or Comedy Picture): Miklos Rozsa, *A Double Life.*

Music (Scoring Musical Picture): Alfred Newman, *Mother Wore Tights.*

Music (Song): Ray Gilbert (Lyrics) and Allie Wrubel (Music), 'Zip-A-Dee-Doo-Dah' from *Song Of The South.*

Short Subjects (Cartoon): *Tweetie Pie*, Warner Bros.

Special Awards: James Baskette, for his able and heart-warming characterization of Uncle Remus in *Song Of The South*, friend and story teller to the children of the world. *Bill And Coo*, in which artistry and patience blended in a novel and entertaining use of the medium of motion pictures. *Shoe Shine*, for the high quality of this film. Colonel William N Selig, Albert E Smith, Thomas Armat and George K Spoor, film pioneers.

For the first time ever the Academy gave a Special Award to a foreign language film, Vittorio de Sica's *Shoe Shine*, the story of a group of children struggling for survival in post war Italy. De Sica's use of a semidocumentary style lent the film objectivity and distance despite the deeply disturbing

OPPOSITE: Ronald Colman won Best Actor for his part as a schizophrenic actor in *A Double Life*.
ABOVE: Best Supporting Actress Celeste Holm in *Gentlemen's Agreement* with Gregory Peck.
RIGHT: Edmund Gwenn with Natalie Wood in *Miracle On 34th Street*.

and highly emotional subject matter of the movie. Clearly post-war Europe was reestablishing a first-rate film industry.

But Hollywood, too, was breaking new ground. Among the movies up for Best Picture was *Gentleman's Agreement* which brought the subject of anti-Semitism out in the open. The movie starred Gregory Peck as a writer who poses as a Jew to learn the extent of discrimination. The cast included Dorothy McGuire, Celeste Holm, and John Garfield. Nominee *Crossfire*, a thriller, also dealt with anti-Semitism. The picture starred Robert Ryan as the bigot and Robert Young as the cop out to solve a murder case where the victim was Jewish. Director Edward Dmytryk was nominated for Best Director for the film.

The Bishop's Wife, was a harmless bit of whimsy starring Cary Grant, Loretta Young, and David Niven. In addition to a Best Picture nomination the film gave director Henry Koster a Best Director nomination. *Miracle On 34th Street* with Natalie Wood, then a child star, was even more whimsical, a delightful fantasy set against the backdrop of New York's Macy's Department Store's annual Thanksgiving Day Parade. Edmund Gwenn's performance was so marvelous he managed to persuade the whole world that yes, Virginia, there indeed was a Santa Claus and his real name was Edmund Gwenn.

The definitive film version of Charles Dicken's *Great Expectations* also received a Best Picture nomination.

Beautifully directed by David Lean who was likewise nominated for Best Director the movie's cast included John Mills, Jean Simmons, Alec Guinness, who was simply super as Pocket, Finlay Currie, and Martita Hunt.

The winner of the Best Picture Oscar was *Gentleman's Agreement* and the film's director Elia Kazan also won the Best Director Award, beating out all the other nominees including George Cukor for *A Double Life*, starring Ronald Colman as a Shakespearean actor gone mad with tragic results for the slender and beautiful Shelley Winters. However, Colman did win the Best Actor Award over nominees Gregory Peck in *Gentleman's Agreement*; John Garfield, a boxer in *Body And Soul*; William Powell, irascible but irresistible in *Life With Father*, and Michael Redgrave, outstanding as Orin in *Mourning Becomes Electra* which also

starred Best Actress nominee Rosalind Russell.

The other nominees for Best Actress were Joan Crawford in *Possessed* with Van Heflin (not a remake of her 1931 film of that name co-starring Clark Gable); Dorothy McGuire in *Gentleman's Agreement*; Susan Hayward, an alcoholic in *Smash-Up, The Story Of A Woman*, and glamorous Loretta Young portraying an unglamorous Swedish farm girl who got a job as a domestic with a congressman played by Joseph Cotton, and went on to win him. Young won the Best Actress Oscar for her performance in *The Farmer's Daughter*.

Best Supporting Actor nominees were Robert Ryan in *Crossfire*; the ever commanding Charles Bickford in *The Farmer's Daughter*; Thomas Gomez as

Brer Rabbit was featured in Walt Disney's *Song Of The South*.

nominations in various categories were *Black Narcissus*, a melodrama set in a Himalayan convent with magnificent color cinematography and a magnificent performance by Deborah Kerr; Charles Chaplin's much underrated *Monsieur Verdoux* with comedienne Martha Raye; *The Ghost And Mrs Muir*, a charming comedy with Rex Harrison; *Green Dolphin Street* with Lana Turner, Van Heflin, and lots of costume changes; *The Bachelor And The Bobby-Soxer* with Cary Grant and Shirley Temple, now all grown up; *Captain From Castile* with Tyrone Power for women to swoon over, and *Forever Amber* with Linda Darnell for men to swoon over.

Song Of The South was a Walt Disney blend of real people and cartoon characters, notable for the cheerful 'Zip-A-Dee-Doo-Dah' which won the Award for Best Song over 'You Do' from the colorful *Mother Wore Tights* which teamed Betty Grable, and song and dance man Dan Dailey. A Special Award went to James Baskette who played Uncle Remus in *A Song Of The South*.

ABOVE: Loretta Young as Katrin Holstrom in *The Farmer's Daughter*.
RIGHT: Betty Grable and Dan Dailey in *Mother Wore Tights*.

the carousel operator in the fine thriller *Ride The Pink Horse* starring Robert Montgomery, and Richard Widmark, a psychopathic killer with a fiendish laugh in *Kiss Of Death*, Widmark's debut film. The movie made Widmark famous but though he stole the picture he couldn't steal the Oscar away from Best Supporting Actor nominee Edmund Gwenn in *Miracle On 34th Street*.

Sultry Gloria Grahame received a Supporting Actress nomination for *Crossfire*; Ethel Barrymore for *The Paradine Case*; Marjorie Main for her comic portrayal of Ma Kettle to Percy Kilbride's Pa Kettle in *The Egg And I*, and Anne Revere in *Gentleman's Agreement*. All lost to the other Best Supporting Actress nominee in *Gentleman's Agreement*, Celeste Holm for her performance as a witty compassionate fashion editor, friend to Gregory Peck.

Among the numerous films up for

1948

Best Picture: *Hamlet*.
Actor: Laurence Olivier, *Hamlet*.
Actress: Jane Wyman, *Johnny Belinda*.
Supporting Actor: Walter Huston, *The Treasure Of The Sierra Madre*.
Supporting Actress: Claire Trevor, *Key Largo*.
Director: John Huston, *The Treasure Of The Sierra Madre*.
Writing (Motion Picture Story): Richard Schweizer and David Wechsler, *The Search*.
Writing (Best Written Screenplay): John Huston, *The Treasure Of The Sierra Madre*.
Cinematography (Black And White): William Daniels, *The Naked City*.
Cinematography (Color): Joseph Valentine, William V Skall, Winton Hoch, *Joan Of Arc*.
Art Director (Black And White): Roger K Furse, *Hamlet*.
Art Director (Color): Hein Heckroth, *The Red Shoes*.

Costume Design (Black And White): Roger K Furse, *Hamlet*.
Costume Design (Color): Dorothy Jeakins and Karinska, *Joan Of Arc*.
Sound Recording: Thomas T Moulton, *The Snake Pit*.
Special Effects: Paul Eagler, J McMillan Johnson, Russell Shearman, Clarence Slifer (Visual), Charles Freeman, James G Stewart (Audible), *Portrait Of Jennie*.
Music (Scoring Dramatic Or Comedy Picture): Brian Easdale, *The Red Shoes*.
Music (Scoring Musical Picture): Johnny Green and Roger Eden, *Easter Parade*.
Music (Song): Jay Livingston, and Ray Evans (Lyrics And Music), 'Buttons And Bows' from *The Paleface*.
Short Subjects (Cartoon): *The Little Orphan*, MGM.
Short Subjects (2-Reel): *Seal Island*, Walt Disney.
Irving G Thalberg Memorial Award: Jerry Wald.
Special Awards: *Monsieur Vincent* (France), outstanding foreign

language film released in the United States during 1948. Ivan Jandl, for the outstanding juvenile performance of 1948 in *The Search*. Sid Grauman, master showman, who raised the standard of exhibition of motion pictures. Adolph Zukor, the father of the feature film in America, for services to the industry. Walter Wanger, for distinguished service to the industry in adding to its moral stature by his production of the picture *Joan Of Arc*.

This was a good year for movies and for the great British actor Laurence Olivier. Although British films had been nominated for Best Picture before, notably Olivier's *Henry V* in 1946 and *Great Expectations* in 1947, this was the first time a British movie won the Award for Best Picture. The movie, of course was *Hamlet*, with Olivier not only directing the film but playing the title role. The movie was exquisitely done, with exceptional camera work, especially in the close-ups during the soliloquies. The movie also won Art Direction, Costume Design, and Set Decoration Awards (Black And White).

The achievement is even more impressive when you consider the competition. *The Red Shoes*, a visually exciting film about backstage life in the world of ballet, culminated in a magnificent dance sequence. Stunningly beautiful red-haired Moira Shearer was the ballerina torn between a career and love and the movie deservedly won the Art Direction and Set Direction Awards (Color). *The Snake Pit*, from a novel by Mary Jane Ward, was Hollywood's latest social problem picture, a study of mental illness with particularly memorable images of life in a mental hospital. Besides a Best Picture nomination *The Snake Pit* brought Olivia de Havilland a Best Actress nomination and Anatole Litvak a Best Director nomination.

Also in contention for Best Picture was *Johnny Belinda* which told the story of a deaf mute who is raped and has a child. Despite the melodramatic and sensational subject matter the movie was handled sensitively. Lew Ayres took a Best Actor nomination for his role as the understanding doctor who helps the girl, Jane Wyman won the Best Actress Academy Award for her role as the deaf mute, Jean Negulesco was nominated for Best Director for

Best Actress Jane Wyman in *Johnny Belinda* with Charles Bickford.

Johnny Belinda and Charles Bickford was nominated for Best Supporting Actor.

The one remaining movie nominated for Best Picture was *The Treasure Of The Sierra Madre*, about the corrosive effects of greed. Walter Huston, as the old prospector looking for gold turned in one of the finest performances in the history of film, winning the Best Supporting Actor Oscar. His son John Huston won the Best Director Oscar defeating the other nominees who included Laurence Olivier for *Hamlet* and Fred Zinnemann for *The Search*, a well-made film about GIs searching for displaced children after the war, starring Montgomery Clift whose performance won him a Best Actor nomination.

John Huston also won the Writing (Best Screenplay) Award for *The Treasure Of The Sierra Madre*. Unfortunately, neither Tim Holt nor Humphrey Bogart received nominations. Bogart was especially fine as Fred C Dobbs, the weak soul who turns vicious under the pressure of gold lust. Two actors who did receive Best Actor nominations were Dan Dailey in *When My Baby Smiles At Me* and Clifton Webb as the deliciously insufferable Mr Belvedere in *Sitting Pretty* with pretty Maureen O'Hara. It was a character he would play again.

RIGHT: *Hamlet* with Laurence Olivier won the Academy Award for Best Picture.
BELOW: Humphrey Bogart and Lauren Bacall in *Key Largo* with Claire Trevor.

Best Actress nominees included Ingrid Bergman in *Joan Of Arc*, a role that had always fascinated Bergman. This version of Joan's story was based on the play *Joan Of Lorraine* by Maxwell Anderson and was directed by Victor Fleming. Jose Ferrer received a Best Supporting Actor nomination for his portrayal of the Dauphin. Irene Dunne was nominated for Best Actress for her performance as the strong and loving Norwegian-American mother in *I Remember Mama* and Oscar Homolka was nominated for Best Supporting Actor for his portrayal of Uncle Chris. Up for Best Supporting Actor, too, was Cecil Kellaway who played a Leprechaun in *The Luck Of The Irish*. A Best Actress nomination went to Barbara Stanwyck for her role as the woman targeted for murder in the thriller *Sorry Wrong Number*.

The Best Supporting Actress nominees were Barbara Bel Geddes in *I*

Best Supporting Actor Walter Huston in *The Treasure Of The Sierra Madre* with Bogart, Tim Holt and Bruce Bennett.

Remember Mama; Ellen Corby, Aunt Trina in *I Remember Mama*; Agnes Moorehead, Jane Wyman's harsh aunt in *Johnny Belinda*; Jean Simmons, a delicate Ophelia in *Hamlet*, and the winner, Claire Trevor, absolutely brilliant as Edward G Robinson's pathetic moll, desperate for drink, in *Key Largo*, which starred Humphrey Bogart and Lauren Bacall.

Other important films of the year included *Red River*, Howard Hawk's impressively done western, starring John Wayne with Montgomery Clift; Mark Hellinger's *Naked City*, a suspense film shot on location in New York City, starring Barry Fitzgerald as a cop with Jules Dassin directing; *The Three Musketeers*, splashy and colorful featuring Gene Kelly as D'Artagnan, with Van Heflin, Gig Young, and Robert Coote. Vincent Price was terrific as the villainous Richelieu. Best of all was the romantic little supernatural spell-

binder, *Portrait Of Jennie* with Joseph Cotton as the artist who falls in love with Jennifer Jones, a girl from the past. The cast included Ethel Barrymore, David Wayne, and Lillian Gish. The movie was directed by William Dieterle. At least it won and deservedly the Special Effects Award.

In the Music category 'Buttons and Bows' from *The Paleface* with Bob Hope and Jane Russell won the Oscar even over 'The Woody Woodpecker Song' from the cartoon *Wet Blanket Policy*.

1949

Best Picture: *All The King's Men.*
Actor: Broderick Crawford, *All The King's Men.*
Actress: Olivia de Havilland, *The Heiress.*
Supporting Actor: Dean Jagger, *Twelve O'Clock High.*
Supporting Actress: Mercedes McCambridge, *All The King's Men.*
Director: Joseph L Mankiewicz, *A Letter To Three Wives.*
Writing (Motion Picture Story): Douglas Morrow, *The Stratton Story.*
Writing (Best Written Screenplay): Joseph L Mankiewicz, *A Letter To Three Wives.*
Writing (Story And Screenplay): Robert Pirosh, *Battleground.*
Cinematography (Black And White): Paul C Vogel, *Battleground.*
Cinematography: (Color): Winton Hoch, *She Wore A Yellow Ribbon.*
Art Director (Black And White): Harry Horner and John Meehan, *The Heiress.*
Art Director (Color): Cedric Gibbons and Paule Groesse, *Little Women.*

Costume Design (Black And White): Edith Head and Gile Steele, *The Heiress.*
Costume Design (Color): Leah Rhodes, Travilla, Marjorie Best, *Adventures Of Don Juan.*
Special Effects: RKO Productions, *Mighty Joe Young.*
Music (Scoring Dramatic Or Comedy Picture): Aaron Copland, *The Heiress.*
Music (Scoring Musical Picture): Roger Edens and Lennie Hayton, *On The Town.*
Music (Song): Frank Loesser (Lyrics And Music), 'Baby, It's Cold Outside' from *Neptune's Daughter.*
Short Subjects (Cartoon): *For Scentimental Reasons,* Warner Bros.
Special Awards: *The Bicycle Thief* (Italy), most outstanding foreign language film released in the United States during 1949. Bobby Driscoll, as the outstanding juvenile actor of 1949. Fred Astaire, for his unique artistry and his contributions to the techniques of musical pictures. Cecil B De Mille, distinguished motion picture pioneer. Jean Hersholt, for distinguished service to the Motion Picture Industry.

All The King's Men, written and directed by Robert Rossen, was a successful film adaptation of Robert Penn Warren's novel, based on the life story of corrupt Louisiana politician Huey Long. Broderick Crawford played Willie Stark, the character modeled on Long, from his early days as a country lawyer on through his election as governor and the years of power and violence that followed until his death by assassination. The movie won Best Picture; Broderick Crawford, Best Actor; narrator John Ireland a Best Supporting Actor nomination, and Mercedes McCambridge won the Best Supporting Actress Oscar for her outstanding performance as a newspaper reporter, her very first screen role. Rossen was nominated but did not win the Best Director Award.

In the running against *All The King's Men* for Best Picture was *Battleground*, the story of World War II's Battle of the Bulge and the brave 101st Airborne Division's place in that battle. *Battleground* brought a Best Supporting Actor nomination to James Whitmore. *The Heiress* was based on a play which was itself an adaptation of Henry James's novel *Washington Square*. Olivia de Havilland played the plain but rich Catherine Sloper, and Montgomery Clift was the charming fortune hunter. The film brought de Havilland the Best Actress Award and British actor Ralph Richardson received a Best Supporting Actor nomination for his role as Dr Sloper.

Marriage and the question of who was unfaithful to whom kept the audience guessing and made Best Picture nominee *A Letter To Three Wives* a popular film. Ironically, not a single member of the cast which included Kirk Douglas, Jeanne Crain, Linda Darnell, Ann Sothern, and Paul Douglas received a nomination for the film but writer and director Joseph L Mankiewicz not only received a nomination for *A Letter To Three Wives* but won the Best Director category and the Best Written Screenplay category as well. Among those losing to him were William Wyler for *The Heiress*; William A Wellman for *Battleground*, and Carol Reed for *The Fallen Idol*, an excellent film version of Graham Greene's novel, with Ralph Richardson brilliant as Baines, the married Embassy butler in

Best Supporting Actress Mercedes McCambridge, John Ireland and Best Actor Broderick Crawford in *All The King's Men.*

TOP: Alice Pearce, Ann Miller, Betty Garrett, Frank Sinatra, Jules Munshin, Gene Kelly: *On The Town.*
ABOVE: Olivia de Havilland: *The Heiress.*

love with a French typist.

Another Best Picture nominee *Twelve O'Clock High* featured Gregory Peck as a commanding officer during World War II who cracked under the strain. The film brought Peck a Best Actor nomination and Dean Jagger the Best Supporting Actor Oscar. *Champion*, about a really nasty boxer, gave nominations to Kirk Douglas for Best Actor and Arthur Kennedy for Best Supporting Actor. British repertory actor Richard Todd received a Best Actor nomination in *The Hasty Heart* and John Wayne was nominated for Best Actor in the war picture *Sands Of Iwo Jima.*

Best Actress nominations included Jeanne Crain as Ethel Waters' granddaughter passing for white in *Pinky*. Both Ethel Waters and Ethel Barrymore received Best Supporting Actress nominations for doing the best they could under the circumstances but in retrospect the picture was absurd, very different from the fine *Intruder In The Dust*, which went straight to the core of Southern racism and which wasn't nominated at all. Susan Hayward was nominated for Best Actress in *My Foolish Heart*, co-starring Dana Andrews and memorable chiefly for the song of the same title which helped make the picture a hit. Nominated, too, were Deborah Kerr, Spencer Tracy's wife driven to drink in *Edward, My Son* and Loretta Young in *Come To The Stable*, a movie about nuns not horses. The picture also brought Supporting Actress nominations to both Celeste Holm and Elsa Lanchester.

One of the most popular movies of the year was *The Stratton Story*, with James Stewart as the heroic baseball player Monte Stratton and June Allyson as his loyal wife. The film took the Writing (Motion Picture Story) Award. June Allyson also appeared as Jo in *Little Women* which earned the Art Direction and Set Direction Awards (Color). *She Wore A Yellow Ribbon* with John Wayne, an outstanding western about the US Cavalry, received the Cinematography (Color) Award and the jolly *Adventures Of Don Juan* with Errol Flynn, the Costume Design (Color) Oscar.

This was a good year for musicals. *The Barkleys Of Broadway* was supposed to team Fred Astaire and Judy Garland but wound up reuniting Astaire with Ginger Rogers. The film won a Cinematography (Color) nomination. Better still was *On The Town* with Gene Kelly, Frank Sinatra, Jules Munshin, Betty Garrett, Ann Miller and Vera Ellen. A zinger of a movie it set the pace for musicals for years to come. It really deserved a Best Picture nomination but at least this tale of three sailors on leave in New York won Scoring Of A Musical Picture. The Best Song Award went to 'Baby, It's Cold Outside' from *Neptune's Daughter* starring Red Skelton and Hollywood's favorite swimmer, Esther Williams. Losing to 'Baby, It's Cold Outside' was 'Lavender Blue' from Walt Disney's *So Dear To My Heart* with this year's winner of a Special Award for outstanding juvenile actor, Bobby Driscoll. *Mighty Joe Young*, a gorrilla following in the footsteps of *King Kong*, brought RKO Productions the Special Effects Award and Cecil B De Mille and dance great Fred Astaire both won much deserved Special Awards.

1950

Best Picture: *All About Eve.*
Actor: Jose Ferrer, *Cyrano de Bergerac.*
Actress: Judy Holliday, *Born Yesterday.*
Supporting Actor: George Sanders, *All About Eve.*
Supporting Actress: Josephine Hull, *Harvey.*
Director: Joseph L Mankiewicz, *All Above Eve.*
Writing (Motion Picture Story): Edna and Edward Anhalt, *Panic In The Streets.*
Writing (Screenplay): Joseph L Mankiewicz, *All Above Eve.*
Writing (Story And Screenplay): Charles Brackett, Billy Wilder, D M Marshman, Jr, *Sunset Boulevard.*
Cinematography (Black And White): Robert Krasker, *The Third Man.*
Cinematography (Color): Robert Surtees, *King Solomon's Mines.*
Art Director (Black And White): Hans Dreier and John Meehan, *Sunset Boulevard.*
Art Director (Color): Hans Dreier and Walter Tyler, *Samson And Delilah.*
Costume Design (Black And White): Edith Head and Charles LeMaire, *All About Eve.*
Costume Design (Color): Edith Head, Dorothy Jeakins, Eloise Jenssen, Gile Steel, Gwen Wakeling, *Samson And Delilah.*
Special Effects: *Destination Moon*, George Pal Productions.
Music (Music Score Of A Dramatic Or Comedy Picture): Franz Waxman, *Sunset Boulevard.*
Music (Scoring Musical Picture): Adolph Deutsch and Roger Edens, *Annie Get Your Gun.*
Music (Song): Ray Evans and Jay Livingston (Lyrics And Music), 'Mona Lisa' from *Captain Carey, USA.*
Short Subjects (Cartoon): *Gerald McBoing-Boing*, UPA, Columbia.
Irving G Thalberg Memorial Award: Darryl F Zanuck.
Special Awards: *The Walls Of Malapaga* (France-Italy), most outstanding foreign language film released in the United States during 1950. George Murphy, for his services in interpreting the film industry to the country at large. Louis B Mayer, for distinguished service to the motion picture industry.

TOP: Judy Holliday as Billie Dawn, in *Born Yesterday.*
RIGHT: George Sanders as Addison de Witt and Anne Baxter as Eve Harrington in *All About Eve.*

The new decade got off to a good start movie wise with five very different films nominated for Best Picture. *All About Eve* crackled with witty dialogue and shone with brilliant performances. Bette Davis was in top form as the aging actress fighting for her career against a treacherous young actress who craved stardom for herself. Anne Baxter portrayed the wicked Eve so well she was

nominated for Best Actress as was Davis herself. Had either actress received the Award it would have looked like a replay of the opening scene from the movie. Thelma Ritter, who played Davis' wise maid, was nominated for Best Supporting Actress in *All About Eve* as was Celeste Holm for her portrayal of a decent loyal wife on the verge of losing her husband to the conniving Eve.

Born Yesterday was a sophisticated comedy starring Broderick Crawford with Judy Holliday as a dumb blonde who turns out to be lots brighter than she looks. Holliday's performance was so good she won the Best Actress Oscar against tough competition including Eleanor Parker in *Caged*, a prison film, and the immortal Gloria Swanson who played Norma Desmond, the silent film star dreaming of a comeback in the bitter and bizarre *Sunset Boulevard*, also nominated for Best Picture. *Father Of The Bride* was a domestic comedy starring Spencer Tracy as the father and Elizabeth Taylor as the bride. The

movie was a major hit and in addition to being nominated for Best Picture it brought Tracy a nomination for Best Actor. Best Picture nominee *King Solomon's Mines*, based on H Rider Haggard's novel, was an adventure movie beautifully filmed on location in Africa with Stewart Granger and Deborah Kerr. An earlier version had been filmed in Britain in 1937 with Cedric Hardwicke.

The winning film was *All About Eve* which brought George Sanders a much deserved Best Supporting Actor Award for his role as Addison de Witt, the cynical drama critic attracted to but not taken in by Eve. Sanders received the Oscar over Edmund Gwenn who played an unusual elderly counterfeiter in *Mister 880*; Sam Jaffe as the safe-cracker in *The Asphalt Jungle*, a crime caper which like *All About Eve* featured a stunning young starlet named Marilyn Monroe; Eric Von Stroheim who played an ex-director now valet-butler still in love with former wife Swanson in *Sunset Boulevard*, and Jeff Chandler who portrayed Indian leader Cochise in *Broken Arrow*, a western starring James Stewart.

In the Best Actor category Jose Ferrer won the Oscar for his role as Cyrano, the elegant, eloquent, long-nosed hero in the romantic *Cyrano de Bergerac*. Among those nominated for Best Actor were Louis Calhern who played Justice Oliver Wendell Holmes in *The Magnificent Yankee*; William Holden, the opportunistic young screenwriter in *Sunset Boulevard*, and James Stewart, perfect in *Harvey*, as the gentle Elwood P Dowd whose best friend is a six-foot-three invisible rabbit. *Harvey* also brought the Best Supporting Actress Oscar to Josephine Hull over the other nominess which included Hope Emerson, the six foot two, two hundred and thirty pound prison matron in *Caged* who also appeared as the circus strongwoman in Story And Screenplay nominee *Adam's Rib*, a Hepburn/Tracy vehicle, and Nancy Olson, the ingenue in *Sunset Boulevard*.

Nominated for Best Director were George Cukor for *Born Yesterday*, John Huston for *The Asphalt Jungle*, Billy Wilder for *Sunset Boulevard*, Joseph Mankiewicz for *All About Eve* (the winner) and Carol Reed for *The Third Man*, a masterful spy story and study of evil starring Joseph Cotton, Valli, Trevor Howard, and Orson Welles as Harry Lime, with a script by Graham Greene. The movie deserved many more nominations than it received. The movie wasn't nominated for Best Picture. Orson Welles wasn't nominated for Best Actor or Greene for Writing. At least the movie should have been nominated in the music category. Never has a zither sounded better.

Other important films nominated in various categories this year included *The Gunfighter*, a mature western with Gregory Peck as an ex-hired gun forced to defend himself even though he's sick of killing; Elia Kazan's *Panic In The Streets* with Richard Widmark as a sympathetic character instead of a villain, and *The Men*, a movie about paraplegic war victims starring Marlon Brando. It was also the year of block-buster *Samson And Delilah* starring Victor Mature and Hedy Lamarr. On the musical front Betty Hutton tore up the screen in *Annie Get Your Gun* while Walt Disney's animated production *Cinderella* lit up the screen. 'Bibbidi-Bobbidi-Boo' from *Cinderella* took a Best Song nomination as did 'Be My Love' from *The Toast Of New Orleans* starring singers Mario Lanza and Kathryn Grayson. All Best Song nominees went down before 'Mona Lisa' from *Captain Carey, USA*, a non-musical war picture with Alan Ladd.

Animator Stephen Bosustow, who helped form UPA (United Productions of America) in 1945 after he and several other artists left the Walt Disney studio, took the Cartoon Award for *Gerald McBoing-Boing*, one of the freshest and most delightful cartoons to appear in years. Bosustow was also up for an Oscar for another nominee, *Trouble Indemnity*, part of the popular Mr Magoo Series. The famous Magoo voice belonged to Jim Backus.

Special Awards were renamed this year. Henceforth they would be Honorary Awards. George Murphy, Louis B Mayer, and *The Walls Of Malapaga*, a Franco-Italian film starring Jean Gabin were the first recipients of the Awards under their new title. The emcee of the Awards Ceremony this year was Fred Astaire, winner of a Special Award last year.

Orson Welles as Harry Lime in *The Third Man*.

1951

Best Picture: *An American In Paris.*

Actor: Humphrey Bogart, *The African Queen.*

Actress: Vivien Leigh, *A Streetcar Named Desire.*

Supporting Actor: Karl Malden, *A Streetcar Named Desire.*

Supporting Actress: Kim Hunter, *A Streetcar Named Desire.*

Director: George Stevens, *A Place In The Sun.*

Writing (Motion Picture Story): Paul Dehn and James Bernard, *Seven Days To Noon.*

Writing (Screenplay): Michael Wilson and Harry Brown, *A Place In The Sun.*

Writing (Story And Screenplay): Alan Jay Lerner, *An American In Paris.*

Cinematography (Black And White): William C Mellor, *A Place In The Sun.*

Cinematography (Color): Alfred Gilks and John Alton, *An American In Paris.*

Art Director (Black And White): Richard Day, *A Streetcar Named Desire.*

Art Director (Color): Cedric Gibbons and Preston Ames, *An American In Paris.*

Costume Design (Black And White): Edith Head, *A Place In The Sun.*

Costume Design (Color): Orry-Kelly, Walter Plunkett, Irene Sharaff, *An American In Paris.*

Special Effects: *When Worlds Collide.*

Music (Music Score Of A Dramatic Or Comedy Picture): Franz Waxman, *A Place In The Sun.*

Music (Scoring Musical Picture): Johnny Green and Saul Chaplin, *An American In Paris.*

Music (Song): Johnny Mercer (Lyrics), Hoagy Carmichael (Music), 'In The Cool, Cool, Cool Of The Evening' from *Here Comes The Groom.*

Short Subjects (Cartoon): *Two Mouseketeers*, MGM.

Documentary (Feature Length): *Kon-Tiki.*

Irving G Thalberg Memorial Award: Arthur Freed.

Special Awards: *Rashomon* (Japan), most outstanding foreign language film released in the United States during 1951. Gene Kelly, actor, singer, director and dancer, and specifically for his brilliant achievements in the art of choreography on film.

This was the year when at long last Humphrey Bogart won a Best Actor Academy Award. He had made many good movies by this time, notably *The Maltese Falcon* (1941) which earned a

Vivien Leigh as Blanche and Karl Malden as Mitch in *A Streetcar Named Desire.*

Best Picture nomination and *Casablanca* (1943) which won the Best Picture Award and earned Bogart a Best Actor nomination. He was outstanding in the 1948 *The Treasure Of The Sierra Madre*, also a Best Picture nominee.

The African Queen was a delicious comedy about the tough skipper of an old wreck of a boat (Bogart) and a prim spinster played by Katharine Hepburn who fell in love on a dangerous journey down an African river in 1915. The picture brought Hepburn a Best Actress nomination and John Huston a Best Director nomination but, oddly enough, didn't receive a Best Picture nomination. At least the movie brought Bogart, who played Charlie Allnut, the boat's captain, the recognition he deserved.

In winning the Best Actor Oscar Bogart pulled off something of a coup since Marlon Brando was expected to win it for his performance as the brutish

Stanley Kowalski in the film adaptation of Tennessee Williams's play *A Streetcar Named Desire*. The movie swept all other acting categories. Vivien Leigh won the Best Actress Oscar for her role as the sensitive genteel Blanche Dubois. Karl Malden received Best Supporting Actor for his portrayal of Mitch, Blanche's suitor, and Kim Hunter won Best Supporting Actress as Stella, torn between her passionate attraction to Stanley and the appeal of Blanche's higher ideals. Director Elia Kazan gained a Best Director nomination for the film.

However, *A Streetcar Named Desire*, though nominated, was not named Best Picture. Among the remaining nominees vying for that honor was *Quo Vadis*. Peter Ustinov stole the picture with his stunning portrayal of Nero,

on the play by Arthur Miller. Fredric March played Willy Loman, the salesman whose dreams have turned to ashes, and received a Best Actor nomination for the role. Mildred Dunnock, who played Willy's wife, was nominated for Best Supporting Actress and Kevin McCarthy gained a Best Supporting Actor nomination for his role as Willy's son Biff. *Bright Victory*, a compelling movie about going blind, brought a Best Actor nomination to Arthur Kennedy.

Dectective Story brought William Wyler a Best Director nomination and Eleanor Parker a Best Actress nomination, with Lee Grant nominated for Best Supporting Actress for her portrayal of a young shoplifter. Kirk Douglas played the intolerant detective and William Bendix was the sympathetic cop.

LEFT: Gene Kelly and Leslie Caron strike a pose in the ballet at the end of *An American In Paris*.
BELOW: Humphrey Bogart and Katharine Hepburn fight through a swamp in *The African Queen.*

Rome's dangerously moody emperor, and received a Best Supporting Actor nomination for the role. Leo Genn who played Gaius Petronius, Nero's counselor was also nominated for Best Supporting Actor. The other films nominated for Best Picture were *Decision Before Dawn* and *A Place In The Sun* based on the novel *An American Tragedy* by Theodore Dreiser. Montgomery Clift received a Best Actor nomination for his excellent performance as the weak young man whose try at the American Dream with beautiful Elizabeth Taylor was endangered by Shelley Winters who was nominated for Best Actress for her performance as the dowdy gullible factory worker seduced by Clift. George Stevens won the Best Direction Oscar for *A Place In The Sun.*

The movie that won Best Picture was a glorious musical, *An American In Paris*, starring Gene Kelly, Leslie Caron, Nina Foch and Oscar Levant. The technicolor was lavish, the Gershwin score great, and the movie made Paris seem like Paradise. Vincente Minnelli received a nomination for directing this exercise in pure fantasy so very well.

Another major motion picture of the year was *Death Of A Salesman*, its own variation of an American tragedy, based

Also nominated were Gig Young for Best Supporting Actor in *Come Fill The Cup*, Jane Wyman for Best Actress in *The Blue Veil*, a movie with Charles Laughton which also brought Joan Blondell a Best Supporting Actress nomination for her role as a fading vaudeville star and Thelma Ritter, up for Best Supporting Actress as a mother-in-law posing as a maid in *The Mating Season*, a comedy with Gene Tierney and John Lund.

Nominated for Cinematography (Black And White) was one of Alfred Hitchcock's best suspense films, *Strangers On A Train* with Farley Granger and Robert Walker. Walker certainly deserved a nomination for one of the finest portrayals of a psychopathic maniac and killer in the history of movie-making.

Other major pictures of the year that received nominations in various categories included *Tales Of Hoffmann*, not as impressive as *The Red Shoes* (1948), but a similar attempt at operatic fantasy; *Show Boat* whose chief claim to fame was Ava Gardner as Julie, after Hollywood proved too timid to cast black singer Lena Horne in the role; *The Great Caruso*, a biography of the immortal singer which was one of Mario Lanza's hits, and *Golden Girl* which boasted the charming and talented Mitzi Gaynor. Edith Head won her fourth Award for Costume Design this year in the Black And White subcategory for *A Place In The Sun*, proving once more that she was Hollywood's superstar seamstress.

When Worlds Collide, a modest sci-fi disaster film won the Special Effects category. *Rashomon*, directed by Japan's Akira Kurosawa and starring Toshiro Mifune and Machiko Kyo, told the tale of a violent crime from different viewpoints. The picture was voted outstanding foreign language film of the year. And Gene Kelly was given an Honorary Award in recognition of his dazzling gifts as a film choreographer.

1952

Best Picture: *The Greatest Show On Earth.*
Actor: Gary Cooper, *High Noon.*
Actress: Shirley Booth, *Come Back Little Sheba.*
Supporting Actor: Anthony Quinn, *Viva Zapata!*
Supporting Actress: Gloria Grahame, *The Bad And The Beautiful.*
Director: John Ford, *The Quiet Man.*
Writing (Motion Picture Story): Fredric M Frank, Theodore St John, Frank Cavett, *The Greatest Show On Earth.*
Writing (Screenplay): Charles Schnee, *The Bad And The Beautiful.*
Writing (Story And Screenplay): T E B Clarke, *The Lavender Hill Mob.*
Cinematography (Black And White): Robert Surtees, *The Bad And The Beautiful.*
Cinematography (Color): Winton C Hoch and Archie Stout, *The Quiet Man.*
Art Director (Black And White): Cedric Gibbons and Edward Carfagno, *The Bad And The Beautiful.*
Art Director (Color): Paul Sheriff, *Moulin Rouge.*
Costume Design (Black And White): Helen Rose, *The Bad And The Beautiful.*
Costume Design (Color): Marcel Vertes, *Moulin Rouge.*
Special Effects: *Plymouth Adventure.*

Music (Music Score Of A Dramatic Or Comedy Picture): Dimitri Tiomkin, *High Noon.*
Music (Scoring Musical Picture): Alfred Newman, *With A Song In My Heart.*
Music (Song): Ned Washington (Lyrics) and Dimitri Tiomkin (Music), 'High Noon' from *High Noon.*
Short Subjects (Cartoon): *Johann Mouse*, MGM.
Irving G Thalberg Memorial Award: Cecil B De Mille.
Honorary Awards: *Forbidden Games* (France), best foreign language film first released in the United States during 1952. George Alfred Mitchell for his continued and dominant presence in the field of cinematography. Joseph M Schenck for long and distinguished service to the motion picture industry. Merian C Cooper for his many innovations and contributions to the art of motion pictures. Harold Lloyd, master comedian and good citizen. Bob Hope for his contribution to the laughter of the world.

Westerns made an impact this year and many of them boasted important stars. One of the best, *High Noon*, concerned a sheriff forced to face a trio of avenging killers alone after attempts to drum up support among the citizens of the town

Gary Cooper as Marshal Will Kane in *High Noon*. Cooper won the award for Best Actor, as the lawman who defends the small town singlehanded, against a gang seeking revenge.

failed. The movie was nominated for a Best Picture Award and the movie's hero, Gary Cooper, won the Best Actor Award. The film's director Fred Zinnemann was nominated for Best Director and a lovely blonde actress named Grace Kelly attracted attention, but no nominations, for her portrayal of Cooper's Quaker wife. The movie's famous song, 'High Noon' ('Do Not Forsake Me, Oh My Darlin''), lyrics by Ned Washington, music by Dimitri Tiomkin, won the Best Song Award. Tiomkin was also responsible for the picture's Award winning score.

In the Supporting Actor category character actor Arthur Hunnicut, a steady sidekick in westerns received a nomination for his role in *The Big Sky* which starred Kirk Douglas. An unusual film nominated for Best Picture was *The Quiet Man*, a fine romantic comedy set in Ireland co-starring John Wayne and Maureen O'Hara with Victor McLaglan and Barry Fitzgerald.

The Quiet Man brought McLaglen a Best Supporting Actor nomination and won John Ford the Best Director Oscar.

Nominated for Best Picture, too, was *Ivanhoe*, a lavish adaptation of Scott's novel with Robert Taylor and Elizabeth Taylor. *Moulin Rouge* was a film interpretation of the life of artist Toulouse-Lautrec. Jose Ferrer played Lautrec on his knees since the painter was a dwarf. He also played Lautrec's father standing up. The movie, nominated for Best Picture, brought Ferrer a Best Actor nomination, Colette Marchand a Best Supporting Actress nomination, and John Huston a Best Director nomination. The movie selected as Best Picture was Cecil B De Mille's *The Greatest Show On Earth*, the story of the Ringling Brothers, Barnum and Bailey Circus. De Mille received a Best Director nomination for the movie which featured a cast of thousands including Betty Hutton, Charlton

Heston, Cornel Wilde, and Dorothy Lamour. Still, despite the glitter, the movie was a puzzling and banal choice.

After all, this was the year of *The Lavender Hill Mob*, the British movie from Ealing Studios which won a Writing (Story And Screenplay) Award and brought Alec Guinness a nomination for Best Actor. Guinness played a bank clerk who organized a bank heist. His improbable crew of cronies included Stanley Holloway and Robert Morley. This was also the year of *Singin' In The Rain*, one of Hollywood's top musicals, starring Gene Kelly, Debbie Reynolds, and wizard of dance Donald O'Connor. Comedienne Jean Hagen received a Best Supporting Actress nomination for her role as the silent film star with the squeaky voice whose career goes down with the coming of sound. Adolph

Anthony Quinn (c) and Marlon Brando (r) as Mexican revolutionaries in *Viva Zapata*.

Green and Betty Comden wrote the wonderful script; Producer Arthur Freed drew on the many numbers he had written with Nacio Herb Brown in the past; Harold Rosson was the cinematographer and Kelly and Stanley Donen directed. They weren't nominated and even the song 'Singin' In The Rain' never made it to the Best Song category.

Viva Zapata! about the Mexican revolutionary earned Marlon Brando a Best Actor nomination for his performance in the title role and Anthony Quinn the Supporting Actor Award for his portrayal of Brando's oldest brother. Kirk Douglas received a Best Actor nomination for *The Bad And The Beautiful*, a movie which also brought sexy Gloria Grahame a Best Supporting Actress Oscar. She was also in the

Alec Guinness and Sydney James in *The Lavender Hill Mob* which won the Oscar for Writing (Story and Screenplay).

thriller *Sudden Fear*, playing the sulky moll for whose sake Jack Palance was ready to bump off Joan Crawford. Palance received a Best Supporting Actor nomination for *Sudden Fear* and Crawford was nominated for Best Actress.

Up for Best Actress, too, was Bette Davis, a fading movie star in *The Star*, Julie Harris, remarkable as a twelve-year-old girl in *Member Of The Wedding*, and Susan Hayward in *With A Song In My Heart*, an idealized version of the life of singer Jane Froman, crippled in an air plane crash during World War II. Thelma Ritter, who played the strong nurse who helped Hayward, received a Supporting Actress nomination for the film. The winner of the Best Actress Award was Shirley Booth, outstanding as the drab but touching wife of Burt Lancaster in *Come Back Little Sheba*, based on the play by William Inge.

The remaining Best Supporting

Actor nominee was Richard Burton in *My Cousin Rachel*, a mystery with gothic overtones, starring Olivia de Havilland. The remaining Best Supporting Actress nominee was Terry Moore, the young girl in *Come Back Little Sheba* and the remaining Best Director nominee was Joseph L Mankiewicz for the excellent *Five Fingers*, which started the post-war boom in spy pictures. *The Man In The White Suit*, one of Alec Guinness's most provocative comedies, received a Screenplay nomination, as did the Tracy/Hepburn vehicle *Pat And Mike* while Danny Kaye's colorful *Hans Christian Andersen* received several nominations including Cinematography (Color).

For the first time the Academy Awards were televised and through 1956 ceremonies were held simultaneously in Los Angeles and New York. This year Bob Hope emceed in Los Angeles and Conrad Nagel was the emcee in New York.

1953

Best Picture: *From Here To Eternity.*
Actor: William Holden, *Stalag 17.*
Actress: Audrey Hepburn, *Roman Holiday.*
Supporting Actor: Frank Sinatra, *From Here To Eternity.*
Supporting Actress: Donna Reed, *From Here to Eternity.*
Director: Fred Zinnemann, *From Here To Eternity.*
Writing (Motion Picture Story): Ian McLellan Hunter, *Roman Holiday.*
Writing (Screenplay): Daniel Taradash, *From Here To Eternity.*
Writing (Story And Screenplay): Charles Brackett, Walter Reisch, Richard Breen, *Titanic.*
Cinematography (Black And White): Burnett Guffey, *From Here To Eternity.*
Cinematography (Color): Loyal Griggs, *Shane.*
Art Director (Black And White): Cedric Gibbons and Edward Carfagno, *Julius Caesar.*
Art Director (Color): Lyle Wheeler and George W Davis, *The Robe.*
Costume Design (Black And White): Edith Head, *Roman Holiday.*
Costume Design (Color): Charles Le Maire and Emile Santiago, *The Robe.*
Special Effects: *The War Of The Worlds.*

Music (Music Score Of A Dramatic Or Comedy Picture): Bronislau Kaper, *Lili.*
Music (Scoring Musical Picture): Alfred Newman, *Call Me Madam.*
Music (Song): Paul Francis Webster (Lyrics) and Sammy Fain (Music), 'Secret Love' from *Calamity Jane.*
Short Subjects (Cartoon): *Toot, Whistle, Plunk And Boom*, Disney, Buena Vista.
Short Subjects (2-Reel): *Bear Country*, Disney, RKO Radio.
Documentary (Short Subject): *The Alaskan Eskimo*, Disney, RKO Radio.
Documentary (Feature Length): *The Living Desert*, Disney, Buena Vista.
Irving G Thalberg Memorial Award: George Stevens.
Honorary Awards: Pete Smith, for witty observations of the American scene in the series, *Pete Smith Specialties.* The Twentieth Century-Fox Film Corporation, in recognition of their imagination, showmanship and foresight in introducing the revolutionary process known as CinemaScope. Joseph I Breen, for his conscientious and open-minded management of the Motion Picture Production Code. Bell and Howell Company, for their pioneering achievements in the advancement of the Motion Picture Industry.

Scientific And Technical Awards: Professor Henri Chretien and Earl Sponable, Sol Halprin, Lorin Grignon, Herbert Bragg and Carl Faulkner of Twentieth Century-Fox Studios for creating, developing and engineering the equipment, processes and techniques known as CinemaScope. Fred Waller, for designing and developing the multiple photographic and projection systems which culminated in Cinerama.

Several of the most charming, most talented, and certainly most beautiful film actresses of the decade vied for Awards this time round. French performer Leslie Caron had been considered mainly a dancer until her portrayal of a sensitive orphan loved by puppeteer Mel Ferrer in *Lili* proved she was much more. The picture earned her a nomination for Best Actress and brought director Charles Walters a Best Director nomination as well. Also nominated for Best Actress was Ava Gardner in *Mogambo*, a remake of *Red Dust* with Gardner playing the role originally played by that earlier siren of the silver screen, Jean Harlow. Grace Kelly also received a Best Supporting Actress nomination for her portrayal of the lady-like blonde who was sheer ice, at least on the surface, in *Mogambo*.

Deborah Kerr became the sex symbol of the year thanks to a notorious beach scene opposite Burt Lancaster in *From Here To Eternity*. The film also brought her a Best Actress nomination but co-star Donna Reed won the Best Supporting Actress Award for her performance as Alma, the 'hostess' at the New Congress Club. The competition included Geraldine Page in *Hondo*, Marjorie Rambeau in *Torch Song*, and Thelma Ritter as the lovable but shady victim in *Pickup On South Street*.

The winner of the Best Actress Award was an irresistible ingenue named Audrey Hepburn who took Hollywood by storm for her role as a princess on vacation from royal responsibilities in *Roman Holiday* with Gregory Peck. Included on the list of actresses losing to Hepburn was Maggie McNamara in the then shocking, now tame, *The Moon Is Blue. Roman Holiday* also picked up a Best Picture nomination, William Wyler a Best

Best Supporting Actor Frank Sinatra as Maggio and Montgomery Clift as Prewitt in *From Here To Eternity.*

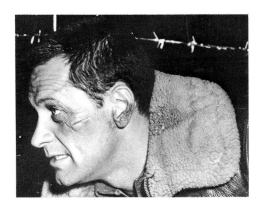

ABOVE: William Holden in *Stalag 17*.
RIGHT: Audrey Hepburn as the princess with Gregory Peck in *Roman Holiday*.

Director nomination, and Eddie Albert a Best Supporting Actor nomination.

Other movies nominated for Best Picture were *Julius Caesar* which brought Marlon Brando a nomination for Best Actor for his portrayal of Mark Antony; *The Robe*, which has the distinction of being the first movie shot in the wide screen process called CinemaScope, a pseudo religious epic with lots of costumes which won Richard Burton a totally undeserved Best Actor nomination; *Shane*, a classic western starring Alan Ladd, and the big winner, *From Here To Eternity*.

Not only did *From Here To Eternity* win the Best Picture Award it brought Burt Lancaster a Best Actor nomination for his performance as the decent Sergeant Warden. Montgomery Clift received a Best Actor nomination for his role as the tough Southerner, Prewitt; Frank Sinatra the Best Supporting Actor Oscar for his role as the tough little soldier, Maggio, and the film won Fred Zinnemann the Best Director Award over, among others, George Stevens for *Shane* and Billy Wilder for *Stalag 17*.

Losing to Sinatra in the Best Supporting Actor category was Jack Palance, magnificent as the villain in *Shane*; Brandon De Wilde, the young boy in *Shane*, and Robert Strauss, who played Animal in *Stalag 17*, a movie about a German POW camp, starring William Holden who received the Best Actor Oscar for his role as the soldier given a raw deal by his fellow prisoners.

On the musical front there was *Call Me Madam*, starring Broadway's leading lady, Ethel Merman; *Calamity Jane*, with pert vivacious Doris Day and the engaging Howard Keel; *The Band Wagon* with Fred Astaire, Cyd Charisse, Oscar Levant and Nanette Fabray, and best of all *Kiss Me Kate*,

Cole Porter's witty take-off on Shakespeare's *Taming Of The Shrew* with Kathryn Grayson, Howard Keel, Ann Miller and Bob Fosse shot in 3-D. Walt Disney received four Oscars, one for cartoon, one for two reel short subject, and two Documentary Awards. A sci-fi thriller *The War Of The Worlds* won a much deserved Special Effects Award.

The big news this year was the introduction of wide screen movies, one Hollywood response to the threat of television. An Honorary Award was given to Twentieth Century-Fox Film Corporation for CinemaScope and a Technical Award went to Professor Henri Chretien, early inventor of the wide screen process, Earl Sponable, Sol Halprin, Lorin Grignon, Herbert Bragg and Carl Faulkner of Twentieth

Century-Fox Studios for creating, developing and engineering the equipment, processes and techniques known as CinemaScope. Other companies soon adopted CinemaScope or produced it under their own trade names. *This Is Cinerama*, nominated in the Music (Scoring Of A Dramatic Or Comedy Picture) category used an extra wide screen system requiring three electronically synchronized projectors. The Cinerama system was developed by Fred Waller who also received a Technical Award. For several years Cinerama resulted mainly in a number of glossy travelogues. It was impressive to look at but too expensive to be practical. Meanwhile, despite CinemaScope, Cinerama and the rest television went marching on.

1954

Best Picture: *On The Waterfront.*
Actor: Marlon Brando, *On The Waterfront.*
Actress: Grace Kelly, *The Country Girl.*
Supporting Actor: Edmond O'Brien, *The Barefoot Contessa.*
Supporting Actress: Eva Marie Saint, *On The Waterfront.*
Director: Elia Kazan, *On The Waterfront.*
Writing (Motion Picture Story): Philip Yordan, *Broken Lance.*
Writing (Screenplay): George Seaton, *The Country Girl.*
Writing (Story And Screenplay): Bud Schulberg, *On The Waterfront.*
Cinematography (Black And White): Boris Kaufman, *On The Waterfront.*
Cinematography (Color): Milton Krasner, *Three Coins In The Fountain.*
Art Director (Black And White): Richard Day, *On The Waterfront.*
Art Director (Color): John Meehan, *20,000 Leagues Under The Sea.*
Costume Design (Black And White): Edith Head, *Sabrina.*
Costume Design (Color): Sanzo Wada, *Gate Of Hell.*
Special Effects: *20,000 Leagues Under The Sea.*

Music (Music Score Of A Dramatic Or Comedy Picture): Dimitri Tiomkin, *The High And The Mighty.*
Music (Scoring Musical Picture): Adolph Deutsch and Saul Chaplin, *Seven Brides For Seven Brothers.*
Music (Song): Sammy Cahn (Lyrics) and Jule Styne (Music), 'Three Coins In The Fountain' from *Three Coins In The Fountain.*
Short Subjects (Cartoon): *When Magoo Flew*, UPA.
Documentary (Feature Length): *The Vanishing Prairie*, Disney, Buena Vista.
Honorary Awards: *Gate Of Hell* (Japan), best foreign language film of 1954. Bausch And Lomb Optical Company, for contributions to the advancement of the motion picture industry. Greta Garbo, for unforgettable performances. Danny Kaye, for his unique talents and his service to the American people. Jon Whitely, for his outstanding juvenile performance in *The Little Kidnappers* (a 1953 British film called *The Kidnappers*, released in the USA in 1954 as *The Little Kidnappers*). Vincent Winter, for his outstanding juvenile performance in *The Little Kidnappers.*

The biggest news of the 1955 Award Ceremony was not who won the Oscar but who lost. Judy Garland was at her magical best in *A Star Is Born* with James Mason, an update of the 1937 Fredric March/Janet Gaynor film. The movie was a tremendous box-office smash and when Best Actress nominee Garland lost to Best Actress nominee Grace Kelly who played a bitter but determined and loving wife trying to deal with an alcoholic husband in *The Country Girl*, Groucho Marx declared it 'the biggest robbery since Brinks.' Also ousted in the Best Actress category was beautiful black actress Dorothy Dandridge, the star of *Carmen Jones*; Audrey Hepburn, charming as the chauffeur's daughter loved by both William Holden and Humphrey Bogart in *Sabrina*, and Jane Wyman in *The Magnificent Obsession*, a three handkerchief movie with Rock Hudson.

With Grace Kelly in *The Country Girl* was Bing Crosby, playing a singer on the skids, a downbeat role for this popular star which earned him a Best Actor nomination. Also nominated for Best Actor was James Mason in *A Star Is Born*, one of the few actors able to appear opposite Garland without fading into the background; Dan O'Herlihy, an Irish actor who turned in a bravura performance in Luis Bunuel's *The Adventures Of Robinson Crusoe*, and

LEFT: Best Actress Grace Kelly with William Holden in *The Country Girl.*
BELOW: Marlon Brando as Terry Malloy in *On The Waterfront*

Matt Mattox performs a solo during the Barn Raising Dance from *Seven Brides For Seven Brothers*.

Humphrey Bogart, memorable as the paranoid yet pathetic Captain Queeg in *The Caine Mutiny*. This movie, basically a courtroom drama about a modern naval mutiny with Van Johnson as a good guy and Fred MacMurray as a cynical troublemaker, won a Best Picture nomination and brought character actor Tom Tully a Best Supporting Actor nomination. But the movie which beat all comers and enshrined 'the method' acting style as the most prestigious style in Hollywood films was *On The Waterfront* which brought Marlon Brando a Best Actor Award.

On The Waterfront, a tale of union corruption and racketeering set on the New York docks, won the Award for Best Picture. The film also brought Elia Kazan the Best Director Oscar and movie newcomer Eva Marie Saint a Best Supporting Actress Award over Nina Foch, sophisticated and chic in *Executive Suite*; Mexican actress Katy Jurado in *Broken Lance*, and Jan Sterling and Claire Trevor, both nominated for *The High And The Mighty*, an

airplane drama starring John Wayne. *On The Waterfront* also brought Supporting Actor nominations to Lee J Cobb, Karl Malden, and Rod Steiger, who played boxer Brando's dishonorable brother brilliantly. The movie took a flock of Awards in other categories as well. The Best Supporting Actor winner, however, was Edmond O'Brien, the press agent in *The Barefoot Contessa*, starring Ava Gardner.

Losing to *On The Waterfront* were Best Picture nominees, *The Country Girl*; *Three Coins In The Fountain*, a three part light romance and travelogue in CinemaScope with Clifton Webb and Dorothy McGuire, and one of the best movie musicals ever made, *Seven Brides For Seven Brothers*. This charming and innocent version of the rape of the Sabine women starred Howard Keel and Jane Powell, with Russ Tamblyn and beautiful Julie Newmar, then Julie Newmeyer. Thanks to the choreography of Michael Kidd, and the talent of such classically trained dancers as Matt Mattox and Jacques d'Amboise, the dancing was superb. Losing to *On The Waterfront* in the direction category were Billy Wilder for *Sabrina*, William Wellman for *The High And The Mighty*, George Seaton for *The Country Girl*,

and Alfred Hitchcock, nominated for the excellent suspense film, *Rear Window*, starring James Stewart and Grace Kelly. Seaton did, however, win the Writing (Screenplay) Oscar for *The Country Girl*.

Nominees in other categories included *The Glenn Miller Story*, about the band leader from the big band era, a quintessential James Stewart/June Allyson picture; *The Egyptian*, with Edmund Purdom and Jean Simmons, a colorful historical epic about monotheism in ancient Egypt; *Brigadoon*, a regrettably static version of the Broadway musical with Gene Kelly who also choreographed the film, and *Desirée* a sweeping costume drama with Jean Simmons and Marlon Brando as Napoleon. The Special Effects Award went to Walt Disney for his *20,000 Leagues Under The Sea*, based on the Jules Verne novel, starring Kirk Douglas, James Mason as Captain Nemo, and a highly impressive giant squid.

Gate Of Hell won Best Foreign Language Film though in the movie's homeland, Japan, it was considered quite ordinary. Two quite extraordinary movie stars received Honorary Awards from the Academy, Greta Garbo and Danny Kaye.

1955

Best Picture: *Marty.*
Actor: Ernest Borgnine, *Marty.*
Actress: Anna Magnani, *The Rose Tattoo.*
Supporting Actor: Jack Lemmon, *Mister Roberts.*
Supporting Actress: Jo Van Fleet, *East Of Eden.*
Director: Delbert Mann, *Marty.*
Writing (Motion Picture Story): Daniel Fuchs, *Love Me Or Leave Me.*
Writing (Screenplay): Paddy Chayefsky, *Marty.*
Writing (Story And Screenplay): William Ludwig and Sonya Levien, *Interrupted Melody.*
Cinematography (Black And White): James Wong Howe, *The Rose Tattoo.*
Cinematography (Color): Robert Burks, *To Catch A Thief.*
Art Director (Black And White): Hal Pereira and Tambi Larsen, *The Rose Tattoo.*
Art Director (Color): William Flannery and Jo Mielziner, *Picnic.*
Costume Design (Black And White): Helen Rose, *I'll Cry Tomorrow.*
Costume Design (Color): Charles Le Maire, *Love Is A Many-Splendored Thing.*
Music (Music Score Of A Dramatic Or Comedy Picture): Alfred Newman, *Love Is A Many-Splendored Thing.*
Music (Scoring Musical Picture): Robert Russell Bennett, Jay Blackton, Adolph Deutsch, *Oklahoma!*, Rodgers and Hammerstein.
Music (Song): Paul Francis Webster (Lyrics) and Sammy Fain (Music), 'Love Is A Many-Splendored Thing' from *Love Is A Many-Splendored Thing.*
Short Subjects (Cartoon): *Speedy Gonzales*, Warner Bros.
Documentary (Short Subject): *Men Against The Arctic*, Disney, Buena Vista.
Honorary Award: *Samurai* (Japan), best foreign language film of 1955.

A young actor destined to become a legend was nominated for Best Actor. His name was James Dean. Another young actor, destined for a long and impressive career in films won his first Oscar in the Supporting Actor category. His name was Jack Lemmon and he received the Award for his comic portrayal of Ensign Pulver in *Mister Roberts*, based on the successful Broadway hit play. The star of the movie (and of the play) Henry Fonda didn't even get a nomination. At least

ABOVE: Ernest Borgnine and Betsy Blair on a date in *Marty.*
LEFT: Anna Magnani and Burt Lancaster in *The Rose Tattoo.*

this engaging movie about the crew of a World War II cargo ship with James Cagney and William Powell included in the cast received a Best Picture nomination.

Cagney was nominated for Best Actor but not for his role as the captain in *Mister Roberts*. He was up for an Oscar for his performance as Doris Day's gangster husband in *Love Me Or Leave Me*, a movie based roughly on the life of singer Ruth Etting. James Dean was nominated for Best Actor for his role as the sensitive boy in the intriguing melodrama *East Of Eden*, based on the novel by John Steinbeck. Raymond Massey played the father and Jo Van Fleet was magnificent as the tough brothel keeper with a soft spot for son Dean. Indeed, she won the Best Supporting Actress Award. Julie Harris, wonderful as Abra the girl loved by Dean, should have been nominated but wasn't. Dean also starred in *Rebel Without A Cause*, about unrest among teenagers in the supposedly placid 1950s, a movie which brought Natalie Wood a Supporting Actress nomination for her role as Dean's girlfriend and Sal Mineo a Best Supporting Actor nomination for his role as the lonely kid named Plato.

The remaining Best Supporting Actor nominees were Arthur Kennedy in *Trial*, Joe Mantell in *Marty*, and veteran character actor Arthur O'Connell in *Picnic*. *Picnic*, nominated for Best Picture and one of the year's hottest movies, starred William Holden as a handsome drifter, Rosalind Russell as a spinster school teacher, and Kim Novak, as an All-American girl low on ingenue charm, but big on sex appeal. The remaining Best Supporting Actress nominees were Betsy Blair in *Marty*, singer Peggy Lee in *Pete Kelly's Blues* and Marisa Pavan, sister of Pier Angeli and wife of Jean-Pierre Aumont in *The Rose Tattoo*.

The overwhelming presence in Best Picture nominee, *The Rose Tattoo*, from a play by Tennessee Williams, was the fiery Italian actress Anna Magnani who won the Best Actress Award over Susan Hayward in *I'll Cry Tomorrow*, based on the life of Lillian Roth and her battle with the bottle; Katharine Hepburn, a spinster having her first and maybe last

affair in *Summertime* with Rossano Brazzi; Jennifer Jones as a Eurasian doctor in *Love Is A Many-Splendored Thing*, with William Holden, and Eleanor Parker in *Interrupted Melody*, the biography of singer Majorie Lawrence, a film which won the Story and Screenplay Award. The movie which won Best Picture and brought a Best Actor Award to Ernest Borgnine and the Best Director Award to Delbert Mann over directors Elia Kazan for *East Of Eden*, David Lean for *Summertime*, John Sturges for the superb suspense film about a racist murder *Bad Day At Black Rock*, and Joshua Logan for *Picnic*, was *Marty*.

Adapted by Paddy Chayefsky from his television play which starred Rod Steiger *Marty*, which brought Chayefsky the Best Screenplay Award, was a touching film about two ordinary lonely people who fall in love. Ironically the

ABOVE RIGHT: Gordon MacRae as Curley and Shirley Jones as Laurey sing 'People Will Say We're In Love,' from *Oklahoma*.
BELOW: William Powell as Doc Daneeka and Best Supporting Actor Jack Lemmon as Ensign Pulver in *Mr Roberts*.

movie, which seemed to condemn those two sacred Hollywood ideals, glamour and beauty, was a kind of anti-Hollywood Hollywood success story. Up against Borgnine in the Best Actor category was Frank Sinatra in *The Man With A Golden Arm*, based on Nelson Algren's novel about a drug addict and Spencer Tracy, the one-armed stranger undeterred by violence who is the catalyst in *Bad Day At Black Rock*.

A wide variety of well-known movies were nominated in several categories. *The Blackboard Jungle* showed that all was not well in inner city schools. Though mild by today's standards the film, starring Glenn Ford as a teacher and Sidney Poitier as a student, dealt with racism and social problems frankly considering the era and so was controversial. One of the best mysteries up for an Award was the ultra glamorous *To Catch A Thief*, with Cary Grant and Grace Kelly, directed by Alfred Hitchcock. The charming French movie *Mr Hulot's Holiday*, starring the amusing Jacques Tati was one of the best comedies.

The great Rodgers and Hammerstein musical *Oklahoma!* appeared on the screen this year, with Gordon MacRae (danced by James Mitchell) and Shirley Jones (danced by Bambi Linn), Gloria Grahame as Ado Annie, and Charlotte Greenwood and Eddie Albert. Despite several nominations the Broadway version was better. In contrast Frank Loesser's *Guys And Dolls* with Marlon Brando as gambler Sky Masterson, Jean Simmons as the Salvation Army lass Sarah Brown, Frank Sinatra as Nathan Detroit and, best of all, Vivian Blaine as the adenoidal Miss Adelaide and Stubby Kaye as Nicely-Nicely was a very nice movie indeed and received nominations in several categories. The Special Effects Award this year went to a war film, *The Bridges Of Toko-Ri*.

1956

Best Picture: *Around The World In Eighty Days.*

Actor: Yul Brynner, *The King And I.*

Actress: Ingrid Bergman, *Anastasia.*

Supporting Actor: Anthony Quinn, *Lust For Life.*

Supporting Actress: Dorothy Malone, *Written On The Wind.*

Director: George Stevens, *Giant.*

Foreign Language Film Award: *La Strada* (Italy).

Writing (Motion Picture Story): Robert Rich (Dalton Trumbo), *The Brave One.*

Writing (Screenplay-Adapted): James Poe, John Farrow, S J Perelman, *Around The World In 80 Days.*

Writing (Screenplay-Original): Albert Lamorisse, *The Red Balloon.*

Cinematography (Black And White): Joseph Ruttenberg, *Somebody Up There Likes Me.*

Cinematography (Color): Lionel Lindon, *Around The World In 80 Days.*

Art Director (Black And White): Cedric Gibbons and Malcolm F Brown (Art Direction), Edwin B Willis and F Keogh Gleason (Set Decoration), *Somebody Up There Likes Me.*

Art Director (Color): Lyle R Wheeler and John DeCuir (Art Direction), Walter M Scott and Paul S Fox (Set Decoration), *The King And I.*

Costume Design (Black And White): Jean Louis, *The Solid Gold Cadillac.*

Costume Design (Color): Irene Sharaff, *The King And I.*

Special Effects: John Fulton, *The Ten Commandments.*

Music (Music Score Of A Dramatic Or Comedy Picture): Victor Young, *Around The World In 80 Days.*

Music (Scoring Musical Picture): Alfred Newman and Ken Darby, *The King And I.*

Music (Song): Ray Evans and Jay Livingston (Lyrics And Music), 'Whatever Will Be Will Be' ('Que Sera, Sera') from *The Man Who Knew Too Much.*

Short Subjects (Cartoon): *Mister Magoo's Puddle Jumper,* UPA.

Short Subjects (2-Reel): *The Bespoke Overcoat.*

Documentary (Feature Length): *The Silent World.*

Irving G Thalberg Memorial Award: Buddy Adler.

Jean Hersholt Humanitarian Award: Y Frank Freeman.

Honorary Award: Eddie Cantor, for distinguished service to films.

This was a good year for big epic movies whether musicals, dramas, or comedies, rich in stars, costumes, and color. The immortal *The King And I*, based on the Broadway Rodgers and Hammerstein musical won a Best Picture nomination, and brought Yul Brynner the Best Actor Oscar for his performance as the exotic king, recreated from his role on stage. Deborah Kerr played Anna (vocals by Marni Nixon), whose western ideas posed a challenge to the king, and was nominated for Best Actress. *Giant*, based on the Edna Ferber novel about Texas, was a gigantic film, a three generation saga which won a Best Picture nomination, a Best Actor nomination for James Dean, aging on screen from a young cowboy to an old and dangerous millionaire, a

Best Actor nomination, too, for Rock Hudson, and a Best Supporting Actress nomination for Mercedes McCambridge. Elizabeth Taylor was the woman married to Hudson and desired by Dean. The movie's enormous success was due in part to Dean's death in an auto accident in 1955 and the subsequent growth of the 'Jimmy Dean legend.'

The Ten Commandments boasted Charlton Heston as Moses. Cecil B de Mille had made a film with the same title in 1923 but only half of it concerned the Bible. In this version de Mille really zoomed in on scripture, or at least his interpretation of it. The movie ran on for hours, stunning the Academy into giving it a Best Picture nomination. Yul Brynner was in the movie as the Pharaoh. On a smaller scale Best Picture nominee *Friendly Persuasion* was a charming film about Quaker farmers during the Civil War with Gary Cooper and Dorothy McGuire in fine form, a lovely song called 'Friendly Persuasion' ('Thee I Love') which picked up a best song nomination, and an excellent perform-

LEFT: Ingrid Bergman in *Anastasia.*
BELOW: James Dean in *Giant.*
RIGHT: Shirley MacLaine as Aouda, David Niven as Phileas Fogg and Cantinflas as Passepartout in *Around The World In Eighty Days.*

ance by a young appealing actor, Anthony Perkins, who received a Best Supporting Actor nomination.

The movie which won the Award for Best Picture was Mike Todd's adaptation of the Jules Verne novel, *Around The World In 80 Days*, a screen-filling globe-trotting movie featuring, apparently, everybody in Hollywood and a number of international stars as well. The cast included David Niven, Cantinflas, Frank Sinatra, Fernandel, Peter Lorre, Charles Boyer, Marlene Dietrich, Buster Keaton and Shirley MacLaine. (The movie had size and scope, but little else to justify its Oscar.)

Lust For Life earned Kirk Douglas a Best Actor nomination for his portrayal of the artist Vincent Van Gogh and brought Anthony Quinn the Best Supporting Actor Award for his portrayal of the painter, Gauguin. Sir Laurence Olivier, brilliant in the title role of *Richard III*, also received a Best Actor nomination. Up for Best Actress was Carroll Baker, as the thumbsucking babyish blonde in Tennessee Williams's

Baby Doll, with Eli Wallach and Karl Malden. It was a movie which helped ease the restrictive Hollywood Production Code.

The remaining nominees for Best Actress were Katharine Hepburn, once again a spinster ready for love, this time in *The Rainmaker*, with Burt Lancaster as the itinerant con artist; Nancy Kelly, the mother in *The Bad Seed*, a movie about an almost supernaturally evil little girl, and Ingrid Bergman in *Anastasia*, a puzzle about the fate of the youngest daughter of the last Russian Tsar. It was Bergman's first American film in years and she won the Oscar for it. The Award was given to her in part as a peace offering to atone for the way America (and Hollywood) had treated her over her 'scandalous' love affair with Roberto Rossellini earlier in the decade.

The Best Supporting Actress Oscar went to Dorothy Malone, sexually insatiable in *Written On The Wind*, a movie which also brought a Best Supporting Actor nomination to Robert

Stack. Malone won her Award over, among others, Eileen Heckart who was also in *Bus Stop* but was nominated in *The Bad Seed*; child actress Patty McCormack, the killer brat in *The Bad Seed*, and Mildred Dunnock, Aunt Rose Comfort in *Baby Doll*. Mickey Rooney received a Best Supporting Actor nomination in the war movie *The Bold And The Brave* and Don Murray a Best Supporting Actor nomination for his role as the smitten cowboy out to win the girl of his dreams one way or another in *Bus Stop*. Best Director nominees were Michael Anderson for *Around The World In 80 Days*, Walter Lang for *The King And I*, King Vidor for *War And Peace* which starred Henry Fonda as Pierre and Audrey Hepburn as Natasha, William Wyler for *Friendly Persuasion* and the winner, George Stevens for *Giant*.

Lots of good movies were nominated in a variety of categories including *High Society*, a musical version of *The Philadelphia Story* (1940), with a lyrical score by Cole Porter. *High Society* starred Grace Kelly, Bing Crosby, Frank Sinatra and Celeste Holm. Also on the list of excellent films nominated

for Awards was the Italian neo-realistic movie *Umberto D* about a lonely old man; the British comedy, *The Lady Killers*, with Alec Guinness, Katie Johnson, and Peter Sellers; the enchanting French fantasy *The Red Balloon*, which won the Award for the Best Original Screenplay; *The Solid*

Gold Cadillac, a comedy with Judy Holliday and Paul Douglas that won only in the Black And White Costume Design category, and Jacques-Yves Cousteau's feature documentary about the sea, *The Silent World*, which took an Oscar. A popular boxing film, *Somebody Up There Likes Me*, also proved an Award winner, for Art Direction (Black And White).

The Best Song Award went to 'Whatever Will Be, Will Be' ('Que Sera, Sera') from Alfred Hitchcock's *The Man Who Knew Too Much*, starring James Stewart and Doris Day, a much altered remake of Hitchcock's original 1934 film which had starred Leslie Banks, Edna Best and Peter Lorre. A new category established this year was the Foreign Language Film Award, and Federico Fellini's *La Strada* with Anthony Quinn, Richard Basehart, and Giulietta Masina won the first Oscar.

This was the last year the Awards Ceremonies were held in both New York and Los Angeles. From now on it would all take place in Los Angeles. The emcee in California this year was comic Jerry Lewis and the emcee in New York was Celeste Holm. To the embarrassment of the Academy a Writing Award went to Robert Rich for *The Brave One*. Rich turned out to be a pseudonym for blacklisted writer Dalton Trumbo.

TOP LEFT: 'Shall We Dance,' Deborah Kerr and Yul Brynner in *The King And I*.
BELOW: Giulietta Masina, Anthony Quinn and Richard Basehart in *La Strada*.

1957

Best Picture: *The Bridge On The River Kwai.*

Actor: Alec Guinness, *The Bridge On The River Kwai.*

Actress: Joanne Woodward, *The Three Faces Of Eve.*

Supporting Actor: Red Buttons, *Sayonara.*

Supporting Actress: Miyoshi Umeki, *Sayonara.*

Director: David Lean, *The Bridge On The River Kwai.*

Foreign Language Film Award: *The Nights Of Cabiria* (Italy).

Writing (Screenplay Adaptation): Pierre Boulle, *The Bridge On The River Kwai.*

Writing (Story And Screenplay Original): George Wells, *Designing Woman.*

Cinematography: Jack Hildyard, *The Bridge On The River Kwai.*

Art Director: Ted Hawarth (Art Direction), Robert Priestley (Set Decoration), *Sayonara.*

Costume Design: Orry-Kelly, *Les Girls.*

Special Effects: Walter Rossi, *The Enemy Below.*

Music (Scoring): Malcolm Arnold, *The Bridge On The River Kwai.*

Music (Song): Sammy Cahn (Lyrics), James Van Heusen (Music), 'All The Way' from *The Joker Is Wild.*

Short Subjects (Cartoon): *Birds Anonymous*, Warner Bros.

Jean Hersholt Humanitarian Award: Samuel Goldwyn.

Honorary Awards: Charles Brackett, for outstanding service to the Academy. B B Kahane, for distinguished service to the Motion Picture Industry. Gilbert M (Broncho Billy) Anderson, motion picture pioneer.

The great British actor Alec Guinness won the Best Actor Award for his role as the British colonel Nicholson in an unusual war movie, *The Bridge On The River Kwai* with William Holden and Jack Hawkins. A film without huge battle scenes and with vast visual beauty *The Bridge On The River Kwai*, set in a Japanese prisoner of war camp during World War II, focused on the inner turmoil of the characters under the pressure of military codes. The movie also captured Best Picture and brought the Best Director Award to David Lean. The Best Screenplay Award went to Pierre Boulle who had also written the novel the movie was based on. Japanese veteran actor Sessue Hayakawa received a Supporting Actor nomination, and the film picked up nominations and Awards in several other categories as well.

Other movies nominated for Best Picture were *Peyton Place*, the film version of Grace Metalious's novel about sex in a small town which gave birth to a sequel, *Return To Peyton Place* in 1961, and spawned a television serial in 1965; *Sayonara*, about a romance between an American air force officer and a Japanese girl after World War II, from a James Michener novel; *Twelve Angry Men*, the film version of a television play about a jury with Henry Fonda, E G Marshall and Lee J Cobb, not one of whom received an Oscar nomination, and the delightful *Witness For The Prosecution*, based on a play by Agatha Christie starring a deceptively icy Marlene Dietrich who deserved a nomination but didn't get one.

Charles Laughton, magnificent as the obstinate QC in *Witness For The Prosecution*, did receive a Best Actor nomination and Elsa Lanchester, also splendid as his persistent nurse, was nominated for Best Supporting Actress.

LEFT: James Donald and Alec Guinness in *The Bridge On The River Kwai.*
BELOW: Joanne Woodward played a woman with multiple personalities in *The Three Faces Of Eve.*

Another Best Actor nominee was Marlon Brando in *Sayonara*. Though Brando didn't win Red Buttons won the Best Supporting Actor Award and Miyoshi Umeki the Best Supporting Actress for their roles as the lovers who marry but are doomed to part in *Sayonara*. Anthony Quinn, an Italian immigrant in *Wild Is The Wind*, received a Best Actor nomination and Anna Magnani a Best Actress nomination for her role in this particular version of the old mail order bride story. Anthony Franciosa was nominated for Best Actor for repeating his successful Broadway role in *A Hatful Of Rain*.

Deborah Kerr received a Best Actress nomination for her portrayal of a nun shipwrecked on a desert island with Robert Mitchum in *Heaven Knows, Mr Allison*. Elizabeth Taylor was nominated for Best Actress as the Southern belle opposite Montgomery Clift in *Raintree County*, a movie memorable chiefly for its costumes. Lana Turner, a sexually repressed widow in *Peyton Place* whose notoriety because of the off-screen Johnny Stompanato scandal helped make the picture a hit also picked up a Best Actress nomination. All these established stars lost to a brilliant young talent, Joanne Woodward, who won the Best Actress Oscar for *Three Faces Of Eve*, a movie based upon an actual psychiatric case of split personality.

A surprise nominee for Best Supporting Actor was Vittorio De Sica in *A Farewell To Arms*, based on the novel by Ernest Hemingway, with Rock Hudson and Jennifer Jones. The 1932 version with Gary Cooper and Helen Hayes, directed by Frank Borzage, was better. Also nominated for Best Supporting Actor were Arthur Kennedy and Russ Tamblyn, both for *Peyton Place*. Carolyn Jones received a Best Supporting Actress nomination for her role in *The Bachelor Party*, another movie adapted from a TV play, in this case one by Paddy Chayefsky, about an unhappy disappointed group of New York City office workers. Nominated, too, for Best Supporting Actress were Hope Lange and Diane Varsi, both for *Peyton Place* with Varsi in the role of Lana Turner's mixed-up daughter. The Best Director nominees included Joshua Logan for *Sayonara*, the movie that proved America and Japan were now friends; Sidney Lumet for *Twelve Angry Men*; Mark Robson for *Peyton Place*, and Billy Wilder for *Witness For The Prosecution*.

Two rather than three Writing Awards were given this year and *Designing Woman*, starring Lauren Bacall and Gregory Peck won the Award for Best Story And Screenplay. This movie was originally meant for Grace Kelly who had retired from the screen to become Princess Grace of Monaco. During the filming Bacall's husband, Humphrey Bogart, died.

Among the films nominated in a variety of categories were *Les Girls* with Gene Kelly as a song-and-dance man; *Pal Joey*, based on the hit Broadway musical, starring Frank Sinatra, Rita Hayworth, and Kim Novak; the fabulously successful western, *Gunfight At*

Miyoshi Umeki and Red Buttons both won awards for *Sayonara*.

The OK Corral, with Burt Lancaster as Wyatt Earp and Kirk Douglas as Doc Holliday, and *Boy On A Dolphin* with Alan Ladd and the dazzlingly beautiful Sophia Loren. 'All The Way' from *The Joker Is Wild* with Frank Sinatra was awarded Best Song. Italian director Fredrico Fellini's *The Nights Of Cabiria* with a touching performance by Giuletta Masina whose expressive face made subtitles unnecessary won the Foreign Language Film Award. The movie became the basis of a Broadway musical, *Sweet Charity*, later a film with Shirley MacLaine. This year's Oscar Ceremony featured a host of hosts, emcees James Stewart, David Niven, Jack Lemmon, Rosalind Russell, Bob Hope, and on film the one and only Donald Duck.

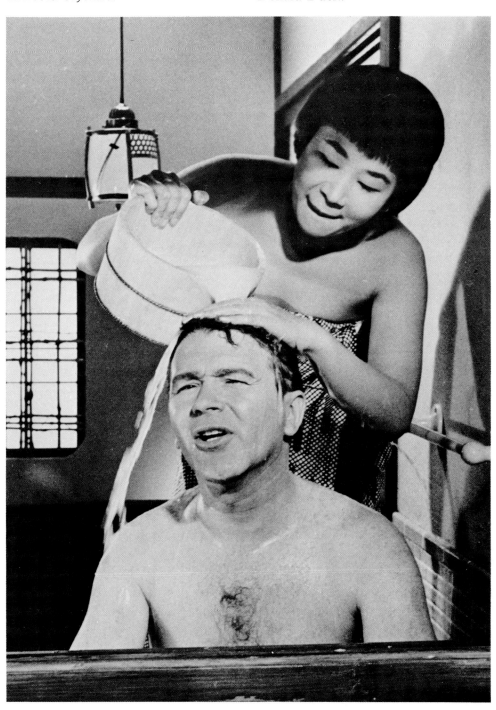

1958

Best Picture: *Gigi.*
Actor: David Niven, *Separate Tables.*
Actress: Susan Hayward, *I Want To Live.*
Supporting Actor: Burl Ives, *The Big Country.*
Supporting Actress: Wendy Hiller, *Separate Tables.*
Director: Vincente Minnelli, *Gigi.*
Foreign Language Film: *My Uncle* (France).
Writing (Screenplay Based On Material From Another Medium): Alan Jay Lerner, *Gigi.*
Writing (Story And Screenplay Written Directly For The Screen): Nathan E Douglas and Harold Jacob Smith, *The Defiant Ones.*
Cinematography (Black And White): Sam Leavitt, *The Defiant Ones.*
Cinematography (Color): Joseph Ruttenberg, *Gigi.*
Art Director: William A Horning and Preston Ames (Art Direction), Henry Grace and Keogh Gleason (Set Decoration), *Gigi.*
Costume Design: Cecil Beaton, *Gigi.*
Special Effects: Tom Howard, *Tom Thumb.*
Music (Music Score Of A Dramatic Or Comedy Picture): Dimitri Tiomkin, *The Old Man And The Sea.*
Music (Scoring Musical Picture): Andre Previn, *Gigi.*
Music (Song): Alan Jay Lerner (Lyrics), Frederick Loewe (Music), 'Gigi' from *Gigi.*
Short Subjects (Cartoon): *Knighty Knight Bugs.*
Documentary (Feature Length): *White Wilderness.*
Irving G Thalberg Memorial Award: Jack L Warner.
Honorary Award: Maurice Chevalier, for his contributions to the world of entertainment for more than half a century.

The man of the hour was Maurice Chevalier who not only received an Honorary Award for his contributions to the world of entertainment for more than half a century but who also enchanted the public with his performance as the old friend of the family in *Gigi*, voted Best Picture. Set in turn-of-the-century Paris, and adapted from a story by Colette, *Gigi* was a musical with a Lerner and Loewe score which told the story of a young girl raised to be a rich man's mistress who plays it smart and becomes a rich man's wife. Leslie

Louis Jourdan, Leslie Caron and Maurice Chevalier starred in *Gigi*.

Caron and Louis Jourdan starred and the movie won Vincente Minnelli the Best Director Oscar.

Among the movies nominated for Best Picture was *Auntie Mame*, about a lively and Bohemian lady with a great zest for life, played by Rosalind Russell who received a Best Actress nomination for the role. The picture also gave Peggy Cass a Best Supporting Actress nomination for her portrayal of the awkward Miss Gooch. Also nominated was Tennessee William's *Cat On A Hot Tin Roof*, a timultous examination of relationships with, though muted, some delving into the subject of homosexuality. *Cat On A Hot Tin Roof* brought Paul Newman a Best Actor nomination for his portrayal of the character Brick, Elizabeth Taylor a Best Actress nomination for her role as Newman's wife, and director Richard Brooks a Best Director nomination. The film's cast included Burl Ives who received the Best Supporting Actor Award this year for another movie, *The Big Country*, a

huge spectacular western about a family feud among ranchers with Gregory Peck and Charlton Heston.

Best Picture nominee *The Defiant Ones* had Tony Curtis and Sidney Poitier as escaped convicts, one white, one black, chained together but divided by racial bigotry and hatred. The movie, which earned Best Actor nominations for both Curtis and Poitier, also brought Theodore Bikel a Best Supporting Actor nomination for his role as the sheriff, Cara Williams a Supporting Actress nomination, and director Stanley Kramer a Directing nomination. Also nominated for Best Picture was *Separate Tables* which allowed David Niven to win the Best Actor Oscar over, among others, Spencer Tracy in the film version of Ernest Hemingway's *The Old Man And The Sea*. Niven portrayed a lonely con artist posing as a retired British major. *Separate Tables*

Susan Hayward won her Oscar for her role as Barbara Graham in *I Want To Live*.

won Wendy Hiller the Best Supporting Actress Academy Award for her portrayal of the kind and understanding hotel manager and brought Deborah Kerr a Best Actress nomination for her role as a spinster crushed by her mother brilliantly played by Gladys Cooper.

The winner of the Best Actress Award was Susan Hayward who played Barbara Graham, a prostitute convicted of murder and sent to the gas chamber, fighting for her life in *I Want To Live*. This film also brought director Robert Wise a Best Director nomination. Nominated for Best Actress, too, was Shirley MacLaine, appealing in the movie version of James Jones's novel *Some Came Running*, starring Frank

Sinatra, a picture which also brought a Best Supporting Actor nomination to Arthur Kennedy and a Best Actress nomination to Martha Hyer. Veteran actor Lee J Cobb received a Best Actor nomination for *The Brothers Karamazov* which starred Yul Brynner.

The remaining nominees in the Supporting Actor and Supporting Actress categories were Gig Young in *Teacher's Pet* and Maureen Stapleton, wonderful in *Lonelyhearts*, her debut film. The remaining nominee for Best Director was Mark Robson for *The Inn Of The Sixth Happiness* which starred Ingrid Bergman as an unofficial missionary in China.

One of the best pictures of the year *The Goddess*, a film biography based on the life of Marilyn Monroe, written by Paddy Chayefsky and starring Kim Stanley who turned in a remarkable performance, should have won many nominations but actually only earned one, in the Writing category, perhaps because the movie revealed a side of Hollywood the industry preferred to ignore. Other notable movies nominated in a variety of categories included the delightful *The Horse's Mouth*, starring Alec Guinness as an artist; *Bell, Book, And Candle*, a comedy about witches, starring James Stewart and Kim Novak with engaging performances by Elsa Lanchester, Hermione Gingold, Jack Lemmon and Ernie Kovacs, and *Vertigo*, also with Stewart and Novak, a suspense film with supernatural overtones directed by Alfred Hitchcock. This was also the year *South Pacific* reached the screen, starring Mitzi Gaynor and Rossano Brazzi. *My Uncle* starring the splendid French actor Jacques Tati, received the Foreign Language Film Award. Bugs Bunny, with the voice of Mel Blanc giving him panache won the Cartoon category, and at the Awards ceremony, the Academy really outdid itself with Bob Hope, Jerry Lewis, comedian Mort Sahl, Tony Randall, Sir Laurence Olivier and David Niven all doing the honors.

ABOVE: Best Actor David Niven as Major Pollock in *Separate Tables*.
BELOW: Sidney Poitier and Tony Curtis in *The Defiant Ones*.

1959

Best Picture: *Ben-Hur.*
Actor: Charlton Heston, *Ben-Hur.*
Actress: Simone Signoret, *Room At The Top.*
Supporting Actor: Hugh Griffith, *Ben-Hur.*
Supporting Actress: Shelley Winters, *The Diary Of Anne Frank.*
Director: William Wyler, *Ben-Hur.*
Foreign Language Film Award: *Black Orpheus* (France).
Writing (Screenplay Based On Material From Another Medium): Neil Paterson, *Room At The Top.*
Writing (Story And Screenplay Written Directly For The Screen): Russell Rouse, Clarence Greene (Story), Stanley Shapiro, Maurice Richlin (Screenplay-Adaptation), *Pillow Talk.*
Cinematography (Black And White): William C Mellor, *The Diary Of Anne Frank.*
Cinematography (Color): Robert L Surtees, *Ben-Hur.*
Art Director (Black And White): Lyle R Wheeler, George W Davis (Art Direction), Walter M Scott, Stuart A Reiss (Set Decoration), *The Diary Of Anne Frank.*
Art Direction (Color): William A Horning, Edward Carfagno, Hugh Hunt (Set Direction), *Ben-Hur.*
Costume Design (Black And White): Orry-Kelly, *Some Like It Hot.*
Costume Design (Color): Elizabeth Haffenden, *Ben-Hur.*
Special Effects: A Arnold Gillespie and Robert MacDonald (Visual), Milo Lory (Audible), *Ben-Hur.*
Music (Score Of A Dramatic Or Comedy Picture): Miklos Rozsa, *Ben-Hur.*
Music (Scoring Musical Picture): Andre Previn and Ken Darby, *Porgy And Bess.*
Music (Song): Sammy Cahn (Lyrics) and James Van Heusen (Music), 'High Hopes' from *A Hole In The Head.*
Short Subjects (Cartoon): *Moonbirds.*
Jean Hersholt Humanitarian Award: Bob Hope.
Honorary Award: Buster Keaton for his unique talents which brought immortal comedies to the screen.

This time round the Academy earned a mark of 'B' for banal for giving the epic *Ben-Hur* no less than eleven Oscars and slighting some pretty impressive films enroute. One of Alfred Hitchcock's best movies in years, *North By Northwest* did not even get a Best Picture nomination nor did the director and cast receive nominations. Yet Cary Grant was absolutely charming in the movie, Eva Marie Saint was cool and pretty, and James Mason made an elegant villain. Though the movie was nominated in several technical categories, it did not pick up a nomination for Costume Design or Special Effects which it certainly deserved. The delightful comedy *Some Like It Hot* fared better. At least Jack Lemmon was nominated for Best Actor and Billy Wilder received a Writing nomination and a Best Director nomination for the film and the picture did win the Award for Best Black and White Costume Design. But this gem of a picture starring Lemmon and Tony Curtis as a couple of musicians in drag with Marilyn Monroe at her sexiest and funniest deserved a whole lot more.

The Four Hundred Blows, written and directed by Francois Truffaut, was a perceptive movie about a young boy. This important 'new wave' film from France received Best Story And Screenplay nominations but not one Foreign Language Film Award. Neither did *Wild Strawberries* by the great Swedish director Ingmar Bergman. Fortunately

BELOW: Jack Lemmon and Tony Curtis in *Some Like It Hot.*

for the Academy's reputation a visually beautiful and celebrated film did win the Foreign Language Film category. This was *Black Orpheus*, written and directed by Marcel Camus. Based on the myth of Orpheus and Eurydice the movie with a black cast starring Marpessa Dawn and Breno Mello was set in Rio during carnival.

A fine British movie, *Room At The Top*, was nominated for Best Picture. Based on John Braine's novel the film told the story of an ambitious young man's climb to the top. It was the first of a series of British movies about working-class life to catch on in America. The movie brought Laurence Harvey a Best Actor nomination, and the great French actress Simone Signoret won the Best Actress Award for her role as the sensual mistress Harvey abandons. British actress Hermione Baddeley received a nomination (Best Supporting Actress) in *Room At The Top* as did the film's director, Jack Clayton, who won in the Best Director category.

LEFT: The chariot race in *Ben-Hur* with Charlton Heston, and Stephen Boyd as Messala.
BELOW: *Black Orpheus* was set in Rio.

ABOVE: Lou Jacobi, Shelley Winters, Richard Beymer and Joseph Schildkraut – *The Diary Of Anne Frank.*
BELOW: Simone Signoret and Laurence Harvey in *Room At The Top.*

A courtroom drama about rape, *Anatomy Of A Murder* received a Best Picture nomination, bringing a Best Actor nomination to James Stewart for his role as the defense attorney, George C Scott a Supporting Actor nomination for his role as the cynical and sarcastic special attorney and a Supporting Actor nomination, too, to Arthur O'Connell. The cast included Ben Gazarra and Lee Remick. Also up for Best Picture was *The Diary Of Anne Frank*, which earned Shelley Winters the Best Supporting Actress Award for her portrayal of Mrs Van Daan, one of the Jews hiding out from the Nazis with the Frank family in an attic in Amsterdam, and *The Nun's Story*, a melodrama with a religious theme, well acted by Audrey Hepburn who received a Best Actress nomination for the movie.

The winner of the Best Picture category was *Ben-Hur*, the story of a Jewish nobleman in the days of ancient Rome. The movie, a remake of the 1925 hit, was notable for a stirring chariot race, and brought a Best Actor Award to Charlton Heston as Ben-Hur, a Best Supporting Actor Award to Hugh Griffith who stole the picture in his role as the Arab sheik, Ilderim, and the Best Director Award to William Wyler. Losing to Heston, along with the other Best Actor nominees, was Paul Muni

who played a cantankerous but kindly doctor in *The Last Angry Man*, his last performance. Losing to Hugh Griffith, along with the other Best Supporting Actor nominees were Ed Wynn who played Mr Dussel the dentist in *The Diary Of Anne Frank*, and Robert Vaughan in *The Young Philadelphians*, whose career really clicked when he starred in the television series *The Man From U.N.C.L.E.* in the mid sixties.

The remaining nominees for Best Actress were Doris Day in *Pillow Talk*, the first of the glamorous and popular comedies which teamed her with Rock Hudson, and Katharine Hepburn and Elizabeth Taylor, both nominated for

Tennessee Williams's shocker, *Suddenly Last Summer*. The Supporting Actress nominees included Susan Kohner and Juanita Moore in *Imitation Of Life*, adapted from Fannie Hurst's romantic novel which was originally filmed in the thirties with Claudette Colbert but which this time round starred Lana Turner, and the incomparable Thelma Ritter, in *Pillow Talk*. Among those who lost in the Direction category were George Stevens for *The Diary Of Anne Frank* and Fred Zinnemann for *The Nun's Story*.

George Gershwin's *Porgy And Bess* starring Sidney Poitier (vocals by Robert McFerrin) and Dorothy Dandrige (vocals by Adele Addison), with Sammy Davis, Jr as Sportin' Life and Pearl Bailey as Maria, won the Award for the Best Musical. The winner of the Best Song category was 'High Hopes' from *A Hole In The Head*, starring Frank Sinatra. One of Hollywood's great clowns from the silent era whose career was once again on the upswing, Buster Keaton, won a well-deserved Honorary Award.

1960

Best Picture: *The Apartment.*
Actor: Burt Lancaster, *Elmer Gantry.*
Actress: Elizabeth Taylor, *Butterfield 8.*
Supporting Actor: Peter Ustinov, *Spartacus.*
Supporting Actress: Shirley Jones, *Elmer Gantry.*
Director: Billy Wilder, *The Apartment.*
Foreign Language Film Award: *The Virgin Spring* (Sweden)
Writing (Screenplay-Adaptation): Richard Brooks, *Elmer Gantry.*
Writing (Screenplay-Original): Billy Wilder, *The Apartment.*
Cinematography (Black And White): Freddie Francis, *Sons And Lovers.*
Cinematography (Color): Russell Metty, *Spartacus.*
Art Director (Black And White): Alexander Trauner, Edward G Boyle (Set Direction), *The Apartment.*
Art Director (Color): Alexander Golitzen, Eric Orbom (Set Decoration), Russell A Gausman and Julia Heron, *Spartacus.*
Costume Design (Black And White): Edith Head and Edward Stevenson, *The Facts Of Life.*

Costume Design (Color): Valles and Bill Thomas, *Spartacus.*
Special Effects: Gene Warren and Tim Baar (Visual), *The Time Machine.*
Music (Score Of A Dramatic or Comedy Picture): Ernest Gold, *Exodus.*
Music (Musical): Morris Stoloff and Harry Sukman, *Song Without End (The Story Of Franz Liszt).*
Music (Song): Manos Hadjidakis (Lyrics And Music), 'Never on Sunday' from *Never On Sunday.*
Short Subjects (Cartoon): *Munro.*
Documentary (Feature): *The Horse With The Flying Tail.*
Jean Hersholt Humanitarian Award: Sol Lesser.
Honorary Awards: Gary Cooper, for his many memorable screen performances. Stan Laurel, for his creative pioneering in the field of cinema comedy. Hayley Mills, for *Pollyanna*, the most outstanding juvenile performance during 1960.

Burt Lancaster as the evangelist in *Elmer Gantry.*

John Wayne's epic, *The Alamo* received a Best Picture nomination as did a movie about itinerant Australian sheepherders called *The Sundowners* which starred Deborah Kerr who received a Best Actress nomination for the film whose cast included Robert Mitchum, Peter Ustinov and Glynis Johns. The ever talented Johns was nominated for Best Supporting Actress for her role as the Cockney barmaid who captures Ustinov. The ever talented Ustinov won the Best Supporting Actor Award for his portrayal of a Roman slaveholder in the vast epic *Spartacus* which starred Kirk Douglas. Best Picture nominee *Sons And Lovers* was a movie adaptation of D H Lawrence's autobiographical novel with Dean Stockwell in the lead. The film brought Trevor Howard, excellent as the father, a Best Actor nomination and Mary Ure a Best Supporting Actress nomination. Unfortunately, Wendy Hiller did not win a Best Actress nomination for her performance as the mother in *Sons And Lovers*.

Also up for Best Picture was *Elmer Gantry*, based on Sinclair Lewis's

satirical novel about a phony evangelist with Burt Lancaster in the title role. Lancaster won the Best Actor Oscar for his performance and Shirley Jones won the Best Supporting Actress Oscar for her role as the hustling prostitute who blackmails the hustling fire and brimstone preacher. The movie that won the Award for the Best Picture was *The Apartment*, a mixture of comedy and pathos which had a lot to say about contemporary life at the time, especially the pursuit of money and sex.

The Apartment starred Jack Lemmon who earned a Best Actor nomination for his portrayal of an ambitious young man eager to get ahead who offers his apartment to executives for romantic assignations. Shirley MacLaine received a Best Actress nomination for her role as the young woman who tries to kill herself after being seduced and betrayed by her boss Fred MacMurray. Spencer Tracy received a Best Actor nomination as Clarence Darrow in *Inherit The Wind*, the movie version of the play based on the famous Scopes 'monkey trial' of the twenties when a school teacher in Tennessee was put on trial for teaching evolution in the classroom. Fredric March played William Jennings Bryan. Laurence Olivier was nominated for Best Actor for his magnificent portrayal of seedy music-hall performer Archie Rice in John Osborne's *The Entertainer*. If justice

TOP: Elizabeth Taylor among her admirers as Gloria Wandrous in *Butterfield 8*.

BELOW: Jack Lemmon strains spaghetti for Shirley MacLaine in *The Apartment*.

prevailed in Hollywood instead of politics Olivier would have won.

Greer Garson was nominated for Best Actress for her portrayal of Eleanor Roosevelt in *Sunrise At Campobello* with Ralph Ballamy as FDR. Greek actress Melina Mercouri received a Best Actress nomination for her role as the fun loving prostitute in *Never On Sunday*, Jules Dassin's delightful movie spoof of American puritanism. The music score by Manos Hadjidakis was innovative and sensational and 'Never On Sunday' won Best Song. The Best Actress Award went to Elizabeth Taylor, a call girl, in *Butterfield 8*, based on John O'Hara's novel. Taylor was given the Award because she'd been ill and the Oscar was the Academy's way of saying 'We're glad you're well.' Unfortunately, this gracious gesture cost Shirley MacLaine, the odds-on

favorite to win, a truly deserved Academy Award.

Nominees for Supporting Actor included Peter Falk in *Murder, Inc*; Jack Kruschen in *The Apartment*; Sal Mineo in *Exodus*, about the establishment of the State of Israel, and Chill Wills, the beekeeper in *The Alamo*. Nominees for Supporting Actress included Shirley Knight in *The Dark At The Top Of The Stairs* and Janet Leigh in the extraordinarily influential mystery and horror film, *Psycho* which starred Anthony Perkins as a mad killer. *Psycho* featured one of the most famous murder scenes ever shown on the screen, a stabbing in a shower. *Psycho*'s director was the master of the suspense genre, Alfred Hitchcock, who received a Best Director nomination for the film. Other directors nominated were Jack Cardiff for *Sons And Lovers;* Jules Dassin for *Never On Sunday*; Fred Zinnemann for *The Sundowners*, and the winner of the Best Director Award, Billy Wilder for *The Apartment*. *The Time Machine*, with Rod Taylor won for Special Effects.

Movies nominated in a variety of categories included the noted anti-war, film *Hiroshima, Mon Amour*; *Visit To A Small Planet*, based on Gore Vidal's play; *Bells Are Ringing*, Judy Holliday's last movie which co-starred Dean Martin; *Can-Can* with the by now ubiquitous Shirley MacLaine. Ingmar Bergman's *The Virgin Spring* won the Foreign Language Film Award and an Honorary Award went to Hollywood legend Gary Cooper who died a month later of cancer. Another Hollywood legend, Stan Laurel also received an Honorary Award as did young British actress Hayley Mills for Walt Disney's sentimental remake *Pollyanna*.

1961

Best Picture: *West Side Story.*
Actor: Maximillian Schell, *Judgment At Nuremberg.*
Actress: Sophia Loren, *Two Women.*
Supporting Actor: George Chakiris, *West Side Story.*
Supporting Actress: Rita Moreno, *West Side Story.*
Director: Robert Wise, Jerome Robbins, *West Side Story.*
Foreign Language Film Award: *Through A Glass Darkly* (Sweden).
Writing (Screenplay-Adaptation): Abby Mann, *Judgment At Nuremberg.*
Writing (Screenplay-Original): William Inge, *Splendor In The Grass.*

Cinematography (Black And White): Eugen Shuftan, *The Hustler.*
Cinematography (Color): Daniel L Fapp, *West Side Story.*
Art Director (Black And White): Harry Horner, (Set Decoration) Gene Callahan, *The Hustler.*
Art Director (Color): Boris Leven, (Set Decoration) Victor A Gangelin, *West Side Story.*
Costume Design (Black And White): Piero Gherardi, *La Dolce Vita.*
Costume Design (Color): Irene Sharaff, *West Side Story.*
Special Effects: *The Guns Of Navarone.*
Music (Score of A Dramatic or Comedy Picture): Henry Mancini, *Breakfast At Tiffany's.*
Music (Musical): Saul Chaplin, Johnny Green, Sid Ramin, Irwin Kostal, *West Side Story.*
Music (Song): Johnny Mercer (Lyrics) and Henry Mancini (Music), 'Moon River' from *Breakfast At Tiffany's.*
Short Subjects (Cartoon): *Ersatz (The Substitute).*
Irving G Thalberg Memorial Award: Stanley Kramer.
Honorary Award: Jerome Robbins, for his brilliant achievements in the art of choreography on film in *West Side Story.*

Richard Beymer (Tony) screams in anguish over the dead bodies of Bernardo (George Chakiris) and Riff (Russ Tamblyn) after the rumble in *West Side Story.*

Movie musicals were practically extinct by the sixties but Leonard Bernstein's *West Side Story*, a contemporary version of the tale of Romeo and Juliet set among rival gangs in New York City came to the screen this year and scooped up many Academy Awards. To begin with *West Side Story* won the Best Picture Oscar. Up against it as a nominee was *Fanny* with Leslie Caron and Charles Boyer who received a Best Actor nomination for the film, based on a stage musical. Only the movie version dropped the songs. Maurice Chevalier was also in the cast.

The Guns Of Navarone a suspenseful war movie and lively spectacle was nominated for Best Picture but won the Award for Special Effects and brought director J Lee Thompson a Best Director nomination. *The Hustler* was a small picture worth a dozen big splashy ones, with Paul Newman as a professional pool player and con man who goes up against Minnesota Fats. Newman received a Best Actor nomination in the movie which also brought a much deserved Best Actress nomination to Piper Laurie who played Newman's crippled girlfriend with sensitivity, a Best Supporting Actor nomination to Jackie Gleason who played Minnesota Fats and a Best Supporting Actor nomination to George C Scott, terrific as the fast-talking promotor, as well as a Best Director nomination to Robert Rosson. Scott shocked and amused a lot of

RIGHT: Anthony Quinn and Gregory Peck in *The Guns of Navarone*.
BELOW: Paul Newman, with Myron McCormick in *The Hustler*.

people by asking that his name be withdrawn from nomination since he considered the Oscar Ceremony 'bull'.

Judgment at Nuremberg, a film about the war crimes trials following World War II received a Best Picture nomination and brought a Best Actor nomination to Spencer Tracy who played a judge, a Best Supporting Actor nomination to Montgomery Clift, outstanding in a small role, a Best Supporting Actress nomination to Judy Garland, for her moving portrayal of a German housewife defending her marriage to a Jew, and a directing nomination to Stanley Kramer. Swiss-born Maximilian Schell won the Award for Best Actor for his role as an intense defense attorney in *Judgment At Nuremberg*. The remaining Best Actor nominee was Stuart Whitman in *The Mark*, a British film about, but somehow still skirting the issue of, child molesting, notable for its sympathy. Maria Schell, Best Actor winner Maximilian Schell's sister was also in the movie.

For the first time in the history of the

Awards an actress appearing in a non-English speaking role was selected as Best Actress. She was Sophia Loren who starred in *Two Women*, about a widow and her daughter in Italy during the war. Eleanora Brown played the daughter. Loren won the Award over, among others, Audrey Hepburn who played Holly Golightly in *Breakfast At Tiffany's*, based on the work by Truman Capote; Geraldine Page in *Summer And Smoke*, based on a play by Tennessee Williams; and Natalie Wood in *Splendor In The Grass*, about teenage love and sex in the nineteen twenties with Warren Beatty. The film brought a Writing Award to William Inge.

The Supporting Actor Award went to George Chakiris, in his first major role, Bernardo, the leader of the Puerto Rican gang in *West Side Story*. The Supporting Actress Award went to the dynamic Rita Moreno who played Bernardo's girlfriend. The remaining nominee in the Best Supporting Actor category was Peter Falk in *A Pocketful of Miracles*, which also starred Bette

ABOVE: Best Actress Sophia Loren in *Two Women*.
LEFT: Audrey Hepburn with George Peppard in *Breakfast at Tiffanys*.

Davis. The film was adapted from the 1933 movie *Lady For A Day*. The remaining Best Supporting Actress nominees were Fay Bainter, the troublemaker's grandmother in the movie version of Lillian Hellman's play about the evils of slander, *The Children's Hour* starring Audrey Hepburn and Shirley MacLaine; Lotte Lenya in *The Roman Spring of Mrs Stone* about a fading beauty and Italian gigolo with Vivien Leigh and Warren Beatty, and Una Merkel, Geraldine Page's mentally disturbed mother in *Summer And Smoke*.

The Best Director Oscar went to director Robert Wise and to Jerome Robbins, who was co-director and choreographer of *West Side Story*. Robbins also took an Honorary Award for choreography. Nominated, too, for Best Director was Federico Fellini for the delicious display of decadence, *La Dolce Vita*. The Foreign Language Film Award, however, went to Ingmar Bergman's *Through A Glass Darkly*, a good but relentlessly grim movie with Max Von Sydow and Harriet Andersson. *The Misfits* starring film legends Clark Gable and Marilyn Monroe went unnominated. It was the last movie for each before their deaths.

1962

Best Picture: *Lawrence Of Arabia.*
Actor: Gregory Peck, *To Kill A Mockingbird.*
Actress: Anne Bancroft, *The Miracle Worker.*
Supporting Actor: Ed Begley, *Sweet Bird Of Youth.*
Supporting Actress: Patty Duke, *The Miracle Worker.*
Director: David Lean, *Lawrence of Arabia.*
Foreign Language Film Award: *Sundays And Cybele* (France).
Writing (Screenplay-Adaptation): Horton Foote, *To Kill A Mockingbird.*
Writing (Screenplay-Original): Ennion De Concini, Alfredo Giannetti, Pietro Germi, *Divorce-Italian Style.*
Cinematography (Black And White): Jean Bourgoin and Walter Wottitz, *The Longest Day.*
Cinematography (Color): Fred A Young, *Lawrence Of Arabia.*
Art Director (Black And White): Alexander Golitzen and Henry Bumstead, (Set Decoration) Oliver Emert, *To Kill A Mockingbird.*

Art Director (Color): John Box and John Stoll, (Set Decoration) Dario Simoni, *Lawrence Of Arabia.*
Costume Design (Black And White): Norma Koch, *What Ever Happened To Baby Jane?*
Costume Design (Color): Mary Wills, *The Wonderful World Of The Brothers Grimm.*
Special Effects: Robert MacDonald (Visual), Jacques Maumont (Audible), *The Longest Day.*
Music (Original Score): Maurice Jarre, *Lawrence Of Arabia.*
Music (Adaptation): Ray Heindorf, Meredith Wilson's *The Music Man.*
Music (Song): Johnny Mercer (Lyrics) and Henry Mancini (Music), 'Days Of Wine And Roses' from *Days Of Wine And Roses.*
Short Subjects (Cartoon): *The Hole.*
Documentary (Short); *Dylan Thomas.*
Documentary (Feature): *Black Fox.*

Lawrence of Arabia starred Peter O'Toole as T E Lawrence.

David Lean, who won an Oscar for directing *The Bridge On The River Kwai* repeated his triumph with this year's big film, *Lawrence of Arabia.* The movie, sweeping in scope and filled with adventure, ran close to four hours in length. Not only did the movie win the Best Picture Oscar but it brought Irish-born actor Peter O'Toole a Best Actor nomination for his outstanding portrayal of the complex, legendary T E Lawrence and the film also brought a Supporting Actor nomination to Omar Sharif who played Lawrence's Arab friend. The excellent cast also included Jack Hawkins, Claude Rains, Arthur Kennedy, Alec Guinness, Anthony Quinn and Jose Ferrer.

Losing to *Lawrence Of Arabia* was Best Picture nominee *The Longest Day*, the story of D-Day 1944, big on action sequences. Also up for Best Picture was Meredith Willson's *The Music Man*, starring Robert Preston repeating his stage role as the endearing con-man Professor Harold Hill with Shirley Jones as Marian the librarian. The movie was a joyous tribute to small

Stroud who became an expert on diseases in birds. The film brought Thelma Ritter a Best Supporting Actress nomination for her portrayal of Lancaster's mother and a Supporting Actor nomination to Telly Savalas who became a star in the seventies thanks to the TV show *Kojak*. Jack Lemmon received a Best Actor nomination and Lee Remick, who played his wife, a Best Actress nomination in *Days Of Wine And Roses*, a chilling and revealing film about alcoholism. Pietro Germi's delightful *Divorce-Italian Style* starred Marcello Mastroianni as a vapid Italian count trying to murder his fat wife because he wanted to marry his pretty cousin. Mastroianni received a Best Actor nomination for the film. Germi was nominated for Best Director and was one of the trio of writers who won the Writing Oscar for the film. Daniela Rocca was terrific as the wife whose moustache was almost as prominent as Mastroianni's.

The nominees for Best Actress included Bette Davis who appeared with Joan Crawford in the horror film *What Ever Happened To Baby Jane?* which brought a Best Supporting Actor nomination to Victor Buono, in his debut movie role; Katharine Hepburn, the tormented drug-addicted mother in *Long Day's Journey Into Night*, and Geraldine Page, as the aging movie star

LEFT: Gregory Peck as Atticus Finch in conversation with Jester Hairston in *To Kill A Mockingbird*.
BELOW: Anne Bancroft as Annie Sullivan and Patty Duke: *The Miracle Worker*.

town America. *Mutiny On The Bounty*, starring Marlon Brando as Fletcher Christian and Trevor Howard as Captain Bligh, received a Best Picture nomination though the film was not as good as the 1935 version starring Clark Gable and the magnificent Charles Laughton. *To Kill A Mockingbird*, nominated for Best Picture, brought Gregory Peck the Best Actor Oscar for his portrayal of Atticus Finch, a small town Southern lawyer who defends a black man accused of rape. The movie also brought a Best Supporting Actress nomination to child actress Mary Badham who played Peck's daughter and a Best Director nomination to Robert Mulligan.

Burt Lancaster received a Best Actor nomination for one of his finest performances in *The Bird Man Of Alcatraz*, the story of imprisoned killer Robert

in *Sweet Bird Of Youth* opposite Paul Newman. Ed Begley who played Boss Finley in that film won the Best Supporting Actor Award over, among others, British actor Terence Stamp in *Billy Budd*, based on the Herman Melville novel. The movie was Stamp's debut film. The winner of the Best Actress Award was Anne Bancroft, forceful, yet sympathetic, in the recreation of her stage role as Annie Sullivan, the teacher of deaf, dumb, and blind Helen Keller in *The Miracle Worker*.

Also recreating her stage role as Helen Keller was Patty Duke who won the Best Supporting Actress Award in

The Miracle Worker. Nominated, too, in the Best Supporting Actress category was Shirley Knight who played Paul Newman's childhood sweetheart Heavenly in *Sweet Bird Of Youth* and Angela Lansbury who played Laurence Harvey's vicious politically conniving mother in *The Manchurian Candidate*. The remaining nominees for Best Director were Arthur Penn for *The Miracle Worker* and Frank Perry for *David And Lisa*, a sensitive movie about mentally ill teenagers.

Among the movies nominated in a wide range of categories were *Freud* with Montgomery Clift, now considered one of Clift's finest films; *Last Year At Marienbad*, written by Alan Robbe-Grillet and directed by Alain

Resnais, a mysterious French film which gained an avant garde following in America; a good British comedy *That Touch Of Mink*; *Two For The Seesaw* with Robert Mitchum and Shirley MacLaine; *Gypsy*, a musical based on a Broadway hit which had starred Ethel Merman, with Rosalind Russell in the lead and Natalie Wood as Gypsy Rose Lee. Other nominees included a superior western, *The Man Who Shot Liberty Valance* with John Wayne and Jimmy Stewart and *The Wonderful World Of The Brothers Grimm*, with Laurence Harvey. The Foreign Language Film Award went to the poignant *Sundays And Cybele*, about the idyllic relationship between a young man with amnesia and a twelve-year-old girl.

American troops on the Normandy beaches in *The Longest Day*.

1963

Best Picture: *Tom Jones.*
Actor: Sidney Poitier, *Lilies Of The Field.*
Actress: Patricia Neal, *Hud.*
Supporting Actor: Melvyn Douglas, *Hud.*
Supporting Actress: Margaret Rutherford, *The V.I.P.s.*
Director: Tony Richardson, *Tom Jones.*
Foreign Language Film Award: Federico Fellini's *8½* (Italy).
Writing (Screenplay-Adaptation): John Osborne, *Tom Jones.*
Writing (Screenplay-Original): James R Webb, *How The West Was Won.*
Cinematography (Black And White): James Wong Howe, *Hud.*
Cinematography (Color): Leon Shamroy, *Cleopatra.*
Art Director (Black And White): Gene Callahan, *America America.*
Art Director (Color): John DeCuir, Jack Martin Smith, Hilyard Brown, Herman Blumenthal, Elven Webb, Maurice Pelling, Boris Juraga, (Set Decoration) Walter M Scott, Paul S Fox, Ray Moyer, *Cleopatra.*
Costume Design (Black And White): Piero Gherardi, *Federico Fellini's 8½.*

Costume Design (Color): Irene Sharaff, Vittorio Nino Novarese, Renie, *Cleopatra.*
Special Visual Effects: Emil Kosa, Jr, *Cleopatra.*
Sound Effects: *It's A Mad, Mad, Mad, Mad World.*
Music (Original Score): John Addison, *Tom Jones.*
Music (Scoring-Adaptation): Andre Previn, *Irma La Douce.*
Music (Song): Sammy Cahn (Lyrics) and James Van Heusen (Music), 'Call Me Irresponsible' from *Papa's Delicate Condition.*
Short Subjects (Cartoon): *The Critic.*
Documentary (Feature Length): *Robert Frost: A Lover's Quarrel With The World.*
Irving G Thalberg Memorial Award: Sam Spiegel.

Raucous, bawdy, and delightful *Tom Jones* not only won Best Picture it *was* the best picture of the year. The movie, set in eighteenth century England, was the first British movie to be named Best Picture since *Hamlet* won the Award in 1948. Romping through the mischievous movie was a superb cast including

Albert Finney who received a Best Actor nomination in the title role and Hugh Griffith who deserved to win the Best Supporting Actor Oscar for his portrayal of the flamboyant squire who loved his daughter Susannah York almost as much as he loved hunting. Though he received a nomination Griffith lost to Melvyn Douglas, an aging rancher and Paul Newman's father, in *Hud.* Nominated for Best Supporting Actress in *Tom Jones* were Diane Cilento, Joyce Redman, memorable in the eating scene, and Dame Edith Evans who played the intrepid aunt. Tony Richardson received the Directing Oscar for the picture and John Osborne won a Writing Award.

Up for Best Picture was *America America*, directed by Elia Kazan who was nominated for Best Director for the movie which was based on his autobiography. The movie, starring Stathis Giallelis, told the tale of a poor Turkish immigrant's struggle to reach America. Nominated, too, for Best Picture was

The Hunt assembles at Squire Western's in *Tom Jones.*

How The West Was Won, the first story film and almost the last in three-lens Cinerama. Visually it was spectacular. Best Picture nominee *Lilies Of The Field* brought the Best Actor Oscar to Sidney Poitier, an important step in the direction of bringing better roles and recognition to black actors. Poitier played a Southern GI who helped five refugee nuns build a chapel and start a new life. German actress Lilia Skala received a Supporting Actress nomination for her role as the Mother Superior.

The most famous yet most disappointing movie nominated was *Cleopatra*, a huge, expensive, and rather dull mess starring Elizabeth Taylor as Cleopatra and Richard Burton as Mark Anthony. Their off-screen romance caused gossips' tongues to wag and did a lot to publicize the movie. Rex

TOP: Melvyn Douglas, Brandon de Wilde and Patricia Neal in *Hud*.
ABOVE: Sidney Poitier and the nuns, in *Lilies Of The Field*.

Harrison, however played Caesar and played him well, receiving a Best Actor nomination for his trouble. Also nominated for Best Actor was Richard Harris, as the British North Country rugby player and rebel in *This Sporting Life*, a movie which also brought British actress Rachel Roberts a Best Actress nomination. Nominated, too, for Best Actor was Paul Newman, in the title role in *Hud*, a strong film about independent cattlemen in Texas. Patricia Neal won the Best Actress Oscar for her portrayal in *Hud* of an earthy woman bruised by men and the drabness of life.

Other actresses nominated for Best

Actress were Leslie Caron, pregnant and lonely in a run-down rooming house in *The L-Shaped Room*; Shirley MacLaine as the Parisian prostitute in *Irma La Douce*, co-starring Jack Lemmon, and Natalie Wood, loved and seduced by a jazz musician played by Steve McQueen in *Love With The Proper Stranger*. The Best Supporting Actress Award went to Margaret Rutherford, fabulous as usual, this time playing a querulous airplane passenger in *The V.I.P.s* which starred Elizabeth Taylor and Richard Burton. The film was a bust but Rutherford certainly deserved recognition for past accomplishments.

Nominees for Supporting Actor included, among others, Nick Adams in *Twilight Of Honor*; Bobby Darin, the shell-shocked GI in *Captain Newman, MD*, with Gregory Peck and Tony Curtis, and John Huston, best known as a director in *The Cardinal*, which won director Otto Preminger a Best Director nomination. The remaining Best Director nominees were Federico Fellini for *8½* which won the Best Foreign Language Film Award and Best Black And White Costume Design, and Martin Ritt for *Hud*.

Other movies with a variety of nominations included *It's A Mad, Mad, Mad, Mad World*, shot in single-lens Cinerama and loaded with stars, car chases, and slapstick; *Bye Bye Birdie* with luscious Ann-Margret; the sophisticated mystery/comedy *Charade*, starring Audrey Hepburn and Cary Grant, and *The Stripper*, a good but underappreciated movie with Richard Beymer, Joanne Woodward, and Claire Trevor. Jackie Gleason starred in *Papa's Delicate Condition*, a comedy about drinking whose 'Call Me Irresponsible' won Best Song. Two new categories were created this year, Special Visual Effects and Sound Effects, in recognition of the fact that the best visual effects and the best audio effects each year do not necessarily occur in the same picture. The single Special Effects Award, therefore, was discontinued. Alfred Hitchcock's excellent supernatural thriller *The Birds* was nominated in the Special Visual Effects category but lost to *Cleopatra*, which scarcely seems fair. *It's A Mad, Mad, Mad, Mad World* took the Sound Effects category. There were no Honorary Awards and no Jean Hersholt Humanitarian Award was given. One of Hollywood's favorite finest actors Jack Lemmon emceed the Ceremonies.

1964

Best Picture: *My Fair Lady.*
Actor: Rex Harrison, *My Fair Lady.*
Actress: Julie Andrews, *Mary Poppins.*
Supporting Actor: Peter Ustinov, *Topkapi.*
Supporting Actress: Lila Kedrova, *Zorba The Greek.*
Director: George Cukor, *My Fair Lady.*
Foreign Language Film Award: *Yesterday, Today And Tomorrow* (Italy).
Writing (Screenplay-Adaptation): Edward Anhalt, *Becket.*
Writing (Screenplay-Original): S H Barnett, Peter Stone, Frank Tarloff, *Father Goose.*
Cinematography (Black And White): Walter Lassally, *Zorba The Greek.*
Cinematography (Color): Harry Stradling, *My Fair Lady.*
Art Director (Black And White): Vassilis Fotopoulos, *Zorba The Greek.*
Art Director (Color): Gene Allen and Cecil Beaton, (Set Decoration) George James Hopkins, *My Fair Lady.*
Costume Design (Black And White): Dorothy Jeakins, *The Night Of The Iguana.*
Costume Design (Color): Cecil Beaton, *My Fair Lady.*
Music (Original Score): Richard M Sherman, Robert B Sherman, *Mary Poppins.*
Music (Adaptation): Andre Previn, *My Fair Lady.*
Music (Song): Music and Lyrics by Richard M. Sherman and Robert B Sherman, 'Chim Chim Cheree' from *Mary Poppins.*
Short Subjects (Cartoon): *The Pink Phink.*
Short Subjects (Live Action): *Casals Conducts.*
Special Visual Effects: Peter Ellenshaw, Hamilton Luske, Eustace Lycett, *Mary Poppins.*
Sound Effects: Norman Wanstall, *Goldfinger.*
Documentary (Feature): *World Without Sun.*
Documentary (Short): *Nine From Little Rock.*
Honorary Award: William Tuttle, for his outstanding make-up achievement for *7 Faces Of Dr Lao.*

The Awards upset of the decade occurred this year. Julie Andrews had become the toast of Broadway thanks to her performance on stage as Eliza in *My Fair Lady.* Yet she was passed over in favor of established film star Audrey Hepburn when it came to making the lavish movie version of the popular musical. Then along came Walt Disney ready to take a chance on Julie Andrews by casting her in the title role in *Mary Poppins.* This debut film performance resulted in Andrews winning the Best Actress Award. *My Fair Lady* received the Best Picture Award but its star Audrey Hepburn, didn't even receive a Best Actress nomination. Hepburn's songs in *My Fair Lady* were sung by Marni Nixon. Andrews could sing her own songs. *My Fair Lady* also brought Rex Harrison the Best Actor Oscar for the role he had made his own, both on stage and on screen, Professor Henry Higgins. *My Fair Lady* picked up awards in many other categories as well.

Up for Best Picture against *My Fair Lady* were *Becket*, based on Jean Anouilh's play, which gained Richard Burton a Best Actor nomination in the title role, Peter O'Toole a Best Actor nomination for his portrayal of Henry II, and John Gielgud a Supporting Actor nomination for his portrayal of King Louis VII of France; Stanley Kubrick's masterpiece, *Dr Strangelove Or: How I Learned To Stop Worrying And Love The Bomb* which brought a Best Actor nomination to Peter Sellers who played three roles in the film, a president of the United States, an RAF officer, and, best of all, an ex (maybe) Nazi scientist, one of the most brilliant characterizations ever done on screen; *Mary Poppins*, a light and fluffy musical version of the famous children's novel, and *Zorba The Greek*

Anthony Quinn received a Best Actor nomination as the lusty, zesty, and larger-than-life Zorba who teaches timid Alan Bates how to live. Lila Kedrova won the Best Supporting Actress Award in *Zorba The Greek*, over

Dick van Dyke and Julie Andrews on a 'Jolly Holiday' in *Mary Poppins.*

Gladys Cooper in *My Fair Lady*; Dame Edith Evans in *The Chalk Garden*; Grayson Hall in *The Night Of The Iguana* based on Tennessee Williams's play, starring Richard Burton and Ava Gardner, and Agnes Moorehead, Bette Davis's slatternly maid in *Hush, Hush, Sweet Charlotte*, a horror film co-starring Olivia de Havilland.

Up for Best Actress was Anne Ban-croft in *The Pumpkin Eater*, based on Penelope Mortimer's novel. Peter Finch and James Mason also turned in fine performances in this early mile-stone in the women's liberation move-ment. Harold Pinter wrote the movie script. Nominated, too, in the Best Actress category was Sophia Loren in *Marriage-Italian Style*, with Marcello Mastroianni who also appeared with her in the three part *Yesterday, Today And Tomorrow*, which won the Foreign Language Film Award. Debbie Rey-nolds played the resiliant woman who became a legend in Colorado mining towns early in the century, in an ex-pensive musical, *The Unsinkable Molly Brown*, a role which won Reynolds a Best Actress nomination. Harve Pres-nell recreated his Broadway role as

Doolittle in *My Fair Lady*; Edmond O'Brien in *Seven Days In May*, a well-paced movie with chilling political overtones about a military attempt to depose a weak American president; Lee Tracy in his final movie, *The Best Man*, and the winner, Peter Ustinov, a sly and clumsy rogue in the lively caper film *Topkapi*. The Best Director nominees

LEFT: Jeremy Brett, Audrey Hepburn, Rex Harrison and Wilfred Hyde-White at Ascot, in *My Fair Lady*.
BELOW: William Tuttle makes-up Tony Randall for *The Seven Faces Of Dr Lao*.
BOTTOM: Maximilian Schell, Melina Mercouri, Gilles Segal, Peter Ustinov, Jess Hahn and Robert Morley conspire in *Topkapi*.

included Michael Cacoyannis for *Zorba The Greek*; Peter Glenville for *Becket*; Stanley Kubrick, who should have won but didn't for *Dr Strangelove Or: How I Learned To Stop Worrying And Love The Bomb*; Robert Stevenson for *Mary Poppins*, and the winner, George Cukor, for *My Fair Lady*.

Other movies nominated in a variety of categories included *Father Goose*, starring Cary Grant and Leslie Caron, which won a Writing Award; the colorful *That Man From Rio*, starring Jean-Paul Belmondo; *The Americanization Of Emily*, with Julie Andrews and James Garner; The Beatles's classic, *A Hard Day's Night*, and the James Bond spy thriller, *Goldfinger*.

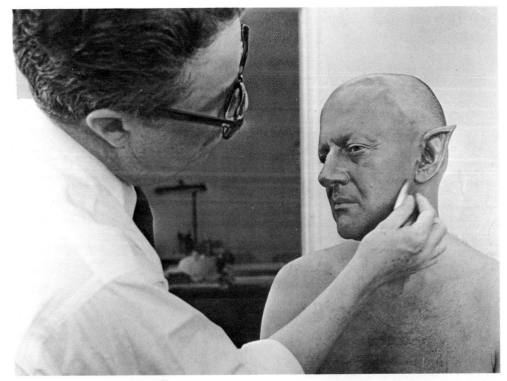

Molly's husband. Kim Stanley was nominated for Best Actress for her brilliant portrayal of a medium in *Seance On A Wet Afternoon*. Richard Attenborough played Stanley's weak-willed husband in this eerie tale about the kidnapping of a child.

Supporting Actor nominees included Stanley Holloway as Eliza's father, the self-serving but persuasive Alfred

1965

Best Picture: *The Sound Of Music.*
Actor: Lee Marvin, *Cat Ballou.*
Actress: Julie Christie, *Darling.*
Supporting Actor: Martin Balsam, *A Thousand Clowns.*
Supporting Actress: Shelley Winters, *A Patch Of Blue.*
Director: Robert Wise, *The Sound Of Music.*
Foreign Language Film Award: *The Shop On Main Street* (Czechoslovakia).
Writing (Screenplay-Adaptation): Robert Bolt, *Doctor Zhivago.*
Writing (Original Screenplay): Frederic Raphael, *Darling.*
Cinematography (Black And White): Ernest Laszlo, *Ship Of Fools.*
Cinematography (Color): Freddie Young, *Doctor Zhivago.*
Art Director (Black And White): Robert Clatworthy, (Set Decoration) Joseph Kish, *Ship Of Fools.*
Art Director (Color): John Box and Terry Marsh, *Doctor Zhivago.*

Costume Design (Black And White): Julie Harris, *Darling.*
Costume Design (Color): Phyllis Dalton, *Doctor Zhivago.*
Music (Original Score): Maurice Jarre, *Doctor Zhivago.*
Music (Score-Adaptation): Irwin Kostal, *The Sound Of Music.*
Music (Song): Paul Francis Webster (Lyrics), Johnny Mandel (Music), 'The Shadow Of Your Smile' from *The Sandpiper.*
Short Subjects (Cartoon): *The Dot And The Line.*
Special Visual Effects: John Stears, *Thunderball.*
Sound Effects: Tregoweth Brown, *The Great Race.*
Documentary (Feature): *The Eleanor Roosevelt Story.*
Documentary (Short Subjects): *To Be Alive!*
Irving G Thalberg Memorial Award: William Wyler.
Honorary Award: Bob Hope, for service to the motion picture industry.

Had *The Sound Of Music* not earned sixty million dollars in paid admissions in its first year it probably wouldn't have won Best Picture. It was the kind of big old-fashioned syrupy musical which had gone out of fashion in Hollywood, though not apparently anywhere else. Based on the hit Broadway musical the movie boasted songs by Richard Rodgers and Oscar Hammerstein II. In turn, both the stage show and the movie were based on the *Story Of The Trapp Family Singers* by Maria Augusta Von Trapp. The film featured beautiful Austrian scenery, a touching story, and a good cast, including Christopher Plummer (vocals by Bill Lee), Julie Andrews as the spunky heroine, a role which brought her a Best Actress nomination, and Peggy Wood, who received a Supporting Actress nomination for her role as the Mother

Julie Andrews and Christopher Plummer and the seven children before they escape at the end of *The Sound Of Music.*

based on Katherine Anne Porter's novel, also had a star-studded cast. Set on a ship filled with Germans and Jews in 1933 the movie was loaded with historic ironies. The film brought a Best Actor nomination to Oskar Werner (Jules in Francois Truffaut's classic *Jules And Jim*) who played the ship's doctor. Simone Signoret was nominated for Best Actress in *Ship Of Fools* for her role as the drug addicted countess having an affair with Werner and the film also brought a Best Supporting Actor nomination to Michael Dunn in his movie role as a compassionate observer of humanity. The remaining Best Picture nominee was the low-budget *A Thousand Clowns*, written by Herb Gardner, which won talented veteran character actor Martin Balsam the Best Supporting Actor Award for his role as Jason Robards's conventional brother.

This was a banner year for Best Actor nominees and it is utterly astonishing to realize that the Academy gave the Oscar to Lee Marvin for his dual role in *Cat Ballou*, an amusing but easily forgettable western spoof with Jane Fonda. The other nominees for Best Actor included Richard Burton, who turned in an excellent performance in *The Spy Who Came In From The Cold*, based on John Le Carre's novel, also featuring Oskar Werner; Laurence Olivier in *Othello*, a movie which brought Frank Finley a Supporting Actor nomination as Iago, Joyce Redman a Supporting Actress nomination as Emilia, and Maggie Smith a Supporting Actress

LEFT: Lee Marvin in *Cat Ballou*, as Kid Shelleen.

BELOW: Julie Christie played an amoral model in *Darling* with Laurence Harvey.

Abbess. The movie also brought Robert Wise the Best Director Oscar.

Darling, about a self-centered model and her negative impact on other people's lives earned a Best Picture nomination, won British actress Julie Christie the Best Actress Award, brought John Schlesinger a Best Director nomination and earned Frederic Raphael a Writing Oscar for his superb script. Christie also starred in *Doctor Zhivago*, based on Boris Pasternak's novel about Russia, which received a Best Picture nomination. The movie brought David Lean a Best Director nomination and Tom Courtenay a Best Supporting Actor nomination. Another Best Picture nominee *Ship Of Fools*,

nomination as Desdemona, and Rod Steiger, in top form in *The Pawnbroker* as an isolated Jewish pawnbroker in Harlem, scarred by his wartime experiences. Steiger was also excellent in *Doctor Zhivago*.

The remaining Best Actress nominees were Samantha Eggar in *The Collector* and Elizabeth Hartman, playing a blind white girl romantically involved with a black man in her debut film, *A Patch Of Blue*. British actor Ian Bannen in *The Flight Of The Phoenix* was the fifth nominee for Best Supporting Actor. The remaining Best Supporting Actress nominees were Ruth Gordon in *Inside Daisy Clover* starring Natalie Wood, and winner Shelley Winters as Hartman's slatternly mother in *A Patch Of Blue*. Nominees for Best Director included, among others, Hiroshi Teshigahara for *Woman Of The Dunes*, a strange and original Japanese movie about a man on a beach trapped into living with a woman in a sandpit, and William Wyler for *The Collector*.

Other movies nominated in a wide range of categories included *Casanova '70*, an Italian film with Marcello Mastroianni as a jaded NATO officer and also starring Virna Lisi and *Those*

Magnificent Men In Their Flying Machines, a lively film about the first London-to-Paris air race. *The Greatest Story Ever Told* with Max Von Sydow as Christ and the state of Utah as Palestine, and *The Agony And The Ecstasy*

BELOW: *Thunderball*, won for special effects.
BOTTOM: *Doctor Zhivago* starred Omar Sharif and Julie Christie.

with Charlton Heston as Michaelangelo and Rex Harrison as Pope Julius were also nominated for technical awards. *The Umbrellas Of Cherbourg*, a charming musical love story from France with a beautiful use of color, is still a masterpiece. Though the film received several nominations in the music category it lost out, in the case of Best Song, to 'The Shadow Of Your Smile' from the Burton/Taylor film, *The Sandpiper*.

Blake Edwards's *The Great Race*, a lavishly spectacular comedy about a 1908 auto race from New York to Paris won the Sound Effects category. The film starred Tony Curtis, Jack Lemmon, Natalie Wood, and Peter Falk. The best movie of all didn't even receive a Best Picture nomination but it did win the Foreign Language Film category. It was *The Shop On Main Street*, a Czechoslovakian movie starring Ida Kaminska and Josef Kroner, brilliantly directed by Jan Kadar and Elmar Klos. The James Bond fantasy film of the year was *Thunderball*, starring Sean Connery, which won the award for Special Visual Effects. Once again Bob Hope won an Honorary Award, this time a gold medal, for his service to the industry and the Academy.

1966

Best Picture: *A Man For All Seasons.*
Actor: Paul Scofield, *A Man For All Seasons.*
Actress: Elizabeth Taylor, *Who's Afraid Of Virginia Woolf?*
Supporting Actor: Walter Matthau, *The Fortune Cookie.*
Supporting Actress: Sandy Dennis, *Who's Afraid Of Virginia Woolf?*
Director: Fred Zinnemann, *A Man For All Seasons.*
Foreign Language Film Award: *A Man And A Woman* (France).
Writing (Screenplay-Original): Claude Lelouch and Pierre Utterhoeven, *A Man And A Woman.*
Writing (Screenplay-Adaptation): Robert Bolt, *A Man For All Seasons.*
Cinematography (Black And White): Heskell Wexler, *Who's Afraid Of Virginia Woolf?*
Cinematography (Color): Ted Moore, *A Man For All Seasons.*
Art Direction (Black And White): Richard Sylbert, (Set Decoration) George James Hopkins, *Who's Afraid Of Virginia Woolf?*
Art Direction (Color): Jack Martin Smith, Dale Hennesy, (Set Decoration) Walter M Scott, Stuart A Reiss, *Fantastic Voyage.*
Costume Design (Black And White): Irene Shareff, *Who's Afraid Of Virginia Woolf?*
Costume Design (Color): Elizabeth Haffenden, Joan Bridge, *A Man For All Seasons.*
Music (Original Score): John Barry, *Born Free.*
Music (Adaptation): Ken Thorne, *A Funny Thing Happened On The Way To The Forum.*
Music (Song): Don Black (Lyrics), John Barry (Music) 'Born Free' from *Born Free.*
Short Subjects (Cartoon): *Herb Alpert and the Tijuana Brass Double Feature.*
Short Subjects (Live Action): *Wild Wings.*
Special Visual Effects: Art Cruickshank, *Fantastic Voyage.*
Documentary (Short): *A Year Toward Tomorrow.*
Documentary (Feature): *The War Game.*
Irving G Thalberg Memorial Award: Robert Wise.
Jean Hersholt Humanitarian Award: George Bagnall.
Special Award: Yakima Canutt, for achievements as a stunt man.

Paul Scofield as Sir Thomas More in *A Man For All Seasons.*

This year the awards were dominated by almost perfect adaptations of two popular and difficult stage dramas. *A Man For All Seasons*, the brilliantly conceived story of the battle between Henry VIII and Sir Thomas More, who refused as a matter of conscience, to sign the Act of Succession which condoned the King's divorce from Catherine of Aragon and marriage to Anne Boleyn. The film gathered prizes all over the world, including six at this Award ceremony.

The film won Best Picture, of course; Paul Scofield who had played the part of More on stage recreated the role for the screen, and won the Oscar. Director Fred Zinnemann took the award for director, and Robert Bolt who wrote the original play, adapted it for the screen in Oscar-winning fashion. There were also some minor awards for Cinematography and Costumes. It was a complete triumph for this very fine film.

The second big winner was *Who's Afraid Of Virginia Woolf?* adapted from Edward Albee's ferocious play. Many believed that this play could never be successfully moved to the screen, but director Mike Nichols did it, and he did it with two of the most famous but unreliable names in films, Richard Burton and Elizabeth Taylor. The pair's appearance together in *Cleopatra* was hardly a good omen. Yet as the drunken college professor, and his frumpy, foulmouthed wife, they were perfect. Burton received a Best Actor nomination

ABOVE: *Born Free* with Bill Travers and Virginia McKenna won two music awards.
RIGHT: Anouk Aimee and Jean-Louis Trintignant in *A Man And A Woman*.

for the role, and Taylor won the Best Actress Award, and she earned it. The visiting young couple, nearly destroyed by the verbal conflict, were played by George Segal, who received a Best Supporting Actor nomination and Sandy Dennis who won the Best Supporting Actress Award. This film was the best vehicle that any of these four performers ever had on screen. It was a magical combination, and the magician may have been director Mike Nichols, who was nominated for Best Director.

Behind the big two in the Best Picture category were some other fine films, *Alfie*, *The Russians Are Coming*, *The Russians Are Coming* and *The Sand Pebbles*.

The nominees for Best Actor, with Scofield and Burton, were Michael Caine, as the immortal, womanizing

Best Director nominees included Michelangelo Antonioni, for *Blow Up*, an ambiguous murder mystery filmed in London and starring Vanessa Redgrave, and Richard Brooks nominated for *The Professionals*. Claude Lelouch was nominated for *A Man And A Woman*, a romantic story about a love affair between a racing car driver and a script girl. *A Man And A Woman* also won the Best Foreign Language Film Award, and the Award for Best Original Screenplay, the first time that a foreign language film had ever won such an Oscar.

ABOVE: The Special Visual Effects Award was won by *Fantastic Voyage*.
RIGHT: Elizabeth Taylor played the frumpish wife in *Who's Afraid Of Virginia Woolf?*

title character in *Alfie*; Alan Arkin, speaking his best pseudo-Russian in *The Russians Are Coming, The Russians Are Coming*, and Steve McQueen, who was beginning to hit the top of his form in *The Sand Pebbles*.

The Redgrave girls both received Best Actress nominations, Vanessa for *Morgan*, a weird, sometimes incomprehensible but very funny comedy and Lynn for *Georgy Girl*, in which she gave a marvelously comic portrayal of a pathetic ugly duckling. Ida Kaminska as the old Jewish woman in *The Shop On Main Street* (which had won the Best Foreign Language Film Award in 1965) was nominated as was the beautiful Anouk Aimée for *A Man And A Woman*.

The Best Supporting Actor Award was won by Walter Matthau, as the ambulance chasing lawyer, 'Whiplash' Willy Gingrich in Billy Wilder's *The Fortune Cookie*, his first real comedy role. He had previously played villains. Robert Shaw was nominated for his performance as Henry VIII in *A Man For All Seasons*. James Mason, as the older man pursuing the dumpy Lynn Redgrave in *Georgy Girl*, was nominated as was Mako for *The Sand Pebbles*.

There were two great actresses contending with Sandy Dennis for Best Supporting Actress, Wendy Hiller, as Thomas More's wife, in *A Man For All Seasons*, and Geraldine Page in *You're A Big Boy Now*. Other nominees were Vivien Merchant for *Alfie* and Jocelyne Lagarde as the Hawaiian Queen in the popular but ponderous *Hawaii*.

1967

Best Picture: *In The Heat Of The Night.*
Actor: Rod Steiger, *In The Heat Of The Night.*
Actress: Katharine Hepburn, *Guess Who's Coming To Dinner.*
Supporting Actor: George Kennedy, *Cool Hand Luke.*
Supporting Actress: Estelle Parsons, *Bonnie And Clyde.*
Director: Mike Nichols, *The Graduate.*
Foreign Language Film Award: *Closely Watched Trains* (Czechoslovakia).
Writing (Screenplay-Original): William Rose, *Guess Who's Coming To Dinner.*
Writing (Screenplay-Adaptation): Stirling Silliphant, *In The Heat Of The Night.*
Cinematography: Burnett Guffrey, *Bonnie And Clyde.*
Art Direction: John Truscott, Edward Carrere, (Set Decoration) John W Brown, *Camelot.*
Costume Design: John Truscott, *Camelot.*
Music (Original Score): Elmer Bernstein, *Thoroughly Modern Millie.*
Music (Adaptation): Alfred Newman, Ken Darby, *Camelot.*
Music (Song): Leslie Bricusse, 'Talk To The Animals' from *Doctor Dolittle.*
Short Subjects (Cartoon): *The Box.*
Short Subjects (Live Action): *A Place To Stand.*
Special Visual Effects: L B Abbott, *Doctor Dolittle.*
Documentary (Short): *The Redwoods.*
Documentary (Feature): *The Anderson Platoon.*
Irving G Thalberg Memorial Award: Alfred Hitchcock.
Jean Hersholt Humanitarian Award: Gregory Peck.

For the first time in the forty-year history of the Academy Awards, the ceremony was postponed. The tragic murder of Dr Martin Luther King and the despair and unease in the nation which followed took a lot of the usual joy and glamour out of the ceremonies when they were presented two days later. The proceedings began with Academy president Gregory Peck presenting a moving tribute to the civil rights leader. Though the voting on the Awards had taken place weeks before the assassination, Academy members seemed to have taken the social upheaval into consideration for several

LEFT: Katharine Hepburn and Spencer Tracy played the parents in *Guess Who's Coming To Dinner?*

salaries as insurance so that he could appear. The film was far from the best that the pair had done, but it was so popular, and so emotionally charged that it could not be ignored by the Academy.

Bonnie And Clyde, based on a couple of real-life Depression-era gangsters was also enormously popular. It broke new ground in the graphic depiction of violence in mainstream Hollywood films. *Bonnie And Clyde* was nominated for a large number of Oscars, but the results were disappointing to the producers, for it was mostly an also-ran.

The Graduate made a star out of Dustin Hoffman, and made former comedian Mike Nichols one of Hollywood's hottest directors, following his success with *Who's Afraid Of Virginia Woolf*. This trendy, funny tale of the 'generation gap' theme became a symbol of its time. It did not, however, win a Best Picture Academy Award, though it was nominated.

The final nominee for Best Picture was *Doctor Dolittle*, an expensive but

LEFT: Sidney Poitier as Detective Virgil Tibbs and Rod Steiger as the Police Chief in *In The Heat Of The Night*.
BELOW: George Kennedy and Paul Newman in *Cool Hand Luke*.

leaden attempt to provide another musical vehicle for Rex Harrison, this time using a series of children's stories as the basis. The film was a major artistic disappointment and a box office turkey, but it was nominated for Best Picture anyway.

Spencer Tracy was nominated for Best Actor. This time sentiment did not prevail and the Award was given to Rod Steiger for his intense portrayal of the sheriff in *In The Heat Of The Night*. Steiger had long been recognized as one of the screen's finest actors, and had been nominated before but this was his first Oscar. The other nominees who also delivered Oscar quality performances were Warren Beatty in *Bonnie And Clyde*, Dustin Hoffman in *The Graduate* and Paul Newman in *Cool Hand Luke*.

Sentiment did prevail in the Best Actress category which was won by Katharine Hepburn for *Guess Who's Coming To Dinner*. She had won her first Academy Award for *Morning Glory* in 1933, this was her second, and others would follow. But between 1933 and 1967 she had delivered many of her finest performances, so recognition at this time was not inappropriate. However other actresses nominated this year had turned in some of their finest per-

films and performances with racial and integration themes were honored.

The surprise winner of the Best Picture Award was *In The Heat Of The Night*, basically a detective story, but given significance because of the conflict between a racist-white Southern police chief and a black detective from the North. Another movie with a racial theme that received a Best Picture nomination was *Guess Who's Coming To Dinner*, a film about a white couple meeting their daughter's black fiancé. That film had more than the racial theme, however. The stars were Spencer Tracy and Katharine Hepburn. Tracy was terminally ill, and there were doubts that he would live long enough to finish the film so Hepburn and director Stanley Kramer put up their

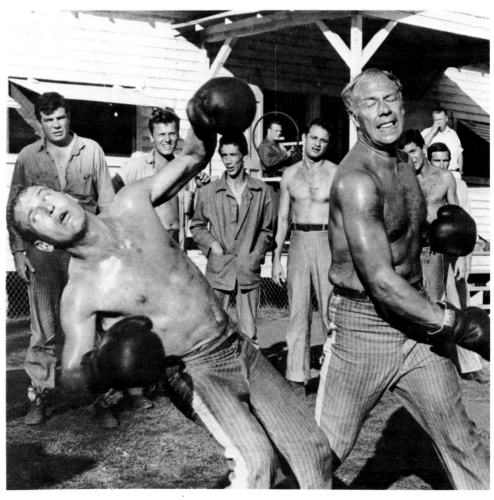

formances ever. The other Hepburn, Audrey, was superb as the blind girl in the chilling *Wait Until Dark*. Anne Bancroft did some of the best work of her very fine career as Mrs Robinson, the cunning, provocative and vaguely evil seducer of Dustin Hoffman in *The Graduate*, and relative newcomer Faye Dunaway made a tremendous impression as the gangster's moll Bonnie, in *Bonnie And Clyde*. Towering above them all in sheer acting skill was Britain's Dame Edith Evans, playing a lonely, old, working class woman living in poverty in *The Whisperers*.

George Kennedy won Best Supporting Actor for an excellent performance in *Cool Hand Luke*. Two actors were nominated from *Bonnie And Clyde*, Gene Hackman and baby-faced Michael J Pollard, either could have won. Nominee John Cassavetes, now best known as the director of controversial films gave a standout performance in the popular war film *The Dirty Dozen*.

Estelle Parsons was an easy winner in the Best Supporting Actress category for *Bonnie And Clyde*, for not only was she good but the competition was weak. Mildred Natwick gave a professional performance as Jane Fonda's mother in the film version of Neil Simon's *Barefoot In The Park*. Carol Channing was, well, Carol Channing in *Thoroughly Modern Millie*. Katherine Ross was as good as she gets as the object of Dustin Hoffman's affections in *The Graduate*, but she looked pale beside more skilled cast members. Beah Richards though good was not truly memorable in *Guess Who's Coming To Dinner*.

Mike Nichols won the Best Director Award for *The Graduate*. Arthur Penn, for *Bonnie And Clyde* and Norman Jewison for *In The Heat Of The Night*, were also in the running. Stanley Kramer's direction of *Guess Who's Coming To Dinner*, like the rest of the film, was merely serviceable. Richard Brooks did a brilliant job filming *In Cold Blood*, Truman Capote's chilling 'non fiction novel' about a mass murder, but the picture was too depressing to gain a wide audience.

Dr Dolittle picked up some minor awards for music and special effects as did another very expensive and very boring musical *Camelot*.

The Thalberg Award for overall excellence was given to Alfred Hitchcock, who certainly earned it.

Dustin Hoffman starred with Anne Bancroft in *The Graduate*, for which Mike Nichols won the award for Best Director.

1968

Best Picture: *Oliver.*
Actor: Cliff Robertson, *Charly.*
Actress: (tie award) Katharine Hepburn, *The Lion In Winter*, Barbra Streisand, *Funny Girl.*
Supporting Actor: Jack Albertson, *The Subject Was Roses.*
Supporting Actress: Ruth Gordon, *Rosemary's Baby.*
Director: Carol Reed, *Oliver.*
Foreign Language Film Award: *War And Peace* (USSR).
Writing (Screenplay-Original): Mel Brooks, *The Producers.*
Writing (Screenplay-Adaptation): James Goldman, *The Lion In Winter.*
Cinematography: Pasqualino De Santis, *Romeo And Juliet.*
Art Direction: John Box, Terence Marsh,

(Set Decoration) Vernon Dixon, Ken Muggleston, *Oliver!*
Costume Designer: Danilo Donati, *Romeo And Juliet.*
Music (Original Score): John Barry, *The Lion In Winter.*
Music (Adaptation): John Green, *Oliver.*
Music (Song): Michel Legrand (Music), Alan and Marilyn Bergman (Lyrics), 'The Windmills Of Your Mind' from *The Thomas Crown Affair.*
Short Subjects (Cartoon): *Winnie The Pooh And The Blustery Day.*
Short Subjects (Live Action): *Robert Kennedy Remembered.*
Special Visual Effects: *2001: A Space Odyssey.*
Documentary (Short): *Why Man Creates.*
Documentary (Feature): *Journey Into Self.*
Jean Hersholt Humanitarian Award: Martha Raye.
Special Awards: John Chambers for his

outstanding make-up achievement for *Planet Of The Apes.* Oona White for her outstanding choreography achievement for *Oliver!*

Innovation is rarely rewarded with an Oscar. Thus in 1968 *Oliver!* a lavish, enjoyable but quite standard film version of a popular London and Broadway musical based on the Charles Dickens book, received a flock of awards. Stanley Kubrick's *2001: A Space Odyssey*, possibly the best science fiction film ever made, and a film that paved the way for the big science fiction spectaculars of the seventies and eighties, received one award – Special Visual Effects.

Oliver was a musical version of Dickens' classic, starring Mark Lester in the title role, and directed by Sir Carol Reed.

OPPOSITE: Katharine Hepburn as Eleanor of Aquitaine in *The Lion In Winter* with Peter O'Toole as Henry II.
ABOVE: Cliff Robertson and Claire Bloom in *Charly*.

It's not that *Oliver!* was a bad film, it was lively, colorful and extremely popular. It represented the first attempt of the distinguished British Director Sir Carol Reed to make a musical, and he did it well enough to earn the Oscar as Best Director.

Oliver! triumphed over such other period-set offerings as *Funny Girl, The Lion In Winter* and *Romeo And Juliet*. The final nominee (and quite possibly the best) was *Rachel, Rachel*, a small film about a spinster schoolteacher, starring Joanne Woodward and produced and directed by her husband Paul Newman.

Cliff Robertson received the Award for Best Actor in *Charly*, the story of a retarded man who temporarily becomes a genius. Robertson had first played the part on television, then he purchased the rights and pushed to have it made as

a film. His efforts were amply rewarded. Robertson's competition was Peter O'Toole, for his vivid portrayal of King Henry II, in *The Lion In Winter*; Ron Moody, a very pleasant Fagin in *Oliver!*; Alan Arkin as a deaf-mute in *The Heart Is A Lonely Hunter*, and Alan Bates as a victim of anti-Semitism in *The Fixer*.

For Oscar trivia buffs 1968 was the year that there was a tie for Best Actress between veteran Katharine Hepburn for her brilliant performance as Eleanor of Aquitaine in *The Lion In Winter*, and a brash newcomer in her first film, Barbra Streisand, recreating her stage success as Fanny Brice in the musical *Funny Girl*. Patricia Neal, returning to films after a series of strokes received a Best Actress nomination for *The Subject Was Roses*. Vanessa Redgrave was triumphant as the innovative dancer in an otherwise lifeless *Isadora*, and Joanne Woodward whose career had been slipping into the shadow of her husband Paul Newman was once again recognized for the fine actress she is, for *Rachel, Rachel*.

Jack Albertson who had begun his long show business career in burlesque was superb as the frustrated, baffled husband and father in *The Subject Was Roses* and won the Best Supporting Actor Oscar. Another show business veteran seventy-one-year-old Ruth Gordon received Best Supporting Actress for her portrayal of the seemingly warm-hearted neighbor in the fine supernatural thriller *Rosemary's Baby*. 'What took you so long,' quipped the irrepressable Gordon when she received her Oscar.

The other candidates for Best Supporting Actor were Seymour Cassel in *Faces*, Daniel Massey as Noël Coward in *Star!*, Jack Wild in *Oliver!* and Gene Wilder in *The Producers*. That film also won an Oscar for writer Mel Brooks.

The nominees for Best Supporting Actress who didn't win were Lynn Carlin for *Faces*, Sondra Locke for *The Heart Is A Lonely Hunter*, Kay Medford for *Funny Girl* and Estelle Parsons for *Rachel, Rachel*.

Stanley Kubrick was nominated for Best Director for *2001: A Space Odyssey*,

but he lost to Carol Reed and *Oliver!* Franco Zeffirelli whose lush and sensual *Romeo And Juliet* received mixed reviews from the critics was also nominated. Anthony Harvey was nominated for his brilliant adaptation of James Goldman's *The Lion In Winter*. The most surprising nomination was that of Gillo Pontecorvo for *The Battle Of Algers*, what we would today call a docudrama about the long war of the French in Algeria. It was a serious, and searing film, and a controversial one for its openly pro-Algerian sympathies.

The film had already been nominated for the Best Foreign Language Film Award in 1966. The winner of the Foreign Language Film Award was *War And Peace*, the massive eight-hour Russian adaptation of Tolstoy's novel which featured believable battle scenes and brilliant performances by a young dancer Ludmila Savalyeva as Natasha, Vyacheslav Tikhonov as Prince Andrei and the director Sergei Bondarchuk as Pierre.

The Academy showed an unusual sense of humor and irreverence when it

The Producers starring Gene Wilder and Zero Mostel, won the award for Best Original Screenplay, written by Mel Brooks, who also directed.

had a chimpanzee present the Special Award for make-up to John Chambers, creator of the make-up for *Planet Of The Apes*.

The most touching moment in the ceremonies came when Bob Hope gave the Jean Hersholt Humanitarian Award to his old companion in comedy Martha Raye.

1969

Best Picture: *Midnight Cowboy.*
Actor: John Wayne, *True Grit.*
Actress: Maggie Smith, *The Prime Of Miss Jean Brodie.*
Supporting Actor: Gig Young, *They Shoot Horses Don't They?*
Supporting Actress: Goldie Hawn, *Cactus Flower.*
Director: John Schlesinger, *Midnight Cowboy.*
Foreign Language Film Award: *Z* (Algeria).
Writing (Screenplay-Original): William Goldman, *Butch Cassidy And The Sundance Kid.*
Writing (Screenplay-Adaptation): Waldo Salt, *Midnight Cowboy.*
Cinematography: Conrad Hall, *Butch Cassidy And The Sundance Kid.*
Art Direction: John DeCuir, Jack Martin Smith, Herman Blumenthal, (Set Decoration) Walter M Scott, George Hopkins, Raphael Bretton, *Hello Dolly!*

Costume Design: Margaret Furse, *Anne Of The Thousand Days.*
Music (Original Score): Burt Bacharach, *Butch Cassidy And The Sundance Kid.*
Music (Adaptation): Lennie Hayton, Lionel Newman, *Hello Dolly!*
Music (Song): Burt Bacharach (Music), Hal David (Lyrics), 'Raindrops Keep Fallin' On My Head' from *Butch Cassidy And The Sundance Kid.*
Short Subjects (Cartoon): *It's Tough To Be A Bird.*
Short Subjects (Live Action): *The Magic Machines.*
Documentary (Short): *Czechoslovakia, 1968.*
Documentary (Feature): *Artur Rubinstein – The Love Of Life.*
Jean Hersholt Humanitarian Award: George Jessel.
Special Award: Cary Grant for his unique mastery of the art of screen acting with the respect and affection of his colleagues.

This was the year that the 'new freedom' really came to Hollywood. It was one of the dominant themes of the Award Ceremonies, and host Bob Hope said that from now on Hollywood would 'hold a mirror up to nature'. That point was driven home by the film voted Best Picture, *Midnight Cowboy* a story set in the world of the Times Square hustler. Though the film may seem tame by today's standards, it was considered a shocking breakthrough in 1969, and it redefined what subject matter was acceptable in Hollywood films.

But it wasn't all new freedoms, for the Academy also paid tribute to one of its old favorites John Wayne who won Best Actor honors for his role as the one-eyed Sheriff Rooster Cogburn in the western *True Grit*. Though he delivered one of his finest performances, Wayne was also known to be suffering from cancer and other ailments, and sentiment doubtless played a part in the voting, for Wayne had never won an Oscar before, though he had been nominated for *Sands Of Iwo Jima* (1949).

Midnight Cowboy beat out two very popular films for the Oscar. *Butch Cassidy And The Sundance Kid*, which teamed Paul Newman and Robert Redford for the first time, had been a huge box office success, though neither Newman nor Redford received Best Actor nominations. *Hello Dolly!*, a lavish screen recreation of the popular Broadway show, was also nominated. It starred Barbra Streisand in the role of Dolly, but possibly miscast, she didn't get a Best Actress nomination. *Anne Of The Thousand Days*, a historical drama and *Z*, a tough and riveting political film rounded out the nominees.

Both Jon Voight, as the Texas-born hustler, and Dustin Hoffman, as the tuburcular 'Ratso' received Best Actor nominations, for *Midnight Cowboy*. Richard Burton had one of his better film outings as Henry VIII in *Anne Of The Thousand Days* and Peter O'Toole did his best in the remake of *Goodbye, Mr. Chips*, but Robert Donat's Oscar winning performance in the original 1939 film was better.

The dark-horse winner in the Best Actress category was Maggie Smith as the Scottish schoolteacher who is ultimately destroyed by one of her pupils in

Dustin Hoffman as Ratso Rizzo in *Midnight Cowboy.*

ABOVE: The musical *Hello Dolly* won awards for Art Direction and Musical Adaptation.
RIGHT: Best Actor John Wayne as the marshal Rooster Cogburn in *True Grit*.

The Prime Of Miss Jean Brodie. Though Smith had made some memorable film appearances before and had received a nomination in 1965 for Best Supporting Actress for her performance as Desdemona in *Othello*, she was known primarily as a stage actress.

Favorite contenders in the Best Actress category had been Jane Fonda as the disillusioned young woman in *They Shoot Horses Don't They?*, and Liza Minnelli in her adult screen debut in *The Sterile Cuckoo*. Jean Simmons had also been nominated for *The Happy Ending*, and Genevieve Bujold, for *Anne Of The Thousand Days*.

It took a British director, John Schlesinger, to effectively portray the underside of American city life in *Midnight Cowboy*, and for that he was given the Best Director Award. It was unlikely that Costa-Gravas would get an Oscar for *Z*, his political thriller based on the assassination of left-wing Greek deputy in Greece in 1953, but the film did gain him a nomination, the Best

Foreign Language Film Oscar and a host of other awards in the US and Europe. George Roy Hill who directed *Butch Cassidy And The Sundance Kid*, Arthur Penn who directed *Alice's Restaurant* and Sidney Pollack who directed *They Shoot Horses Don't They?* all received nominations for their efforts, and the nominations were well deserved.

Gig Young, normally a journeyman actor who appeared in light comedy won the Best Supporting Actor Award for *They Shoot Horses Don't They?* in a better role than he was usually given, as the cynical emcee of a dance marathon. Jack Nicholson had his best role to date as the middle class guy who joins up with a couple of free-wheeling hippies in *Easy Rider*, a film that started a vogue

for youth-oriented movies. It got Nicholson the first of his many Oscar nominations. Elliott Gould virtually stole *Bob & Carol & Ted & Alice* and received a Supporting Actor nomination for it. Also nominated in this category were Anthony Quayle as Cardinal Wolsey in *Anne Of The Thousand Days* and Rupert Crosse in *The Reivers*.

Until her Best Supporting Actress Oscar for *Cactus Flower* Goldie Hawn was best known as the giggling dumb blonde on TV's 'Rowan and Martin's Laugh-in.' She had only made one film, a small part in a minor Disney effort *The One And Only Genuine Original Family Band* (1968). No one expected that she would be able to match and almost outshine such established talents as

Ingrid Bergman and Walter Matthau, but as the infatuated young woman, she did just that. Susannah York was good in *They Shoot Horses Don't They?* and Sylvia Miles was even better as the woman who out-hustles the hustler in *Midnight Cowboy*. Rounding out the Best Supporting Actress field were Catherine Burns in *Last Summer* and Dyan Cannon in *Bob & Carol & Ted & Alice*.

Cary Grant who unaccountably had never won an Oscar for any of his brilliant comedy work was given an Honorary Award.

'Raindrops Keep Falling On My Head' from *Butch Cassidy And The Sundance Kid* won the Award for Best Song of 1969.

1970

Best Picture: *Patton*.
Actor: George C Scott, *Patton*.
Actress: Glenda Jackson, *Women In Love*.
Supporting Actor: John Mills, *Ryan's Daughter*.
Supporting Actress: Helen Hayes, *Airport*.
Director: Franklin J Schaffner, *Patton*.
Foreign Language Film Award: *Investigation Of A Citizen Above Suspicion* (Italy).
Writing (Screenplay-Original): Francis Ford Coppola, Edmund H North, *Patton*.
Writing (Adaptation): Ring Lardner, Jr, *M*A*S*H*.
Cinematography: Freddie Young, *Ryan's Daughter*.
Art Direction: Urie McCleary, Gil Parrondo, (Set Decoration) Antonio Mateos, Pierre-Louis Thevenet, *Patton*.
Costume Design: Nino Novarese, *Cromwell*.

Music (Original Score): Francis Lai, *Love Story*.
Music (Original Song Score): The Beatles, *Let It Be*.
Music (Song): Fred Karlin (Music), Robb Royer, James Griffin (Lyrics). 'For All We Know' from *Lovers And Other Strangers*.
Short Subjects (Cartoon): *Is It Always Right To Be Right?*
Short Subjects (Live Action): *The Resurrection Of Broncho Billy*.
Special Visual Effects: *Tora! Tora! Tora!*
Documentary (Short): *Interviews With My Lai Veterans*.
Documentary (Feature): *Woodstock*.
Irving G Thalberg Memorial Award: Ingmar Bergman.
Jean Hersholt Humanitarian Award: Frank Sinatra.
Special Awards: Lillian Gish, for superlative artistry and for distinguished contribution to the progress of motion pictures. Orson Welles, for superlative artistry and versatility.

Everyone knew George C Scott's attitude toward the Academy Awards, he had already received two nominations for Best Supporting Actor, and the second time he asked that his name be withdrawn, though the request was refused. When he was nominated as Best Actor for *Patton* he made the same request, and he was again refused. It was generally agreed that Scott's towering performance as the brilliant and eccentric warrior was worthy of an Oscar, but how would the voting members of the Academy react to his scorn for them? They simply ignored it, and gave him the Best Actor Award anyway, though he wasn't there to pick it up.

Patton was the biggest winner this year. It also received the Best Picture and Best Director Awards; in addition there were some minor Oscars includ-

Best Actor George C Scott as the title character in *Patton*.

ing one for the script's writers, Edmund H North, and Francis Ford Coppola, who would soon be heard from again.

The two big box office successes in 1970 were *Patton* and the embarrassingly weepy *Love Story*, which was also nominated for Best Picture. *Five Easy Pieces* the film that propelled Jack Nicholson to stardom was another nominee, as was Robert Altman's *M★A★S★H* which was to spawn the long

running TV series. *Airport* a popular, star-stuffed, disaster film was the fifth nominee.

If the Academy had not decided to overlook the rebuff, and give the Oscar to someone other than George C Scott, it probably would have gone to Jack Nicholson whose portrayal of a drifter returning to his rich family in *Five Easy Pieces* was a triumph. James Earl Jones was also triumphant in *The Great White*

Elliot Gould, Tom Skerritt and Donald Sutherland stop their golf game to read an X-ray in *M★A★S★H*.

Hope where he recreated his stage role of the first black boxing champion Jack Johnson. Melvin Douglas may have given the finest performance of his long and distinguished career in *I Never Sang For My Father*, as a selfish and domineering father, who sabotages his son's efforts at closeness. Ryan O'Neal was nominated for *Love Story*, and he almost managed to hold the film together.

Glenda Jackson, best known as a London stage actress became known to American movie goers when she won a Best Actress Oscar for *Women In Love*, based on the novel by D H Lawrence.

Another British actress to get a nomination this year was Sarah Miles, very effective in the beautiful but slow film, *Ryan's Daughter*. Carrie

BELOW: Lillian Gish, here in *Night Of The Hunter* (1955) was honored for her films. RIGHT: Glenda Jackson, Jennie Linden in *Women In Love*.

Snodgrass had a superb film debut as the housewife in *Diary Of A Mad Housewife*. Jane Alexander had a strong and effective role in *The Great White Hope* as Johnson's white wife. Ali McGraw was critically panned for *Love Story*, but the public turned out to see the film, and she got a Best Actress nomination anyway.

John Mills won Best Supporting Actor for his role as the mute village idiot in *Ryan's Daughter* which was far from the finest work of this very skilled actor, but then the competition wasn't all that great either. Gene Hackman was

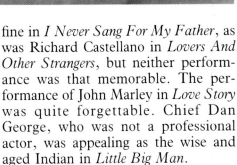

portant film. Maureen Stapleton was also nominated for *Airport*. The actress who was nominated and should have won was Sally Kellerman, who created the role of 'Hot Lips' in *M★A★S★H*. The other nominees were Karen Black at her very best as Nicholson's waitress-girlfriend in *Five Easy Pieces* and Lee Grant who was beginning to reestablish her film career after being blacklisted for years, for *The Landlord*.

Franklin J Schaffner won the Best Director Oscar for *Patton*. Robert Altman was nominated for *M★A★S★H*, his best directoral effort ever. Ken Russell may also have been at the top of his form when he received a nomination for *Women In Love*. Fedrico Fellini was not at the top of his form, but his films are always fascinating, and he got a nomination for the bizarre *Fellini Satyricon*. Arthur Hiller was nominated for *Love Story*.

Screenwriter Ring Lardner, Jr, who had not only been blacklisted, but had

been jailed during the McCarthy era received an Oscar for *M★A★S★H*.

The Documentary film award went to *Woodstock*, a film about the rock concert that gave its name to a generation.

For the first time the Irving G Thalberg Memorial Award for consistently excellent filmmaking was given to the director of foreign language films, Ingmar Bergman, who certainly deserved it. The Jean Hersholt Humanitarian Award was given to Frank Sinatra who had recently announced the first of his many retirements. He was presented with the award by Gregory Peck who described Sinatra as 'a soft touch.' More well-deserved honors were given to Lillian Gish and Orson Welles.

Trevor Howard as the priest and Best Supporting Actor John Mills as the village idiot in *Ryan's Daughter*.

fine in *I Never Sang For My Father*, as was Richard Castellano in *Lovers And Other Strangers*, but neither performance was that memorable. The performance of John Marley in *Love Story* was quite forgettable. Chief Dan George, who was not a professional actor, was appealing as the wise and aged Indian in *Little Big Man*.

Helen Hayes received the Best Supporting Actress Award for *Airport*, clearly a show of respect for past performances primarily on stage rather than acknowledgment of any special merit for her appearance in this unim-

1971

Best Picture: *The French Connection.*
Actor: Gene Hackman, *The French Connection.*
Actress: Jane Fonda, *Klute.*
Supporting Actor: Ben Johnson, *The Last Picture Show.*
Supporting Actress: Cloris Leachman, *The Last Picture Show.*
Director: William Friedkin, *The French Connection.*
Foreign Language Film Award: *The Garden Of The Finzi-Continis* (Italy).
Writing (Screenplay-Original): Paddy Chayefsky, *The Hospital.*
Writing (Screenplay-Adaptation): *The French Connection.*
Cinematography: Oswald Morris, *Fiddler On The Roof.*
Art Direction: John Box, Ernest Archer, Jack Maxted, Gil Parrondo, (Set Decoration) Vernon Dixon, *Nicholas And Alexandra.*

Costume Design: Yvonne Blake, Antonio Castillo, *Nicholas And Alexandra.*
Music (Original Score): Michel Legrand, *Summer Of '42.*
Music (Adaptation): John Williams, *Fiddler On The Roof.*
Music (Song): Isaac Hayes, 'Theme From Shaft' from *Shaft.*
Short Subjects (Cartoon): *The Crunch Bird.*
Short Subjects (Live Action): *Sentinels Of Silence.*
Special Visual Effects: Alan Maley, Eustace Lycett, Danny Lee, *Bedknobs And Broomsticks.*
Documentary (Short): *Sentinels Of Silence.*
Documentary (Feature): *The Hellstrom Chronicle.*
Honorary Award: Charles Chaplin for the incalculable effect he has had in making motion pictures the art form of this century.

Roy Scheider with Best Actress Jane Fonda in *Klute.*

The big event at the forty-fourth annual awards ceremony was the appearance of Charlie Chaplin to receive an Honorary Award. Chaplin had been in exile from America for twenty years because of his political views. Indeed when he returned, then president Richard Nixon declined to meet him. But Chaplin's reception in Hollywood was very different. The Little Tramp, then over eighty received a four-minute standing ovation from the nearly three thousand guests in the Dorothy Chandler Pavilion of the Los Angeles County Music Center. Chaplin, responded quietly: 'Words are so futile, so feeble. I can only say thank you for the honor of inviting me here. You are wonderful, sweet people.'

Otherwise 1971 was a fairly mediocre year for the Awards. *The French Connection*, a superior cops and robbers or in this case cops and drug dealer film, featuring a memorable auto chase was awarded Best Picture. A far better film

Best Actor Gene Hackman as Detective 'Popeye' Doyle in *The French Connection*.

Stanley Kubrick's *A Clockwork Orange* a riveting and nightmarish vision of the future based on Anthony Burgess' novel, was nominated but did not win, perhaps because it was too strong. *The Last Picture Show*, about being young in a tiny Texas town, and shot in black and white was a deserving nominee. *Fiddler On The Roof* a too respectful and plodding version of the great Broadway musical, and *Nicholas And Alexandra* a slow moving costume drama about the lives of the last Tsar of Russia and his wife were also nominated.

Gene Hackman received the Best Actor Oscar for his role as the crazy detective Popeye Doyle in *The French Connection*. Both Peter Finch, a homosexual doctor in *Sunday, Bloody Sunday* and George C Scott, a suicidal doctor in *The Hospital*, were nominated for first rate performances in films that did not attract the audiences they deserved. Walter Matthau was excellent as always but the film for which he was nominated, *Kotch*, wasn't. The Israeli actor, Topol, looked like Tevye, but lacked life in *Fiddler On The Roof*, but he received a nomination anyway. Zero Mostel who created the role on stage should have been given the part. Amazingly Malcolm McDowell, who was absolutely brilliant as Alex the thuggish main character in *A Clockwork Orange*, wasn't even nominated. Perhaps Academy members simply found his character too repellant.

Jane Fonda had her best role to date as the threatened hooker in *Klute*, and

ABOVE: Topol as Tevye celebrates in *Fiddler On The Roof*.

RIGHT: Best Supporting Actor Ben Johnson in *The Last Picture Show*.

she won the Best Actress Award for it. Glenda Jackson was nominated again, this time for *Sunday, Bloody Sunday*. Vanessa Redgrave used all of her awesome talents in the title role of *Mary Queen Of Scots*, but the film still failed to get off the ground. Janet Suzman tried the same for *Nicholas And Alexandra*, with the same results. Julie Christie attracted critical attention and an Oscar nomination as the madame in Robert Altman's slow moving *McCabe And Mrs Miller*.

Ben Johnson received a Best Supporting Actor Award for his portrayal of the philosophical pool-hall owner in *The Last Picture Show*. Cloris Leachman won the Best Supporting Actress as the aging and frustrated wife of the Texas town's gym coach in the same film. Also from *The Last Picture Show* Jeff Bridges received a Best Supporting Actor nomination and Ellen Burstyn one for Best Supporting Actress.

The other Best Supporting actor

nominees were Leonard Frey for *Fiddler On The Roof*, Richard Jaeckel for *Sometimes A Great Notion* and Roy Scheider for *The French Connection*. The other Best Supporting Actress nominees were Barbara Harris in *Who Is Harry Kellerman, And Why Is He Saying Those Terrible Things About Me*, Margaret Leighton in *The Go-Between*, and one time sex-symbol Ann-Margaret

who surprised practically everyone by turning in a memorable performance in Mike Nichols' *Carnal Knowledge*, a landmark film that the Academy almost completely ignored.

William Friedkin, a young, former TV documentary director who had never directed a major feature before, won the Award for Best Director for *The French Connection*. Another young director Peter Bogdanovich, got a lot of attention and a Oscar nomination for *The Last Picture Show*. John Schlesinger deserved his nomination for *Sunday, Bloody Sunday*, Norman Jewison didn't deserve his for *Fiddler On The Roof*. And finally Stanley Kubrick was nominated for *A Clockwork Orange*, and although he didn't win he certainly deserved to.

Italian director Vittorio de Sica's best film in years, *The Garden Of The Finzi-Continis*, a penetrating and moving study of anti-Semitism in pre-World War II Italy, won the Best Foreign Language Film Award.

The Hospital, a film that wonderfully evoked the craziness of New York City received little attention, but did win an Oscar for its writer Paddy Chayefsky.

1972

Best Picture: *The Godfather.*
Actor: Marlon Brando, *The Godfather.*
Actress: Liza Minnelli, *Cabaret.*
Supporting Actor: Joel Grey, *Cabaret.*
Supporting Actress: Eileen Heckart, *Butterflies Are Free.*
Director: Bob Fosse, *Cabaret.*
Foreign Language Film Award: *The Discreet Charm Of The Bourgeoisie* (France).
Writing (Screenplay-Original): Jeremy Larner, *The Candidate.*
Writing (Screenplay-Adaptation): Mario Puzo, Francis Ford Coppola, *The Godfather.*
Cinematography: Geoffrey Unsworth, *Cabaret.*
Art Direction: Rolf Zehetbauer, Jurge Kiebach, (Set Decoration) Herbert Strabel, *Cabaret.*

Costume Design: Anthony Powell, *Travels With My Aunt.*
Music (Original Score): Charles Chaplin, Raymond Rasch, Larry Russell, *Limelight.*
Music (Adaptation): Ralph Burns, *Cabaret.*
Music (Song): Al Kasha And Joel Hirschhorn, 'The Morning After' from *The Poseidon Adventure.*
Short Subjects (Animated): *A Christmas Carol.*
Short Subjects (Live Action): *Norman Rockwell's World.*
Documentary (Short): *This Tiny World.*
Documentary (Feature): *Marjoe.*
Jean Hersholt Humanitarian Award: Rosalind Russell.
Honorary Award: Edward G Robinson, who achieved greatness as a player, a patron of the arts and a dedicated citizen . . . in sum, a Renaissance man. From his friends in the industry he loves.

It had been said that Marlon Brando was all washed up, a brilliant actor, but too undisciplined and too eccentric to work effectively in films any more. Francis Ford Coppola had to fight to get Brando the part of Don Vito Corleone, in *The Godfather*. It was a gamble, but one that payed off brilliantly as Brando turned in an Oscar-winning perform-ance as the aging Mafia chief. Brando, however, did have a little surprise for the Academy. It had been widely rumored that he would turn down the Award as George C Scott had done before. Scott merely failed to turn up. Brando sent a young Indian woman, Sacheen Littlefeather to refuse the award for him, and to publicize the plight of Native Americans. The result

Best Actress Liza Minnelli as Sally Bowles and Best Supporting Actor Joel Grey as 'Emcee' in the musical *Cabaret.*

was confusion and near pandemonium, on live television before an audience of about eighty million.

The Godfather also won the award for Best Picture, but the other big box office hit of the year *Cabaret*, a musical that had its origins in Christopher Isherwood's *Berlin Stories*, set in Germany at the time of the rise of the Nazis, picked up even more awards, including a Best Actress Award for Liza Minnelli who played the role of the singer Sally Bowles.

The Godfather and *Cabaret* were the two main contenders for Best Picture. *Deliverance*, a brutal and terrifying tale of four civilized men on a river trip with some barely civilized good-old-boys, had a certain notoriety. The other two nominees were *The Emigrants*, about the hard life of Scandinavian immigrants in America, and *Sounder*, a gentle tale of growing up black in the South.

Brando didn't have a lot of real competition for Best Actor. Both Laurence Olivier and Michael Caine were nominated for the mystery thriller *Sleuth*, but mystery thrillers, and the actors appearing in them rarely win Oscars. Peter O'Toole was nominated for *The Ruling Class*, giving an excellent performance in a brilliant picture that few people ever went to see, and Paul Winfield was nominated for *Sounder*.

Liza Minelli was equally dominant in the Best Actress category. Two black actresses had been nominated, a first for the Academy Awards. Cicely Tyson was excellent in *Sounder*. Diana Ross, however, was miscast as Billy Holiday in *The Lady Sings The Blues*. Liv Ullmann was beautiful and effective in *The Emigrants*, and Maggie Smith was fun in the film based on the Graham Greene novel *Travels With My Aunt*.

Eileen Heckart, won Best Supporting Actress as the mother trying to cope with her son's blindness in *Butterflies Are Free*. Her selection was popular, perhaps because the rest of the nominees gave forgettable performances in forgettable films. They were Jeannie Berlin for *The Heartbreak Kid*, Geraldine Page, usually wonderful, but ultimately done in by the material in *Pete 'n' Tillie*. Susan Tyrrell received a nomination for *Fat City* and Shelley Winters gave the best performance in

BELOW: Robert Redford as *The Candidate* with Karen Carlson as his wife.
OPPOSITE: Marlon Brando as Don Vito Corleone the aging Mafia gang leader in *The Godfather*.

The Award for Foreign Language Film went to Luis Buñuel's *The Discreet Charm Of The Bourgeoisie*, a surreal fable.

the disaster film *The Poseidon Adventure*, but that wasn't saying much. In any event it earned her a nomination.

The Best Supporting Actor category this year was quite different for it honored a number of memorable performances, including three from *The Godfather*. Al Pacino was nominated for his role as Michael, really more of a starring than a supporting part. Other nominees included Robert Duvall as the Corleone family lawyer, and James Caan as the hot-headed, slow-witted Sonny. None of them won, because song and dance man Joel Grey turned in a masterpiece of a performance as the MC in *Cabaret*, a role he first created on Broadway, and also more of a starring than a supporting part. The fifth contender, Eddie Albert, was nominated for *The Heartbreak Kid*.

Bob Fosse, who had always been better known as a dancer and choreographer received the Best Director Award for *Cabaret*, and it was the musical scenes that made this film work. In between the numbers *Cabaret* was rather dull and ordinary. Francis Ford Coppola probably should have won the Best Director Award for *The Godfather*. John Boorman did an excellent job with *Deliverance*, Jan Troell's *The Emigrants* was a spare, chilly, but ultimately a very moving film. Joseph L Mankiewicz did a more than competent job of translating *Sleuth* from stage to screen, but in the end it was still the sort of entertainment that works better on stage.

Master satirist Luis Buñuel won the Best Foreign Language Film Award for one of the very best films of his long career, *The Discreet Charm Of The Bourgeoisie*.

1973

Best Picture: *The Sting.*
Actor: Jack Lemmon, *Save The Tiger.*
Actress: Glenda Jackson, *A Touch Of Class.*
Supporting Actor: John Houseman, *The Paper Chase.*
Supporting Actress: Tatum O'Neal, *Paper Moon.*
Director: George Roy Hill, *The Sting.*
Foreign Language Film Award: *Day For Night* (France).
Writing (Screenplay-Original): David S Ward, *The Sting.*
Writing (Screenplay-Adaptation): William Peter Blatty, *The Exorcist.*
Cinematography: Sven Nykvist, *Cries And Whispers.*
Art Direction: Harry Bumstead, (Set Decoration) James Payne, *The Sting.*
Costume Design: Edith Head, *The Sting.*
Music (Original Score): Marvin Hamlisch, *The Way We Were.*

Music (Adaptation): Marvin Hamlisch, *The Sting.*
Music (Song): Marvin Hamlisch (Music), Allan and Marilyn Bergman (Lyrics), 'The Way We Were' from *The Way We Were.*
Short Subjects (Animated): *Frank Film.*
Short Subjects (Live Action): *The Bolero.*
Documentary (Short): *Princeton: A Search For Answers.*
Documentary (Feature): *The Great American Cowboy.*
Jean Hersholt Humanitarian Award: Lew Wasserman.
Irving G Thalberg Memorial Award: Lawrence Weingarten.
Honorary Awards: Henri Langlos, for his devotion to the art of film, his massive contributions in preserving its part and his unserving faith in its future. Groucho Marx, in recognition of his brilliant creativity and for the achievements of the Marx Brothers in the art of motion picture comedy.

There was little suspense as to what picture would be the big winner this year. Everyone expected *The Sting*, a fast, stylish comedy starring one of Hollywood's favorite couples Paul Newman and Robert Redford, to sweep the awards just as it had swept the box office. And it did, winning Best Picture, Best Director, Best Original Screenplay and some minor awards as well, including one for its wonderful musical score adapted by Marvin Hamlisch.

The competition was by no means insignificant. There was *American Graffiti*, a popular film about growing up in California in the sixties, directed by a talented young director named George Lucas. *The Exorcist*, a truly terrifying film which reinvigorated the entire genre of horror films, and was a huge box office success, was also nomi-

Paul Newman and Robert Redford starred in *The Sting.*

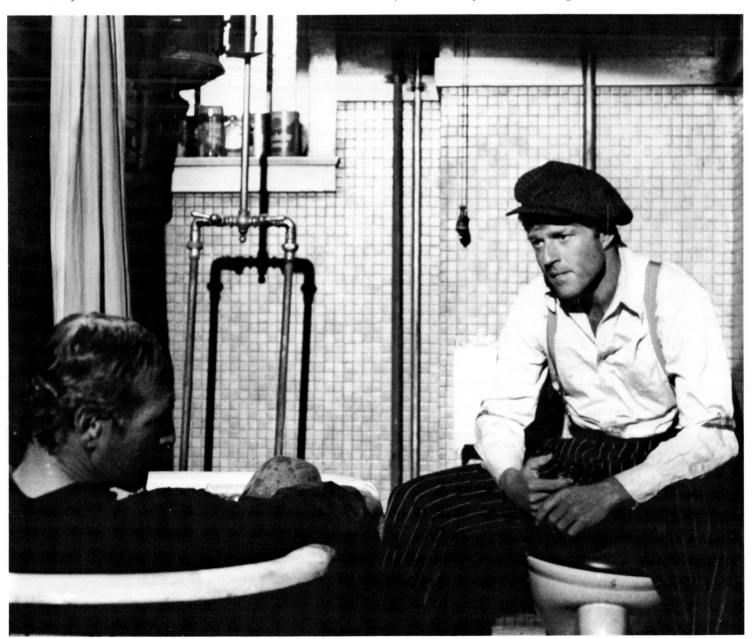

nated. *Cries And Whispers*, an absolutely harrowing film about love, pain, death and spiritual anguish, was too depressing to be a serious contender. It was, however one of the great director Ingmar Bergman's finest films and had already received other more highbrow awards. Had it been nominated in the Foreign Language Film category it doubtless would have won. Also nominated was *A Touch Of Class*, a bitingly funny film with an Oscar winning performance by Glenda Jackson.

Robert Redford was nominated for Best Actor for his performance as the Depression-era con man in *The Sting*.

OPPOSITE: *The Way We Were* starred Barbra Streisand.
BELOW: *A Touch Of Class* with Glenda Jackson and George Segal.

The other nominees were Al Pacino for the police drama *Serpico*, based on the experiences of a New York cop; Marlon Brando for *Last Tango In Paris*, a controversial film because of its very explicit sex, and Jack Nicholson who played a softhearted sailor in *The Last Detail*. The winner, however, was Jack Lemmon for his powerful portrayal of a middle-aged dress manufacturer facing ruin in *Save The Tiger*.

Glenda Jackson received the Best Actress Award, her second in three years for *A Touch Of Class*, a comedy which represented quite a change of pace from her previous films. Marsha Mason, in her pre-Neil Simon days was nominated for her part as a prostitute trying to change her life in *Cinderella Liberty*, as was Ellen Burstyn for her performance as the terrified mother of

the possessed girl in *The Exorcist*. Barbra Streisand, in what was surely her best dramatic role ever, was nominated for her part as the radical girl in love with the very square Robert Redford, in *The Way We Were*. The unlikely combination clicked resulting in one of the best romantic films made in recent years. Joanne Woodward, always excellent was excellent once again in a small film, *Summer Wishes, Winter Dreams*.

John Houseman, a veteran actor, director and teacher of acting was an extremely popular choice as the winner of the Best Supporting Actor Award, for *The Paper Chase* in which he played a very demanding law professor. A couple of accomplished character actors also received Best Supporting Actor nominations, Jack Gilford nominated

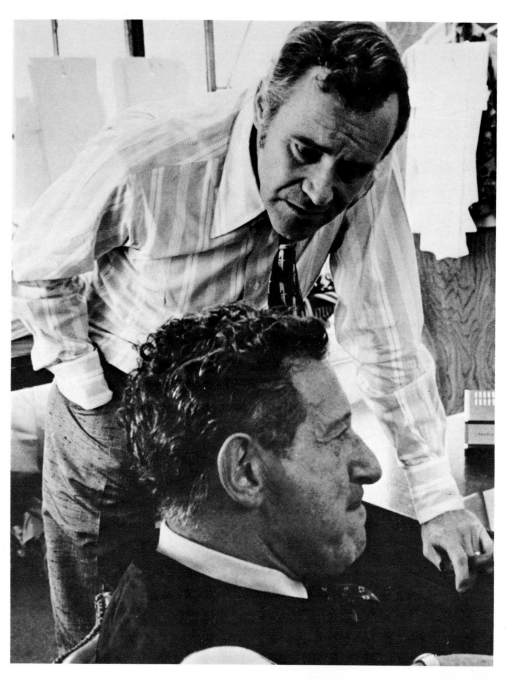

American Graffiti, Madeline Kahn for *Paper Moon* and Sylvia Sydney for *Summer Wishes, Winter Dreams*.

George Roy Hill, who directed *The Sting* at such a snappy pace, was given the Oscar in that category. Competition had been stiff. William Friedkin was generally acknowledged to have done a superior job with *The Exorcist*. Ingmar Bergman's *Cries And Whispers* was too grim, and Bernardo Bertolucci *The Last Tango In Paris* too explicit, to gain them Oscars, but both were recognized as masters of their craft. Then there was a young director named George Lucas whose pleasant little film *American Graffiti* was extremely popular. It gave his career a tremendous boost and he would be heard from again in Hollywood, but not for little films.

Probably the biggest winner of the evening was Marvin Hamlisch who walked away with three well deserved Oscars in the music field, the Best Original Score, *The Way We Were*, the best musical adaptation, *The Sting*, and the Best Song, 'The Way We Were.' The name Marvin Hamlisch, quite unknown to the general public before the ceremony, was a household word afterward.

One name that was not unknown was Groucho Marx. He was given a Special Award recognizing the magnificent achievements of the Marx Brothers.

LEFT: Best Actor Jack Lemmon in *Save The Tiger* with Jack Gilford.
BELOW: Ryan O'Neal with his daughter Tatum, the Best Supporting Actress in *Paper Moon*.

for *Save The Tiger*, and Vincent Gardenia for the excellent baseball film *Bang The Drum Slowly*. Playwright Jason Miller was nominated for *The Exorcist*, and Randy Quaid received his nomination for the part of the sailor going off to jail in *The Last Detail*.

Two very young performers received nominations for Best Supporting Actress, and the youngest won. She was Tatum O'Neal, the ten-year-old daughter of actor Ryan O'Neal, who showed exceptional maturity as the young con artist in *Paper Moon*. At one time the Academy would have given her a miniature statuette but times had changed. The contrast of the 71-year-old Houseman and the 10-year-old O'Neal was striking. The other young girl to receive a nomination was Linda Blair, the possessed girl in *The Exorcist*. Also nominated were Candy Clark for

1974

Best Picture: *The Godfather, Part II.*
Actor: Art Carney, *Harry And Tonto.*
Actress: Ellen Burstyn, *Alice Doesn't Live Here Anymore.*
Supporting Actor: Robert de Niro, *The Godfather, Part II.*
Supporting Actress: Ingrid Bergman, *Murder On The Orient Express.*
Director: Francis Ford Coppola, *The Godfather, Part II.*
Foreign Language Film Award: *Amarcord* (Italy).
Writing (Screenplay-Original): Robert Towne, *Chinatown.*
Writing (Screenplay-Adaptation): Francis Ford Coppola, Mario Puzo, *The Godfather, Part II.*
Cinematography: Fred Koenkamp, *The Towering Inferno.*
Art Direction: Dean Tavoularis, Angel Graham, (Set Decoration) George R Nelson, *The Godfather, Part II.*
Costume Design: Theoni V Aldredge, *The Great Gatsby.*
Music (Original Score): Nino Rota, Carmine Coppola, *The Godfather, Part II.*
Music (Adaptation): Nelson Riddle, *The Great Gatsby.*
Music (Song): Al Kasha, Joel Hirschorn, 'We May Never Love Like This Again' from *The Towering Inferno.*
Short Subjects (Animated): *Closed Mondays.*
Short Subjects (Live Action): *One-Eyed Men Are Kings.*
Documentary (Short): *Don't.*
Documentary (Feature): *Hearts And Minds.*
Jean Hersholt Humanitarian Award: Arthur Krim.
Special Achievement Award, Visual Effects: Frank Brendel, Glen Robinson, Albert Whitlock, *Earthquake.*
Special Awards: Jean Renoir, for his outstanding contributions to the world of Film. Howard Hawks, for his career-long directorial genius.

The conventional Hollywood wisdom is that sequels are never as good as the original. Therefore most of the experts agreed that *The Godfather, Part II,* good as it was, would never win the award for Best Picture because *The Godfather* had won back in 1972. Be-

Best Actor Art Carney and his feline co-star in *Harry and Tonto.*

sides argued the experts Marlon Brando wasn't in Part II. This time the experts were wrong. *The Godfather, Part II*, not only won, it swept six Oscars. Director Francis Ford Coppola's father even won (with Nino Rota) for the Best Original Score. It did better in the Awards than the original.

The biggest surprise of the evening was in the Best Actor category. The early favorite had been Jack Nicholson, as the private eye in *Chinatown*. Then there was Al Pacino of *Godfather II*, picking up where he had left off as Michael Corleone, and perhaps better in the second part than the first. Dustin Hoffman was sensational as the doomed comedian Lenny Bruce in *Lenny*, and Albert Finney had a splendid time as

ABOVE: Robert de Niro played young Vito Corleone in *The Godfather, Part II*.
RIGHT: Diane Ladd and Ellen Burstyn in *Alice Doesn't Live Here Anymore*.

Agatha Christie's detective Hercule Poirot in *Murder On The Orient Express*. The winner was none of the above, it was Art Carney, best known as Jackie Gleason's sidekick on television, in a gentle story of an old man and his cat, *Harry And Tonto*.

Ellen Burstyn received the Best Actress Award for *Alice Doesn't Live Here Anymore*, the story of a newly widowed woman trying to cope with economic survival and building a new life for herself and her son in modern America. The main competition had

ABOVE: Best Supporting Actress Ingrid Bergman one of the suspects in *Murder On The Orient Express*.

been Faye Dunaway, the troubled rich girl in *Chinatown*, and Valerie Perrine, memorable as Lenny Bruce's drug addicted, sexually obsessed wife in *Lenny*. Also nominated were Gena Rowlands for *A Woman Under The Influence*, and Diahann Carroll for *Claudine*.

Three of the five nominees for Best Supporting Actor had appeared in *Godfather II*. The winner was Robert de Niro, an exceedingly talented young actor who played the future Mafia chieftain as a young man. Also nominated from the film were Michael V Gazzo, and Lee Strasberg, more famous as an acting coach than an actor. Nominees from other films were Jeff Bridges for *Thunderbolt And Lightfoot* and Fred Astaire, no longer dancing, but still effective as an actor in *The Towering Inferno*.

Two of Francis Ford Coppola's films had been nominated for Best Picture, *The Godfather, Part II*, which he directed, won. The other nominee was *The Conversation* which Coppola also produced. It was a brilliant, though non-commercial film, of which Coppola himself was very proud. *Chinatown*, was the biggest disappointment of the evening, an early favorite it received 11 nominations, including one for Best

Federico Fellini's *Amarcord* won the award
for Best Foreign Language Film.

Picture, but won only a single award.
Robert Towne received it for his original screenplay.

Ingrid Bergman won her third Oscar
– her first in a supporting role – as the
Swedish missionary in *Murder On The
Orient Express*. Though she was excellent this award seemed more of an
expression of affection for the actress
than recognition of a particular performance. Her main competition was
pre-Rocky Talia Shire in *The Godfather, Part II* and Madeline Kahn,
hilarious in Mel Brook's wonderful
Blazing Saddles, which unaccountably

did not receive a Best Picture nomination. Nor did another Brooks film of
that year the brilliant *Young Frankenstein*. Diane Ladd in *Alice Doesn't Live
Here Anymore* and Valentina Cortese in
Day For Night were also nominated for
Best Supporting Actress.

France's Francois Truffaut, was
nominated for Best Director for *Day
For Night*, possibly the most affection-
ate account of making a film ever re-
corded on film. Dancer, choreographer
turned director Bob Fosse got a well
deserved nomination for the entirely
non-musical *Lenny*. Maverick director
John Cassavetes, was nominated for *A
Woman Under The Influence*. And
finally there was Roman Polanski, who

many believed really deserved the
Oscar for his stylish *Chinatown*.

A major disappointment of the year
was *The Great Gatsby*, based on the
F Scott Fitzgerald novel, which starred
Robert Redford in the title role. The
film turned out to be dull and plodding,
but the costumes were great and Theoni
V Aldredge received an Oscar for them.

Two big 'disaster' films of the year,
The Towering Inferno and *Earthquake*,
both received awards in minor categories.

Federico Fellini's *Amarcord* won the
Award as the Best Foreign language
Film, and Fellini himself was to be
nominated for Best Director for the
very same film in 1975.

1975

Best Picture: *One Flew Over The Cuckoo's Nest*

Actor: Jack Nicholson, *One Flew Over The Cuckoo's Nest.*

Actress: Louise Fletcher, *One Flew Over The Cuckoo's Nest.*

Supporting Actor: George Burns, *The Sunshine Boys.*

Supporting Actress: Lee Grant, *Shampoo.*

Director: Milos Forman, *One Flew Over The Cuckoo's Nest.*

Foreign Language Film Award: *Dersu Uzala* (USSR).

Writing (Screenplay-Original): Frank Pierson, *Dog Day Afternoon.*

Writing (Screenplay-Adaptation): Bo Goldman, *One Flew Over The Cuckoo's Nest.*

Cinematography: John Alcott, *Barry Lyndon.*

Art Direction: Ken Adam, Roy Walker, (Set Decoration) Vernon Dixon, *Barry Lyndon.*

Costume Design: Ulla-Britt Sonderlund, Milena Canonero, *Barry Lyndon.*

Music (Original Score): John Williams, *Jaws.*

Music (Adaptation): Leonard Rosenman, *Barry Lyndon.*

Music (Song): Keith Carradine, 'I'm Easy' from *Nashville.*

Short Films (Animated): *Great.*

Short Films (Live Action): *Angel And Big Joe.*

Documentary (Short): *The End Of The Game.*

Documentary (Feature): *The Man Who Skied Down Everest.*

Irving G Thalberg Memorial Award: Mervyn LeRoy.

Special Achievement Awards, Visual Effects: Carlo Rambaldi, Glen Robinson, Frank Van Der Veer, *The Hindenburg.*

Sound Effects: Peter Berkos, *The Hindenburg.*

Honorary Award: Mary Pickford, in recognition of her unique contributions to the film industry and the development of film as an artistic medium.

One Flew Over The Cuckoo's Nest swept the forty-eighth Annual Academy Awards. It won all four major Oscars, Best Picture, Best Actor, Best Actress and Best Director, the first time that had happened since 1934 when the feat was accomplished by *It Happened One Night.*

Yet despite the dominance of *One Flew Over The Cuckoo's Nest*, and its stars, the evening really belonged to George Burns who won the Best Supporting Actor Award for his role in Neil Simon's *The Sunshine Boys.* Burns was a veteran of vaudeville, burlesque, radio, television and films, and at age 80 he was making his first movie since 1939. The role of the retired vaudeville performer was originally to go to Jack Benny, who died before the film was made. Burns was certainly the oldest nominee that evening and possibly the oldest Oscar winner ever. In his accept-

Best Supporting Actor George Burns with Walter Matthau in *The Sunshine Boys.*

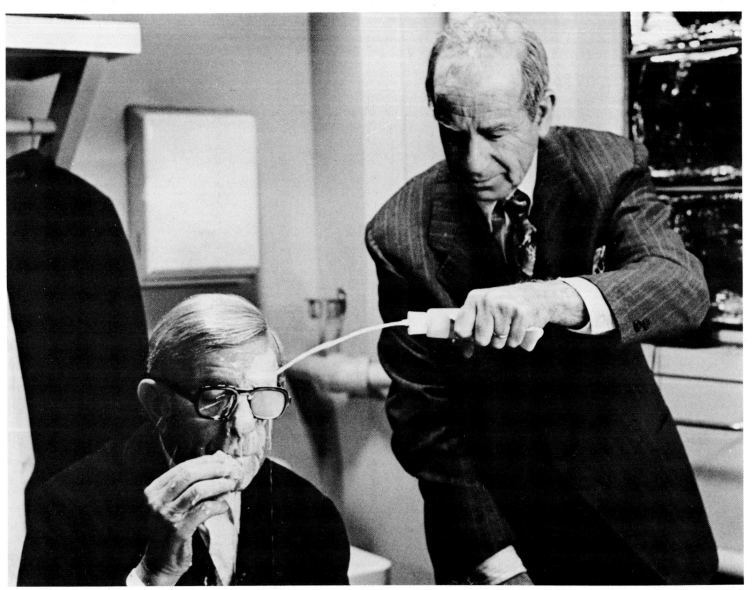

ABOVE: Best Actor Jack Nicholson in *One Flew Over The Cuckoo's Nest.*
RIGHT: Best Supporting Actress Lee Grant with Warren Beatty in *Shampoo.*

ance speech he quipped, 'I've been in show business all my life, and if you stay around long enough you get to be new again.'

Jack Nicholson won a Best Actor Oscar for his role as the misfit prisoner who inspires patients in a mental hospital to rebel against tyrannical nurse Louise Fletcher, who won the Best Actress Award. Nicholson had received three previous nominations. This was Fletcher's first.

This year the nominees for Best Picture were an interesting and worthwhile lot. There was *Barry Lyndon*, director Stanley Kubrick's leisurely but gorgeous excursion into eighteenth century England. *Dog Day Afternoon* featured a fantastic performance by Al Pacino, as a crazed would-be bank robber. The film was all the more impressive because it was based on a real incident. *Nashville* was Robert Alt-

Jaws starred Roy Schieder, Richard Dreyfuss and Robert Ryan.

man's interesting if not altogether successful look at country music. It featured some wonderful scenes and memorable performances. Then there was the picture that almost everybody went to see that year, *Jaws*, directed by a relatively unknown young man named Steven Spielberg.

Walter Matthau received a Best

Actor nomination as George Burns' sometime partner in *The Sunshine Boys* as did Al Pacino for *Dog Day Afternoon*. *The Man In The Glass Booth* adapted from a play about the trial of Adolph Eichman, earned Maximilian Schell a nomination. *Give 'em Hell Harry!* a filmed one-man show about Harry Truman, earned James Whitmore a nomination for his portrayal of the feisty president.

The nominees for Best Actress were

an unusual group. Glenda Jackson was nominated for *Hedda*, a film version of the Ibsen play. Carol Kane was nominated for *Hester Street*, a small independent film about immigrant Jews on the Lower East Side of Manhattan. *The Story of Adele H*, a French film about Victor Hugo's youngest daughter's obsession with an English army officer, earned Isabelle Adjani a Best Actress nomination for a riveting and disturbing performance. Then there was Ann-

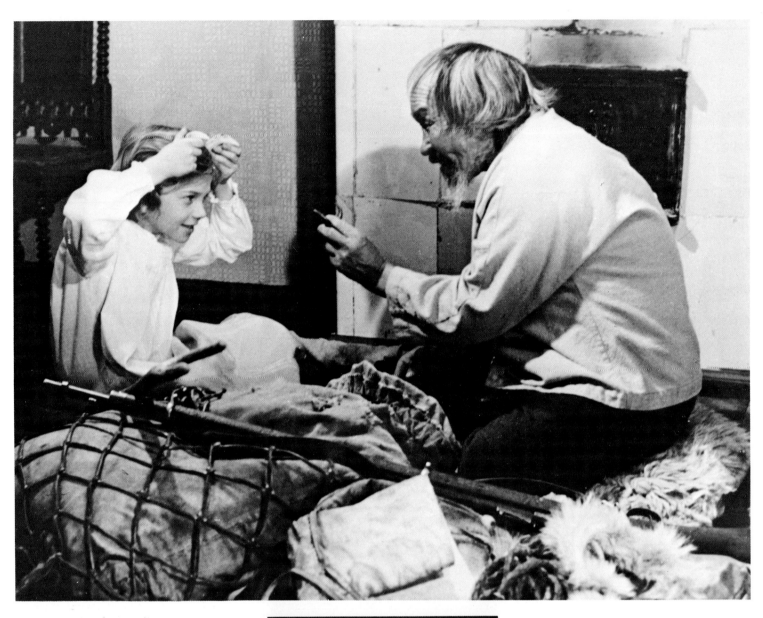

Margaret, who got a nomination for her part in Ken Russell's very loud version of the Who's rock opera *Tommy*.

One Flew Over The Cuckoo's Nest didn't win the Award for Best Supporting Actor, but Brad Dourif did receive a nomination for his part in the film. Two film veterans also got nominations, Burgess Meredith for *The Day Of The Locust* and Jack Warden for *Shampoo*. Nominee Chris Sarandon was excellent as the gay lover in *Dog Day Afternoon*.

Both Ronee Blakley and Lily Tomlin received Best Supporting Actress nominations for *Nashville*. Sylvia Miles was nominated for *Farewell, My Lovely*, an attempt to evoke the hard-boiled detective films of the thirties and forties. Unaccountably Brenda Vaccaro was nominated for Jacqueline Susann's *Once Is Not Enough*, a film without any redeeming features. The winner was Lee Grant for her performance as the neurotic wife in *Shampoo*.

The nominees for Best Director read

ABOVE: Best Foreign Film was *Dersu Uzala*. LEFT: Mary Pickford was honored for her film making. (*The Little American* 1917.)

like an honor role of great directors: Milos Forman, the winner for *One Flew Over The Cuckoo's Nest*, Robert Altman, then at the top of his form for *Nashville* and Stanley Kubrick for *Barry Lyndon*. Sidney Lumet received a nomination for *Dog Day Afternoon*, and Federico Fellini one for *Amarcord*, the great director's recollections of his youth in provincial Italy. One name not on the list was Steven Spielberg, director of *Jaws*.

Barry Lyndon received many of the awards for cinematography, costumes and art direction. It even won an Award for Adapted Musical Score. But the Award for the Best Original Score went to John Williams for *Jaws*.

The Academy also took time out to honor America's Sweetheart, Mary Pickford with a Special Award, and a short retrospective of her films.

1976

Best Picture: *Rocky*.
Actor: Peter Finch, *Network*.
Actress: Faye Dunaway, *Network*.
Supporting Actor: Jason Robards Jr, *All The President's Men*.
Supporting Actress: Beatrice Straight, *Network*.
Director: John G Avildsen, *Rocky*.
Foreign Language Film: *Black And White in Color* (Ivory Coast).
Writing (Screenplay-Original): Paddy Chayefsky, *Network*.
Writing (Screenplay-Adaptation): William Goldman, *All The President's Men*.
Cinematography: Haskell Wexler, *Bound For Glory*.
Art Director: George Jenkins, (Set Decoration) George Gaines, *All The President's Men*.
Costume Design: Danilo Donati, *Fellini's Casanova*.
Film Editing: Richard Halsey, Scott Conrad, *Rocky*.
Music (Original Score): Jerry Goldsmith, *The Omen*.
Music (Adaptation): Leonard Roseman, *Bound For Glory*.
Music (Song): Barbra Streisand (Music), Paul Williams (Lyrics), 'Evergreen' from *A Star Is Born*.
Short Films (Animated): *Leisure*.
Short Films (Live Action): *In The Region Of Ice*.
Documentary (Feature): *Harlan County, USA*.
Documentary (Short): *Number Our Days*.
Special Awards, Visual Effects: *King Kong*, *Logan's Run*.

This was the year that an underdog from south Philadelphia named Rocky Balboa won his big match both on the screen and in the Academy Awards. The popular film *Rocky* which a virtual unknown named Sylvester Stallone wrote and starred in, came out of nowhere to beat such heavy favorites as *All The President's Men*, the Watergate story starring Robert Redford and Dustin Hoffman, and *Network*, a scathing indictment of television. Also nominated were *Bound For Glory*, the story of folksinger Woody Guthrie, and Martin Scorsese's grim and gritty *Taxi Driver*.

Rocky's director John G Avildsen also beat out some hefty competition to win the Oscar in that category. The other nominees were Ingmar Bergman for *Face To Face*, Sidney Lumet for *Network*, Alan J Pakula for *All The President's Men* and one of the very few women directors with an international reputation, Italy's Lina Wertmuller for *Seven Beauties*.

Stallone was nominated both in Best Actor and Original Screenplay categories, but received neither award. The anger that showed on his face was evident to millions of television viewers.

The Best Actor Award was a sad first. It was given to Peter Finch for his bravura portrayal of a crazed TV commentator in *Network*, whose immortal line was 'I'm mad as Hell, and I'm not going to take it anymore.' Finch had died while on a publicity tour for

Best Actor Peter Finch as the mentally disturbed newscaster in *Network* won his award posthumously.

the film and thus became the first actor to win the Award posthumously. Both Spencer Tracy and James Dean had previously received posthumous Best Actor nominations.

Network was the big winner in the major awards categories. Finch had to best another *Network* star, William Holden who had also received a Best Actor nomination, as did Robert de Niro in *Taxi Driver*, Giancarlo Giannini in *Seven Beauties* and, of course, 'Rocky' Stallone.

Network's leading lady Faye Dunaway, won the Best Actress Award playing the icy television executive for whom success means more than sex. Also nominated were Rocky's girl friend Talia Shire; the great Liv Ullmann for *Face To Face*; Sissy Spacek, the repressed teenager with horrifying psychokenetic powers, in *Carrie*, the adaptation of Stephen King's novel, and French star Marie-Christine Barrault in *Cousin, Cousine*.

The biggest surprise of the year came

OPPOSITE: *Fellini's Casanova* starring Donald Sutherland won the Costume award.
RIGHT: Sylvester Stallone wrote and starred in *Rocky*, with Talia Shire.
BELOW: Robert Redford, Jack Warden, Jason Robards Jr, Dustin Hoffman in *All The President's Men.*

in the Supporting Actress category which was won by Beatrice Straight for her very brief role as the deserted wife in *Network*. Her competition had included Jane Alexander in *All The President's Men*, Lee Grant in *Voyage Of The Damned*, Jodie Foster in her fateful role as the teen-age hooker in *Taxi Driver* and Piper Laurie as *Carrie*'s religiously obsessed mother.

Jason Robards, Jr received a well-deserved Oscar as Best Supporting Actor for his portrayal of *Washington Post* editor Ben Bradlee, in *All The*

President's Men. Bradlee was a pivotal figure in exposure of the Watergate scandal that ultimately led to the resignation of President Richard Nixon. Also nominated were Burgess Meredith and Burt Young, both for *Rocky*, Ned Beatty for *Network*, and Laurence Olivier, who was absolutely chilling as a sadistic Nazi dentist in *Marathon Man*.

Former TV writer Paddy Chayefsky who had turned on his old medium with fury in *Network*, was a highly popular winner of the Best Original Screenplay Award. William Goldman who adapted Bob Woodward and Carl Bernstein's book *All The President's Men* for the screen, won an Oscar for that task.

Barbra Streisand, who starred in a critically panned remake of *A Star Is Born*, did win an Oscar for 'Evergreen' the song that she wrote for the film with Paul Williams. Dino De Laurentiis' expensive, highly publicized remake of *King Kong* was a disaster that was almost completely shut out of the awards, though it did manage to pick up a Special Award for Visual Effects which was shared with *Logan's Run*, an expensive science-fiction flop. Far, far better was the low budget winner of the feature length Documentary Award, *Harlan County, USA* about life and death in the coal mining country of West Virginia.

1977

Best Picture: *Annie Hall.*
Actor: Richard Dreyfuss, *The Goodbye Girl.*
Actress: Diane Keaton, *Annie Hall.*
Supporting Actor: Jason Robards, Jr, *Julia.*
Supporting Actress: Vanessa Redgrave, *Julia.*
Director: Woody Allen, *Annie Hall.*
Foreign Language Film Award: *Madame Rosa* (France).
Writing (Screenplay-Original): Woody Allen and Marshall Brickman, *Annie Hall.*
Writing (Screenplay-Adaptation): Alvin Sargent, *Julia.*
Cinematography: Vilmos Zsigmond, *Close Encounters Of The Third Kind.*
Art Director: John Barry, Norman Reynolds, Leslie Dilley, (Set Decoration) Roger Christian, *Star Wars.*
Costume Design: John Mollo, *Star Wars.*
Film Editing: Paul Hirsch, Marcia Lucas, Richard Chew, *Star Wars.*
Music (Original Score): John Williams, *Star Wars.*
Music (Song): Joseph Brooks for 'You Light Up My Life' from *You Light Up My Life.*
Music (Adaptation): Jonathan Tunick, *A Little Night Music.*
Short Films (Animated): *Sand Castles.*
Short Films (Live Action): *I'll Find A Way.*
Sound: Don MacDougall, Ray West, Bob Minkler, Dereck Ball, *Star Wars.*
Visual Effects: John Stears, John Dykstra, Richard Edmund, Grant McCune, Robert Blalack, *Star Wars.*
Documentary (Feature): *Who Are The DeBolts: And Where Did They Get Nineteen Kids?*
Documentary (Short): *Gravity Is My Enemy.*
Irving G Thalberg Memorial Award: Walter Mirsch.
Jean Hersholt Humanitarian Award: Charlton Heston.
Special Achievement Awards:
Sound Effects: Benjamin Burt, Jr for creating the alien creature and robot voices in *Star Wars.*
Sound Effects Editing: Frank Warner, *Close Encounters Of The Third Kind.*

The ceremony marking the fiftieth anniversary of the Academy Awards, wasn't quite what the Academy hoped it might be. The big winner of the evening, America's most original film-maker, Woody Allen, didn't even bother to show up. Allen's dislike of Hollywood was well known, indeed the town was satirized in *Annie Hall*, the film that he wrote, directed and starred in. The film itself won Best Picture, and Diane Keaton, who had the title role received the Award for Best Actress and Allen took both writing and directing honors. But he stayed in New York and ignored the whole ceremony.

It's not as if there was no competition this year. Also nominated for Best Picture were Neil Simon's *The Goodbye Girl*, *Julia* based on an episode in Lillian Hellman's autobiography, *The Turning Point* which had two Oscar quality performances, and the film that was the biggest box office grosser to date, *Star Wars*, but *Annie Hall* beat them all.

About the only award Woody Allen didn't win was the Best Actor, though he was nominated, along with such competition as Richard Burton in the film adaptation of the play *Equus*, Italian star Marcello Mastroianni for *A Special Day*, and a little known former television actor, John Travolta in a film that capitalized on the disco craze, *Saturday Night Fever*. The winner however, was Richard Dreyfuss as the temperamental actor in *The Goodbye Girl.*

Diane Keaton's competition in the Best Actress category had also been formidable. There were Anne Bancroft and Shirley MacLaine from *The Turning Point*, the story of two dancers, one who had pursued a career, the other who had opted for home and family. Jane Fonda was at her intense and nervous best in

Best Actor Richard Dreyfuss meditating in *The Goodbye Girl.*

ABOVE: Best Actress Diane Keaton in the title role of *Annie Hall*, with Woody Allen, who won the award for Best Director.
RIGHT: Best Supporting Actress Vanessa Redgrave in *Julia* with Jane Fonda.

Julia. Marsha Mason, then wife of Neil Simon was also nominated for her role in Simon's *The Goodbye Girl*.

Both Jason Robards, Jr and Maximilian Schell were nominated for Best Supporting Actor for their roles in *Julia*, Schell was good but it was Robards as the writer Dashiell Hammett who won. It was his second Supporting Actor Oscar in as many years. Dancer Mikhail Baryshinikov was, what else, a dancer in *The Turning Point*, his movie debut, and Peter Firth was the deeply troubled young man in *Equus*. Then there was Alec Guinness, who had appeared in so many memorable films for which he was not nominated, he received a nomination for the brief but

pivotal role in *Star Wars*, that of the old Jedi Obi-wan Kenobi.

The first award given at the ceremonies that evening was for Best Supporting Actress. The winner was Vanessa Redgrave who once again

TOP: George Lucas's *Star Wars* won six technical awards, including Visual Effects. BELOW: *A Little Night Music* with Diana Rigg, Laurence Guittard, Elizabeth Taylor and Len Cariou won the Music (Adaptation) award.

proved she is one of the finest film actresses of her time, with her marvelous performance as the anti-Nazi activist in *Julia*. But when she went up to accept the award she made a statement about her difficulties making a documentary, *The Palestinians*. People regarded it as a political statement, and it wasn't the sort of thing that the glittering audience in the huge Dorothy Chandler Pavilion or the estimated 80 million TV viewers wished to hear.

Then there was the embarrassing stream of Allen non-appearances. He wasn't there to collect the Directing Oscar. Here he had beaten out Steven Spielberg for *Close Encounters Of The Third Kind*, George Lucas for *Star Wars*, Fred Zinnemann for *Julia*, and Herbert Ross for *The Turning Point*.

Once again it was the absent Allen who dominated the scene for along with co-author Marshall Brickman he won the Best Original Screenplay Oscar, from Neil Simon for *The Goodbye Girl*, George Lucas for *Star Wars*, Arthur Laurents for *The Turning Point*, and Robert Benton for *The Late Show*, a wonderful but sadly unappreciated film with Art Carney and Lily Tomlin.

Though *Star Wars* didn't receive any of the major awards, it dominated the minor ones, winning six Oscars, and a Special Award. The epic won for Best Sound, Best Visual Effects, Best Costumes, Best Original Score, Best Art Direction and Best Film Editing. The other big science fiction epic, Spielberg's UFO tale, *Close Encounters of The Third Kind* was well deserved runner up in many of these categories and did win the Oscar for Cinematography.

The Best Foreign Language Film was France's *Madame Rosa* with Simone Signoret in one of her most memorable roles.

1978

Best Picture: *The Deer Hunter.*
Actor: Jon Voight, *Coming Home.*
Actress: Jane Fonda, *Coming Home.*
Supporting Actor: Christopher Walken, *The Deer Hunter.*
Supporting Actress: Maggie Smith, *California Suite.*
Director: Michael Cimino, *The Deer Hunter.*
Foreign Language Film Award: *Get Out Your Handkerchiefs* (France).
Writing (Screenplay-Original): Nancy Dowd, *Coming Home.*
Writing (Screenplay-Adaptation): Oliver Stone, *Midnight Express.*
Cinematography: *Days Of Heaven.*
Art Director: Paul Sylbert, Edwin O'Donovan, *Heaven Can Wait.*
Costume Design: Anthony Powell, *Death On The Nile.*
Music (Original Score): Giorgio Muroder, *Midnight Express.*
Music (Song): 'Last Dance' from *Thank God It's Friday.*
Short Films (Animated): *Special Delivery.*
Short Films (Live Action): *Teenage Father.*
Documentary (Short): *The Flight Of The Gossamer Condor.*
Documentary (Feature Length): *Scared Straight.*
Special Achievement Award, Visual Effects: Les Bowie, Colin Chilvers, Denys Coop, Roy Field, Derek Meddings and Zoran Persic, *Superman.*
Jean Hersholt Humanitarian Award: Leo Jaffe.
Honorary Awards: Walter Lantz, for bringing joy and laughter to every part of the world through his unique animated motion pictures. Laurence Olivier, for the full body of his work. King Vidor, for his incomparable achievements as a cinematic creator and innovator.

The Vietnam war was the subject of two films which dominated the awards this year. The films, expressing very different attitudes toward Vietnam seemed to mirror the nation's divided feelings about the long war. *The Deer Hunter* which stood to the right politically won Best Picture. Its more left wing rival, *Coming Home*, was also nominated as was *Heaven Can Wait*, Warren Beatty's delightful remake of *Here Comes Mr Jordan* (1941) and *Midnight Express*, a

Jane Fonda and Jon Voight both won acting awards for *Coming Home.*

graphically brutal true story of a young American in a Turkish prison. The fifth nominee *An Unmarried Woman*, with Jill Clayburgh as a betrayed wife who has an affair with an artist (Alan Bates), was praised as a realistic film, but it was really a romantic fantasy.

In the acting categories *Coming Home*

OPPOSITE: Robert de Niro was one of the stars of *The Deer Hunter*.
BELOW: Warren Beatty starred in and directed *Heaven Can Wait* which won the Art Direction Award.

came out ahead with Jon Voight winning the Best Actor Oscar for his portrayal of a paralyzed Vietnam vet. Jane Fonda received the Best Actress Award as well for *Coming Home*. Off screen Fonda had been outspoken in her opposition to the war and her win, particularly for this film, created considerable controversy.

The Deer Hunter's Robert de Niro was nominated for a Best Actor Award, as was Warren Beatty for *Heaven Can Wait*. A longshot nominee was Gary Busey for *The Buddy Holly Story*, the

film biography of a rock 'n' roll pioneer. Laurence Olivier who had received a nomination for his portrayal of a Nazi in *Marathon Man* got another for playing a Nazi hunter in the thriller *The Boys From Brazil*.

An exceptionally fine group of actresses were nominated this year. Ingrid Bergman was honored for her role as the concert pianist in *Autumn Sonata*, her best performance in years. Ellen Burstyn was nominated for the filmed version of the popular play *Same Time Next Year*. Geraldine Page, who

was starting to pile up an impressive number of nominations received another for *Interiors*, and Jill Clayburgh got one for playing the unmarried woman in *An Unmarried Woman*.

Both Christopher Walken from the *Deer Hunter* and Bruce Dern from *Coming Home* were up for Best Supporting Actor. Walken won. Better than either was John Hurt in *Midnight Express*, who was nominated but didn't win. Veteran character actor Jack Warden got a well deserved nomination for his part as the puzzled coach in *Heaven Can Wait*. The longshot of the year was Richard Farnsworth in *Comes A Horseman*.

Meryl Streep had a small part in *The Deer Hunter*, and received the first of many Oscar nominations, this one for Best Supporting Actress. From *Coming Home* there was Penelope Milford. Dyan Cannon was truly hilarious as the woman who just can't seem to kill off

her rich husband in *Heaven Can Wait*. Maureen Stapleton was marvelous, as always, in *Interiors*. But none of them won, because Maggie Smith took her part in Neil Simon's popular attempt at rewriting *Plaza Suite* in a California setting, and turned it into a comedic gem.

Michael Cimino received the Oscar for directing *The Deer Hunter*, which gave the young director the reputation of Hollywood's new boy wonder. On the strength of his success he was given almost unlimited power to direct a new epic, *Heaven's Gate* (1981) which turned into Hollywood's most expensive and best-publicized disaster.

Hal Ashby had been nominated for directing *Coming Home*. Warren Beatty and Buck Henry were both nominated for their directorial work on *Heaven Can Wait*, and Alan Parker was nominated for *Midnight Express*. Woody Allen received a nomination for *Inter-*

iors, an unusual Allen film, for it wasn't a comedy, and he didn't star in it. It was generally considered one of his less successful efforts.

The big splashy extravaganza of the year was *Superman – The Movie*. It didn't take any major awards, or even major nominations, but it did pick up a Special Achievement Award for Visual Effects, which the film certainly deserved.

Days Of Heaven, about workers who harvest wheat was slow, but exquisitely photographed, and took an award for Cinematography. And from France came *Get Out Your Handkerchiefs* a thoroughly original comedy.

BELOW: Christopher Reeve as *Superman* which won a special achievement award for its effects.
OPPOSITE: David Niven and Bette Davis with Peter Ustinov as Hercule Poirot in *Death On The Nile*.

1979

Best Picture: *Kramer Vs Kramer.*
Actor: Dustin Hoffman, *Kramer Vs Kramer.*
Actress: Sally Field, *Norma Rae.*
Supporting Actor: Melvyn Douglas, *Being There.*
Supporting Actress: Meryl Streep, *Kramer Vs Kramer.*
Director: Robert Benton, *Kramer Vs Kramer.*
Foreign Language Film Award: *The Tin Drum* (Germany).
Writing (Screenplay-Original): Steve Tesich, *Breaking Away.*
Writing (Screenplay-Adaptation): Robert Benton, *Kramer Vs Kramer.*
Cinematography: *Apocalypse Now.*
Art Director: Philip Rosenberg, Tony Walton, *All That Jazz.*
Costume Design: Albert Wolsky, *All That Jazz.*
Music (Original Score): *A Little Romance.*

Music (Song): David Shire (Music), Norman Gimbel (Lyrics) 'It Goes Like It Goes' from *Norma Rae.*
Short Films (Animated): *Every Child.*
Short Films (Live Action): *Board And Care.*
Documentary (Short): *Paul Robeson: Tribute To An Artist.*
Documentary (Feature Length): *Best Boy.*
Special Visual Effects: *Alien.*
Jean Hersholt Humanitarian Award: Robert Benjamin.
Irving G Thalberg Memorial Award: Ray Stark.
Honorary Award: Alec Guinness, for advancing the art of screen acting through a host of memorable and distinguished performances.

Kramer Vs Kramer, a film based on a true story of separation, divorce and child custody in the modern world was the big winner in this year's ceremony, gathering four of the six major awards.

However, the award that attracted the most attention went to Sally Field for Best Actress. Field had been the cute, button-nosed star of such television series as *Gidget* and *The Flying Nun*. Now over thirty she had made a major career switch in *Norma Rae*, an uncute, unglamorous story of an ordinary woman helping to organize a union in a southern textile mill.

Kramer Vs Kramer won Best Picture over *Norma Rae*, *All That Jazz*, *Breaking Away* and Francis Ford Coppola's *Apocalypse Now*. Coppola's epic on Vietnam adapted roughly from Joseph Conrad's *Heart Of Darkness* had been in production for years; there had been rumors of endless problems, and when the film finally appeared, while it wasn't

BELOW: Dustin Hoffman and Meryl Streep in *Kramer Vs Kramer*.
OPPOSITE: Best Actress Sally Field as the militant factory worker in *Norma Rae*.

LEFT: *Apocalypse Now*, was an adaptation of Joseph Conrad's *Heart Of Darkness*.
ABOVE: Shirley MacLaine with Best Supporting Actor Melvyn Douglas in *Being There*.

quite a dud, it wasn't what had been expected from the director of *The Godfather*.

Dustin Hoffman, the father suddenly forced to care for his child in *Kramer Vs Kramer* won best actor in a walk. The competition was, Jack Lemmon for *China Syndrome*, Al Pacino for . . . *And Justice For All* and Roy Scheider in *All That Jazz*. Peter Sellers nominated for the performance of his career in the dark comedy *Being There*, also might have won the Oscar.

Jane Fonda received a Best Actress nomination for her part as the television reporter in *China Syndrome*, a film about a possible nuclear accident that was released shortly before the Three Mile Island incident in Pennsylvania. The film had a tremendous impact for it seemed to anticipate the headlines. Jill Clayburgh was nominated for *Starting Over*, and Marsha Mason for *Chapter Two* written by her husband Neil Simon, and based on their marriage.

Bette Midler received a nomination for her sensational dramatic film debut as a character based on the tragic rock singer Janis Joplin in *The Rose*.

The veteran Melvyn Douglas was given a Best Supporting Actor Oscar, as much for his long years in the business as for his performance as the millionaire in *Being There*. Mickey Rooney received a nomination for *The Black Stallion* but undoubtedly sentiment for the old trooper played a part. Robert Duvall in *Apocalypse Now*, Frederic Forrest in *The Rose* and Justin Henry, the child in *Kramer Vs Kramer*, rounded out the Supporting Actor nominees.

Meryl Streep won her first Oscar, for Supporting Actress, as the wife in *Kramer Vs Kramer*. Jane Alexander also received a supporting actress nomination for the film. Young Mariel Hemingway was nominated for her part as Woody Allen's teenage girlfriend in *Manhattan*. Barbara Barrie was at her long suffering best as the mother of a boy who wants to be a bicycle racer in *Breaking Away*, and Candice Bergen was nominated for *Starting Over*.

Robert Benton won the directing award for *Kramer Vs Kramer*. Francis Ford Coppola was also nominated for directing *Apocalypse Now*. Other nominees were director/dancer/choreographer Bob Fosse for the roughly autobiographical *All That Jazz*, Peter Yates for *Breaking Away*, the low-budget sleeper of the year, and there was a rare nomination for the director of a French film, Edouard Molinaro for the delightful *La Cage Aux Folles*. Woody Allen didn't even get a nomination for *Manhattan*. Perhaps Academy members figured out that's where he would be on Award night.

The Tin Drum a quite literal adaptation of Gunter Grass's famous and grotesquely fantastic novel of the decay of Germany won the Award for Best Foreign Language Film.

One of the high points of the ceremony was the presentation of a Special Award to Alec Guinness for 'advancing the art of screen acting,' an honor that he certainly deserved.

RIGHT: *The Tin Drum* won the Award for Best Foreign Language Film.

BELOW: Bob Fosse's imaginative musical *All That Jazz* won the Costume Design Award.

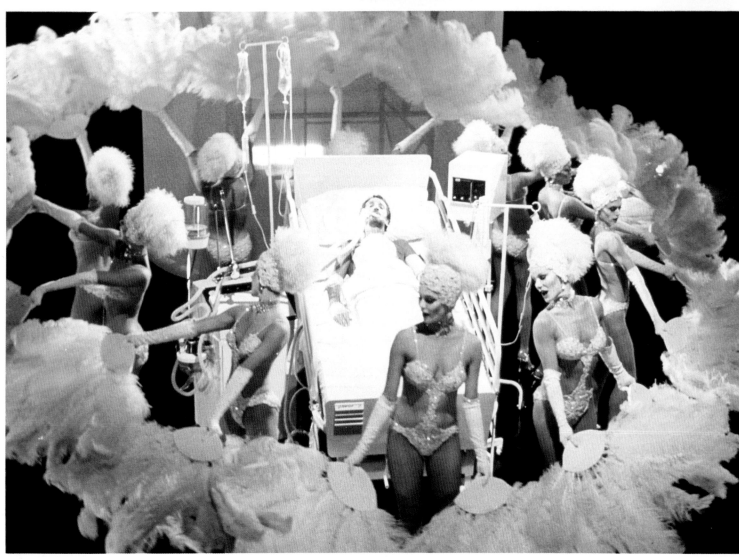

1980

Best Picture: *Ordinary People.*
Actor: Robert de Niro, *Raging Bull.*
Actress: Sissy Spacek, *Coal Miner's Daughter.*
Supporting Actor: Timothy Hutton, *Ordinary People.*
Supporting Actress: Mary Steenburgen, *Melvin And Howard.*
Director: Robert Redford, *Ordinary People.*
Foreign Language Film Award: *Moscow Does Not Believe In Tears* (USSR).
Writing (Screenplay-Original): Bo Goldman, *Melvin And Howard.*
Writing (Screenplay-Adaptation): Alvin Sargent, *Ordinary People.*
Cinematography: Geoffrey Unsworth and Ghislain Cloquet, *Tess.*
Art Director: Pierre Guffroy, Jack Stephens, *Tess.*
Special Achievement Award, Visual Effects: Brian Johnson, Richard Edlund, Dennis Muren, Bruce Nicholson, *The Empire Strikes Back.*
Music (Scoring): Michael Gore, *Fame.*
Music (Song): Michael Gore, 'Fame' from *Fame.*

Short Films (Animated): *The Fly.*
Short Films (Live Action): *The Dollar Bottom.*
Documentary (Short): *Karl Hess: Toward Liberty.*
Documentary (Feature Length): *From Mao To Mozart: Isaac Stern In China.*
Honorary Award: Henry Fonda, the consummate actor, in recognition of his brilliant accomplishments and enduring contribution to the art of motion pictures.

One of Hollywoods biggest sex symbols won an Oscar without ever appearing on screen. Robert Redford proved that he wasn't just another pretty face by receiving the Award as Best Director for *Ordinary People*, the film that also won Best Picture. Ironically Redford has yet to win an Oscar for his acting.

Ordinary People, the story of a family unable to cope with the death of one child and its result on their deeply troubled son, also earned a Best Supporting Actor Award for Timothy Hutton, who played the remaining son. Mary Tyler Moore, best known as the chipper Mary of televison fame, was a bold choice for the part of the icy mother who refuses to face reality. She proved that she was more than a sitcom star, and picked up a well deserved Best Actress nomination for the role.

There were no big spectaculars, no blockbusters among the Best Picture nominees, but they were all good solid films. Biographies dominated: *Coal Miner's Daughter* was the story of country singer Loretta Lynn, *Raging Bull* the story of boxer Jake La Motta and *The Elephant Man*, the moving story of the hideously deformed John Merrick. *Tess* was Roman Polanski's version of the Thomas Hardy novel.

Robert de Niro played Jake La Motta as a vicious brutal man. The performance was so raw that it may have alienated audiences, but it won de Niro the Best Actor Award. Most of the other nominees gave award quality performances as well. John Hurt was nearly miraculous as a man of inhuman ap-

Best Supporting Actress Mary Steenburgen in *Melvin and Howard* which also won the Award for Best Original Screenplay.

pearance striving to be treated as a human being in *Elephant Man*. Robert Duvall was totally convincing as the brutally macho military man in *The Great Santini*, a critically acclaimed film all but ignored by audiences. Peter O'Toole gave one of his best performances in *The Stunt Man*, a film that may have been a bit too strange to attract a mass audience. The weakest nominee was Jack Lemmon whose performance

in *Tribute* was merely very good.

Usually when actresses play singers their songs are dubbed, but Sissy Spacek who started as a country singer did her own singing and won the Best Actress Award for *Coal Miner's Daughter*. Goldie Hawn was immensely funny and appealing as the pampered woman who finds herself trapped in the army in *Private Benjamin*. Ellen Burstyn in *Resurrection* and Gena

ABOVE: Timothy Hutton with Donald Sutherland in *Ordinary People*.
OPPOSITE: Sissy Spacek as country singer Loretta Lynn in *A Coal Miner's Daughter*.

Rowlands in *Gloria* also received nominations for first rate performances in films that were commercial failures.

Timothy Hutton won a Supporting Actor Award for playing the son in *Ordinary People*, but Judd Hirsch who

Irene Cara, Bruno Curreri and the other young stars of *Fame*.

played his psychiatrist was also nominated. Jason Robards, Jr made a brief but memorable appearance as billionaire Howard Hughes in *Melvin And Howard* and picked up another Supporting Actor nomination. Michael O'Keefe from *The Great Santini* and Joe Pesci from *Raging Bull* were also nominated.

Mary Steenburgen seemed to come out of nowhere to take the Best Supporting Actress Award for her hilarious portrayal of the wife in *Melvin And Howard*. The great Eva Le Gallienne was also given a nomination, perhaps as much for past performances as for her role in *Resurrection*. Eileen Brennan was memorably funny as the sergeant in *Private Benjamin*, and like everything else about *Raging Bull*, Cathy Moriarty looked and sounded absolutely right.

The fifth nominee Diane Scarwid was the best thing about *Inside Moves*.

Redford had some stiff competition in winning his directing Oscar. Martin Scorsese had *Raging Bull* shot in black and white, to give it the quality of a newsreel of the forties. David Lynch took what might have been a thoroughly repellent subject and turned *The Elephant Man* into a moving film. Richard Rush made *The Stunt Man* visually and emotionally startling.

Roman Polanski who has avoided the US and England because of legal troubles, made *Tess* in Europe and his cameras lingered long and lovingly over the beautiful scenery, and even longer on the beautiful Nastassia Kinski.

None of the films nominated for major awards were big box office smashes. The film of 1980 that was, *The Empire Strikes Back* won no major awards, and received very few nominations, but it did get a well deserved Special Award for Visual Effects.

Fame the best musical Hollywood made in years, swept the music awards. One of the most unheralded films of the year *Melvin And Howard* based on a supposed meeting between Howard Hughes and Melvin Dummar a small-time hustler and loser with big dreams, picked up a couple of Oscars including one for writer Bo Goldman.

LEFT: Robert de Niro as boxer Jake La Motta in *Raging Bull*.
BELOW: Mark Hamill as Luke Skywalker with R2-D2 in *The Empire Strikes Back*.

1981

Best Picture: *Chariots Of Fire.*
Actor: Henry Fonda, *On Golden Pond.*
Actress: Katharine Hepburn, *On Golden Pond.*
Supporting Actor: John Gielgud, *Arthur.*
Supporting Actress: Maureen Stapleton, *Reds.*
Director: Warren Beatty, *Reds.*
Foreign Language Film Award: *Mephisto* (Hungary).
Writing (Screenplay-Original): Colin Welland, *Chariots Of Fire.*
Writing (Screenplay-Adaptation): Ernest Thompson, *On Golden Pond.*
Cinematography: Vittorio Storaro, *Reds.*
Art Director: Norman Reynolds, Leslie Dilley, (Set Decoration) Michale Ford, *Raiders Of The Lost Ark.*
Makeup: Rick Baker, *An American Werewolf In London.*
Special Visual Effects: *Raiders Of The Lost Ark.*
Music (Original Score): *Chariots Of Fire.*
Music (Song): Burt Bacharach, Carole Bayer Sager, Christopher Cross, Peter Allen, 'Best That You Can Do' from *Arthur.*
Short Films (Animated): *Crac.*
Short Films (Live Action): *Violet.*
Documentary (Short): *Close Harmony.*
Documentary (Feature Length): *Genocide.*
Jean Hersholt Humanitarian Award: Danny Kaye.
Irving G Thalberg Memorial Award: Albert R Broccoli.
Honorary Award: Barbara Stanwyck, for superlative creativity and unique contribution to the art of screen acting.

This was Henry Fonda's year. The legendary actor was too ill to attend the ceremonies. Everyone in Hollywood knew that he was dying, yet he had made one final picture *On Golden Pond*, a story about growing old and facing death. Though Fonda had been presented with an Honorary Award in 1980, he had never won a Best Actor Award despite his many fine performances. *On Golden Pond* was one of his best and there was never the slightest doubt that he would get the Oscar he had so often deserved before. His co-star, another screen legend, Katharine Hepburn won the Best Actress Award, her fourth.

The Best Picture Award was a surprise, it went to *Chariots Of Fire*, a British film about British runners in the 1924 Olympics in Paris. Though the film was beautifully acted and photographed, it was a small film, with no well-known stars. A stirring score, which also won an Oscar was an additional advantage.

On Golden Pond was also nominated for Best Picture, as was *Atlantic City*, Louis Malle's look at an aging gambler. Other nominations went to two of the year's big films, *Reds* the Warren Beatty epic about American radical John Reed, and the biggest film of the year *Raiders Of The Lost Ark*.

Standing very much in Fonda's shadow this year were Warren Beatty, who did everything for *Reds* including star in it; Burt Lancaster, surprisingly sensitive in *Atlantic City*; Dudley Moore, playing the title role of the poor-little drunk rich boy in *Arthur*, and Paul Newman who had been much better

Henry Fonda and Katharine Hepburn both won Awards for *On Golden Pond*.

than he was in *Absence Of Malice*.

Standing in Hepburn's shadow were Diane Keaton, as Louise Bryant, Reed's lover and fellow radical in *Reds*; Susan Sarandon, who delivered an exceptional performance in *Atlantic City*; Meryl Streep, as the mysterious heroine of the very slow moving *The French Lieutenant's Woman*, and Marsha Mason who unaccountably was nominated for *Only When I Laugh*.

The supporting role awards were more interesting because there was some suspense. John Gielgud who had spent decades on the stage as a leading classical actor had begun a new career playing small comic parts in films. His role as the butler in *Arthur* was by far

the best thing in the film and won him a Best Supporting Actor Award. However, Ian Holm, as the trainer Sam Musabini in *Chariots Of Fire* probably should have won. Jack Nicholson was an odd choice to play Eugene O'Neill in *Reds* but his performance earned him a nomination anyway. Howard E Rollins, Jr was the black piano player fighting for dignity in *Ragtime*. James Coco mugged his way through *Only When I Laugh*.

Maureen Stapleton won Best Supporting Actress for her solid and believable portrayal of anarchist Emma Goldman in *Reds*. Elizabeth McGovern was both appealing and repellent as showgirl Evelyn Nesbit in *Ragtime*. Neither Melinda Dillon in *Absence Of*

LEFT: Best Supporting Actor Sir John Gielgud, in *Arthur* with Dudley Moore.
BELOW: *Chariots Of Fire* starred Nigel Havers (l), Ian Charleson (c) and Ben Cross (r).

Malice or Joan Hackett in *Only When I Laugh*, were particularly memorable. The sentimental favorite in this category was Jane Fonda, who had arranged to get the rights to *On Golden Pond* for her father and appeared in it with him, as his daughter.

Warren Beatty may have expected

OPPOSITE: Special Effects were a high point of *Raiders Of The Lost Ark*.
BELOW: Warren Beatty won the Best Director Award for *Reds*.

more, but he did get the Award for Best Director for *Reds*, a project which had obsessed him for years. *Reds* was serious and well made but the subject may have been too controversial for Academy members. Competition was stiff in the directing category. Louis Malle did an excellent job with *Atlantic City*, as did Hugh Hudson with *Chariots Of Fire*. Mark Rydell's direction of *On Golden Pond* was competent, but not much more. However, the man who probably should have won the

award was Steven Spielberg, director of *Raiders Of The Lost Ark*, one of the best adventure films ever made, and one of the most popular.

Raiders did win the Art Direction Award, the very least the Academy could do for this truly wonderful film. This was the first year that a separate award was given for makeup and the very deserving winner was *An American Werewolf In London*, a film which revolutionized the cinematic view of the werewolf.

1982

Best Picture: *Gandhi*.
Actor: Ben Kingsley, *Gandhi*.
Actress: Meryl Streep, *Sophie's Choice*.
Supporting Actor: Louis Gossett, Jr, *An Officer And A Gentleman*.
Supporting Actress: Jessica Lange, *Tootsie*.
Director: Richard Attenborough, *Gandhi*.
Foreign Language Film Award: *Volver A Empezar (To Begin Again)* (Spain).
Writing (Screenplay-Original): John Briley, *Gandhi*.
Writing (Screenplay-Adaptation): Costa-Gavras, Donald Stewart, *Missing*.
Cinematography: Billy Williams, Ronnie Taylor, *Gandhi*.
Art Director: Stuart Craig, Bob Laing, *Gandhi*.
Special Visual Effects: *ET The Extra-Terrestrial*.
Music (Original Score): *ET The Extra-Terrestrial*.
Music (Song): Jack Nitzsche, Buffy Sainte-Marie (Music), Will Jennings (Lyrics), 'Up Where We Belong' from *An Officer And A Gentleman*.
Short Film (Animated): *Tango*.
Short Film (Live Action): *A Shocking Accident*.
Documentary (Short): *If You Love This Planet*.
Documentary (Feature Length): *Just Another Missing Kid*.
Honorary Award: Mickey Rooney, in recognition of his 60 years of versatility in a variety of memorable film performances.

One Los Angeles columnist quipped, '*Gandhi* was everything the voting members of the Academy would like to be: moral, tan and thin.' The film about the life of the great Indian leader took most of the major awards at the Fifty-fifth Academy Awards Ceremony. The sweep came as a surprise to most people and probably as a shock to Steven Spielberg who had been expected to dominate this year with *ET The Extra-Terrestrial*, far and away the most popular film of the year and the biggest box office grosser to date. *ET* took only a few minor awards, and some people in the industry wondered if this was a deliberate rebuke to the young director, who had made some of the most successful films in Hollywood history, but had never won a major award.

Still *Gandhi* was a good, if somewhat stuffy film, and there could be no argument at all about giving the Best Actor Award to Ben Kingsley, a newcomer to films whose portrayal of Mahatma Gandhi was little short of miraculous.

Gandhi not only beat out *ET*, it also

OPPOSITE: Best Actor Ben Kingsley as Mahatma Gandhi in *Gandhi*.
BELOW: Jessica Lange and Dustin Hoffman in *Tootsie*.

beat the extremely popular *Tootsie*. Two other films, *Missing* and *The Verdict* though both excellent treatments of important topics, never really stood a chance.

In any other year Dustin Hoffman would have been a shoo-in as best actor for his wonderful portrayal of an actor forced to impersonate a woman in *Tootsie*. Paul Newman gave his best performance in years as the alcoholic lawyer who refuses to be corrupted in *The Verdict*; Peter O'Toole was also in top form as an alcoholic Errol Flynn-type of actor in *My Favourite Year*, so was Jack Lemmon in *Missing*, as a father searching for his son amid the violence of Central America. It was a good year for the actors.

Meryl Streep was awarded the Best Actress Oscar for her dazzling performance as the doomed survivor of the Nazi camps in *Sophie's Choice*. Julie Andrews, moving ever farther from Mary Poppins had a transvestite role in the hilarious *Victor/Victoria*. Sissy Spacek believable as the wife of the

drill sergeant in *An Officer And A Gentleman*. What with *Tootsie* and *Victor/Victoria* this was a big year for tales of confusion of sexual identity. Screen veteran Robert Preston received a Best Supporting Actor nomination for his bravura performance as a flaming queen in *Victor/Victoria* and John Lithgow got one for playing a football player who had become a woman in *The World According To Garp*. James Mason had a more conventional role as a cynical, scheming lawyer in *The Verdict*. Charles Durning did his usual professional job, but nothing could save *The Best Little Whorehouse In Texas*.

Jessica Lange who was nominated for Best Actress and didn't win was also nominated for Best Supporting Actress, and this time she did win, for her role in

LEFT: Louis Gossett Jr with Richard Gere and David Keith in *An Officer And A Gentleman*.
BELOW: Meryl Streep and Kevin Kline in *Sophie's Choice*.

Tootsie. Lange was beautiful and competent but it was a creampuff part, and this looked more like a consolation prize. Teri Garr, also nominated for *Tootsie* was better and so was Kim Stanley who played Lange's mother in *Frances*. Lesley Ann Warren almost stole *Victor/Victoria* from a very good cast with her portrayal as a gangster's moll. Glenn Close, a skillful actress, was excellent as Robin William's mother in *The World According To Garp*.

ET did pick up a number of well deserved special effects awards and Spielberg could console himself with the knowledge that his film made more money than all the top winners combined.

Mickey Rooney whose career had been boosted by his Broadway success *Sugar Babies*, was given a special Honorary Award, his second. He had previously been awarded a Special miniature Oscar in 1938.

missing man was nominated for *Missing*. Debra Winger was nominated for her performance in the year's surprise hit *An Officer And A Gentleman*. Jessica Lange played Frances Farmer, in an interesting but flawed biography of the actress' tragic life, *Frances*.

Louis Gossett, Jr was chosen Best Supporting Actor for his hard-nosed

1983

Best Picture: *Terms Of Endearment.*
Actor: Robert Duvall, *Tender Mercies.*
Actress: Shirley MacLaine, *Terms Of Endearment.*
Supporting Actor: Jack Nicholson, *Terms Of Endearment.*
Supporting Actress: Linda Hunt, *The Year Of Living Dangerously.*
Director: James L Brooks, *Terms of Endearment.*
Foreign Language Film Award: *Fanny And Alexander* (Sweden).
Writing (Screenplay-Original): Horton Foote, *Tender Mercies.*
Writing (Screenplay-Adaptation): James L Brooks, *Terms Of Endearment.*
Cinematography: Sven Nykvist, *Fanny And Alexander.*
Art Direction: Anna Asp, *Fanny And Alexander.*
Costume Design: Marik Vos, *Fanny And Alexander.*
Special Achievement Awards, Visual Effects: Richard Edlund, Dennis Muren, Ken Ralston, Phil Tippett, *Return Of The Jedi.*
Music (Original Score): Michel Legrand, Alan and Marilyn Bergman, *Yentl.*
Music (Song): Giorgio Moroder (Music), Keith Forsey and Irene Cara (Lyrics) 'What A Feeling' from *Flashdance.*
Short Films (Animated): *Sundae In New York.*
Short Films (Live Action): *Boys And Girls.*
Documentary (Short): *Flamenco At 5:15.*
Documentary (Feature): *He Makes Me Feel Like Dancing'*
Jean Hersholt Humanitarian Award: M J Frankovich.
Honorary Award: Hal Roach, in recognition of his unparalleled record of distinguished contributions to the motion picture art form.

Terms Of Endearment, a well played, but weepy drama of a mother and daughter swept the awards this year. It had proved popular with the public, and popular with the voting members of the Academy as well. Most of all the film was a triumph for Shirley Mac-Laine. MacLaine who had started as a dancer, entered films in 1955. Her career had its ups and downs, but in recent years she had been on a hot streak and as Debra Wingers' mother in *Terms Of Endearment*, she showed that at age 50, a time when many other once-cute actresses can't even get roles, she was better than ever.

The Big Chill about a group of former 60s radicals gathering at the funeral of a friend was also nominated. It featured some fine ensemble acting by some of America's better young actors and actresses. Though it was nominated for Best Picture *The Right Stuff*, about the early days of the US space program, must have been a disappointment to its producers. The critics had praised it but people stayed away, real space was

OPPOSITE: Best Actress Shirley MacLaine in *Terms Of Endearment.*
BELOW: Ingmar Bergman's *Fanny and Alexander* won the Award for Best Foreign Language Film.

not nearly as interesting to movie goers as the science fiction galaxies of George Lucas. Also nominated were *Tender Mercies*, a small, well-made film about an alcoholic ex-country singer, and *The Dresser* set in a broken down touring British rep company during World War II, and adapted from a successful play.

Four Englishmen and an American were nominated for Best Actor, and the American won. Robert Duvall received the Oscar for *Tender Mercies* and probably for many past excellent performances as well. Michael Caine, with his best role in years, was nominated for the part of the drunken professor in *Educating Rita*. Tom Conti was a drunken poet in *Reuben, Reuben*. Tom

LEFT: Robert Duvall in *Tender Mercies*.
BELOW: Best Supporting Actress Linda Hunt as Billy Kwan in *The Year Of Living Dangerously*.

Jennifer Beals played a steel worker who wants to be a dancer in *Flashdance*.

Courtenay was the dresser, in *The Dresser*. He also drank. Albert Finney the aging actor in *The Dresser* didn't drink, but he did give his usual splendid performance.

Debra Winger received a Best Actress nomination for the part of the daughter in *Terms Of Endearment* but MacLaine was a clear favorite. Meryl Streep was splendid as the nuclear plant worker who believes she has been contaminated by radioactivity in *Silkwood*, which was based on a real incident. Newcomer Julie Walters made an impressive screen debut as the cockney girl who wants an education in *Educating Rita*. Jane Alexander's performance in *Testament*, the most shattering film about the aftermath of a nuclear war ever made, was almost unbearably touching.

Jack Nicholson, a star who doesn't scorn small parts took one in *Terms Of Endearment*, and won the Best Supporting Actor Oscar for it. John Lithgow, rapidly maturing into one of the most eccentric and best character actors in America received a Supporting Actor

nomination for the same film. The playright and actor Sam Shepard, played test pilot Chuck Yeager in *The Right Stuff*. Rip Torn stood out in the surprisingly bland *Cross Creek*, and Charles Durning was a very funny Nazi in Mel Brook's remake of the 1941 Jack Benny film, *To Be Or Not To Be*. All received Best Supporting Actor nominations.

There was an unusually interesting group of nominees for Best Supporting Actress. One was the singer Cher in her dramatic debut in *Silkwood*. She surprised all the critics by turning in a first rate performance. Glenn Close was nominated for *The Big Chill*, though all of the actresses in that film were equally deserving. Amy Irving got a nomination for the Barbra Streisand vehicle, *Yentl*, and Alfre Woodward was nominated for *Cross Creek*. The winner, however, was Linda Hunt the four-foot-nine actress who played a male Eurasian dwarf, in the brilliant Australian film *The Year of Living Dangerously*. Her acceptance speech was a high point of the Awards ceremony.

The best film of the year won the Foreign Language Film Award. Ingmar Bergman's *Fanny And Alexander* was a lush sometimes frightening, sometimes funny film about childhood. It represented a major break from the great director's string of small and very bleak films of madness, illness and death. The film received a host of awards for cinematography, design and costumes.

Bergman was nominated for Best Director, but lost to James L Brooks of *Terms Of Endearment*. Mike Nichols was nominated for *Silkwood*, Peter Yates for *The Dresser* and Bruce Beresford for *Tender Mercies*.

The biggest film of the year, *Return Of The Jedi*, third in the *Star Wars* series, received few nominations or awards, but it did win a Special Achievement Award for Visual Effects, which were, as might be expected, spectacular.

1984

Best Picture: *Amadeus.*
Actor: F Murray Abraham, *Amadeus.*
Actress: Sally Field, *Places In The Heart.*
Supporting Actor: Haing S Ngor, *The Killing Fields.*
Supporting Actress: Peggy Ashcroft, *A Passage To India.*
Director: Milos Forman, *Amadeus.*
Foreign Language Film Award: *Dangerous Moves* (Switzerland).
Writing (Screenplay-Original): Robert Benton, *Places In The Heart.*
Writing (Screenplay-Adaptation): *Amadeus.*
Cinematography: Chris Menges, *The Killing Fields.*
Art Direction: Patrizia Von Brandenstein, (Set Direction) Karel Cerny, *Amadeus.*
Costume Design: Theodore Pistek, *Amadeus.*
Special Visual Effects: Dennis Muren, Michael McAlister, Lorne Peterson, George Gibbs, *Indiana Jones And The Temple Of Doom.*
Special Achievement Awards, Sound Effects Editing: Kay Rose, *The River.*

Makeup: Paul LeBlanc, Dick Smith, *Amadeus.*
Music (Original Score): Maurice Jarre, *A Passage To India.*
Music (Original Song Score): Prince, *Purple Rain.*
Music (Song): Stevie Wonder 'I Just Called To Say I Love You' from *The Woman In Red.*
Short Films (Animated): *Charade.*
Short Films (Live Action): *Up.*
Documentary (Short): *The Stone Carvers.*
Documentary (Feature Length): *The Times Of Harvey Milk.*
Jean Hersholt Humanitarian Award: David L Wolper.
Honorary Award: James Stewart, for his fifty years of memorable performances. For his high ideals both on and off the screen. With the respect and affection of his colleagues.

A film adapted from a Broadway play about composer Wolfgang Amadeus Mozart would seem an unlikely Oscar winner in the 1980s, yet this year *Amadeus* swept the Awards, and the film was a popular winner as well.

Amadeus appealed to the lovers of classical music, and to the lovers of rock music – clips from the film were incorporated in a popular rock video. It was grand and stirring entertainment. It won Best Picture, Best Actor and Milos Forman, the man most responsible for making the film a success was voted Best Director. *Amadeus* also captured a flock of minor awards for costumes, makeup and art direction, all well deserved.

Other films nominated for Best Picture were *A Passage To India*, an intelligent and lavish adaptation of the E M Forster novel; *Places in The Heart*, about a young widow trying to save her farm; *A Soldier's Story*, set in a segregated Southern Army Camp during World War II, and *The Killing Fields*, a horrifying true story of an American reporter in Cambodia at the time of the take-over by the Khmer Rouge.

BELOW: Haing S Ngor and Sam Waterston in *The Killing Fields.*
OPPOSITE: F Murray Abraham as the jealous composer Antonio Salieri in *Amadeus.*

The Best Actor Award was won by F Murray Abraham, an actor better known in New York than Hollywood, who played Mozart's great enemy, Antonio Salieri, a mediocre but fashionable composer. Also nominated for Best Actor was Tom Hulce of *Amadeus* who played Mozart. The always brilliant Albert Finney was brilliant again as the doomed alcoholic in *Under The Volcano*. Sam Waterston was nominated for his part as the reporter in *The Killing Fields*, and Jeff Bridges for his part as an extra-terrestrial in the above average science fiction film *Starman*.

It was the year of country girls among the Best Actress nominees. Sally Field won as the widow in *Places In The Heart*. Her competition included Jessica Lange trying to save her farm in *Country*, and Sissy Spacek trying to save hers in *The River*. Vanessa Redgrave was splendid, as always, as the suffragette trying to save her protégée from the wiles of Christopher Reeve in the adaptation of Henry James' *The Bostonians*. Judy Davis as a young Englishwoman confronting the mysteries of India in *A Passage To India*, also de-

livered an award caliber performance.

Far and away the most unusual winner of an Oscar in this or any other year was Haing S Ngor, a Cambodian refugee doctor who had never acted before. He received the Best Supporting Actor Award for *The Killing Fields*. The film was, in many respects the story of his life, and an emotional peak was reached when he stepped up to take the statuette at the Awards ceremony.

John Malkovich, recognized as one of America's finest young actors, on stage or screen was nominated for his part as the blind man in *Places In The Heart*. Adolph Caesar received his nomination as the tough officer hated by his men in *A Soldier's Story*, and Noriyuki 'Pat' Morita as the old man who changes a boy's life in *The Karate Kid*. Ralph Richardson, who had recently died was nominated for his role as Tarzan's grandfather in *Greystroke: The Legend Of Tarzan*. The nomination may have been based on sentiment for the great actor rather than on his performance in this particular film.

Peggy Ashcroft, another legend of the British stage, won Best Supporting Actress for *Passage To India*, an award

Judy Davis as Adela Quested and Best Supporting Actress Dame Peggy Ashcroft as Mrs Moore in *A Passage To India*.

that no one could quarrel with. Geraldine Page, a legend of the Broadway stage was nominated for her part in *The Pope Of Greenwich Village*. In a small role she stole the show. Christine Lahti was the best thing about the generally disappointing Goldie Hawn vehicle *Swing Shift*. Glenn Close as usual was good in *The Natural*, which featured Robert Redford as the world's greatest baseball player. The last nominee was Lindsay Crouse in *Places In The Heart*.

Milos Forman's direction of *Amadeus*, was towering. He turned a successful play into an even more successful film, a task accomplished only rarely. His strongest competition was probably David Lean who directed *Passage To India*, but it should have been Woody Allen, who made *Broadway Danny Rose*, a small comedic gem, and one of his best films. Roland Joffee director of *The Killing Fields*, and Robert Benton, director of *Places In The Heart* also received nominations.

Once again the big, spectacular

adventure film, this time *Indiana Jones And The Temple Of Doom*, did not fare well with the voting members of the Academy but it did receive a Special Award for Visual Effects.

The Academy also honored one of its own favorite sons, Jimmy Stewart.

The greatest impression at the ceremonies was made by rock singer Prince, resplendent in sequined robe, who received an award for his score for *Purple Rain*.

RIGHT: Best Actress Sally Field played a widow trying to hold on to her family farm in *Places In The Heart*.
BELOW: Special Effects heightened the excitement in *Indiana Jones And The Temple Of Doom*.

1985

Best Picture: *Out Of Africa.*
Actor: William Hurt, *Kiss Of The Spider Woman.*
Actress: Geraldine Page, *The Trip To Bountiful.*
Supporting Actor: Don Ameche, *Cocoon.*
Supporting Actress: Anjelica Huston, *Prizzi's Honor.*
Director: Sydney Pollack, *Out Of Africa*
Foreign Language Film Award: *The Official Story* (Argentina).
Writing (Screenplay-Original): William Kelley, Pamela Wallace, Earl W Wallace, *Witness.*
Writing (Screenplay-Adaptation): Kurt Luedtke, *Out Of Africa.*
Cinematography: David Watkin, *Out Of Africa.*

Art Direction: Stephen Grimes, (Set Direction) Josie MacAvin, *Out Of Africa.*
Costume Design: Emi Wada, *Ran.*
Editing: Thom Noble, *Witness.*
Sound: Chris Jenkins, Gary Alexander, Larry Stensvold, Peter Handford, *Out Of Africa.*
Special Visual Effects: Ken Ralston, Ralph McQuarrie, Scott Farrar, David Berry, *Cocoon.*
Sound Effects Editing: Charles L Campbell, Robert Rutledge, *Back To The Future.*
Makeup: Michael Westmore, Zoltan Elek, *Mask.*
Music (Original Score): John Barry, *Out Of Africa.*
Music (Song): Lionel Ritchie, 'Say You, Say Me' from *White Nights.*
Short Films (Animated): *Anna And Bella.*

Short Films (Live Action): *Molly's Pilgrim.*
Documentary (Short); *Witness To War: Dr Charlie Clements.*
Documentary (Feature Length): *Broken Rainbow.*
Jean Hersholt Humanitarian Award: Charles (Buddy) Rogers.
Honorary Awards: Paul Newman, in recognition of his many memorable and compelling screen performances and for his personal integrity and dedication to his craft. Alex North, in recognition of his brilliant artistry in the creation of memorable music for motion pictures.

BELOW: *Out Of Africa,* starring Meryl Streep, won the award for Best Picture.
OPPOSITE: Best Actor William Hurt played an imprisoned homosexual in *Kiss Of The Spider Woman.*

ABOVE: Don Ameche (left) won the award for Best Supporting Actor for *Cocoon*

OPPOSITE TOP: Best Actress Geraldine Page (right) with Rebecca de Mornay in *The Trip To Bountiful*.

OPPOSITE BELOW: *Prizzi's Honor* starring Jack Nicholson, Kathleen Turner and Anjelica Huston was nominated for Best Picture, as was the director John Huston for Best Director. Only Anjelica Huston won an award for Best Supporting Actress.

RIGHT: *The Color Purple* starring Whoopi Goldberg, was nominated for eleven awards but did not win any of them.

PICTURE CREDITS

All photos from The Bison Picture Library, with the following exceptions: Academy of Motion Picture Arts and Sciences: 2 center, 4
Life Magazine: 2 left center, Leslie Winter © 1960 Time Inc.; 3 center btm, Peter Stackpole © 1940 Time Inc.
Museum of Modern Art/Film Stills Archive: 6 below, 14, 15, 23, 24 top, 27 top, 28 top, 30 top, 45 top, 51 top, 55 bottom, 57, 58, 62, 77, 91, 110, 119, 148 bottom.
National Film Archives: 9 top, 67 bottom, 83, 85 top, 124 both, 125, 164 bottom, 168.
Phototeque: 7 both, 8 top, 9 bottom, 10, 11 bottom, 16 bottom, 21 top, 29, 31, 32, 33 top, 34, 35, 40, 54 top, 55 top, 59 bottom, 64, 72 bottom, 73 bottom, 75, 81 right, 87 top, 90, 95 bottom, 96 bottom, 105, 141, 142-43, 150, 153 bottom, 184, 186, 187, 188 top.

ACKNOWLEDGMENTS

The author and publisher would like to thank the following people for their help: Ron Callow for the design, Elizabeth Montgomery for the editing, Mary Raho and Donna Cornell for the picture research and Karla Knight for the index.